LAW AND ORDER LEVIATHAN

Law and Order Leviathan

AMERICA'S EXTRAORDINARY
REGIME OF POLICING
AND PUNISHMENT

DAVID GARLAND

PRINCETON UNIVERSITY PRESS
PRINCETON & OXFORD

Copyright © 2025 by Princeton University Press

Princeton University Press is committed to the protection of copyright and the intellectual property our authors entrust to us. Copyright promotes the progress and integrity of knowledge created by humans. By engaging with an authorized copy of this work, you are supporting creators and the global exchange of ideas. As this work is protected by copyright, any reproduction or distribution of it in any form for any purpose requires permission; permission requests should be sent to permissions@press.princeton.edu. Ingestion of any PUP IP for any AI purposes is strictly prohibited.

Published by Princeton University Press
41 William Street, Princeton, New Jersey 08540
99 Banbury Road, Oxford OX2 6JX

press.princeton.edu

GPSR Authorized Representative: Easy Access System Europe - Mustamäe tee 50, 10621 Tallinn, Estonia, gpsr.requests@easproject.com

All Rights Reserved

ISBN 978-0-691-27119-4
ISBN (e-book) 978-0-691-27121-7

Library of Congress Control Number: 2024056580

British Library Cataloging-in-Publication Data is available

Editorial: Rachael Levay, Erik Beranek, and Tara Dugan
Production Editorial: Karen Carter
Jacket/Cover Design: Karl Spurzem
Production: Erin Suydam
Publicity: William Pagdatoon
Copyeditor: Martin Schneider

Jacket/Cover Image: © Bennett Fuhrman

This book has been composed in Arno

Printed in the United States of America

10 9 8 7 6 5 4 3 2 1

"Non est potestas Super Terram quae Comparetur ei"
(No power on earth compares to it)

—THOMAS HOBBES, LEVIATHAN (1651)

CONTENTS

	Prologue: From Tocqueville to Hobbes	1
1	Challenging Leviathan	6
2	Toward a Structural Explanation	14
3	America's Penal State	31
4	The Control Imperative	44
5	America's Political Economy	58
6	Political Economy and Social Disorder	75
7	Political Institutions and Crime Control	88
8	Social Sources of Indifference	102
	Epilogue: Constraints and Possibilities	119

Acknowledgments 137
Notes 139
Bibliography 171
Index 209

LAW AND ORDER LEVIATHAN

Prologue

FROM TOCQUEVILLE TO HOBBES

IN THE EARLY 1830S, Alexis de Tocqueville, the first and still best-known theorist of American society, formulated a paradox about the young nation. America was, he said, a land "of the most extended liberty," and yet its prisons "offer the spectacle of the most complete despotism." Freedom and unfreedom were juxtaposed in a way that surprised the French visitor and struck him as ironic.[1] Nearly two centuries later, commentators still find it puzzling that liberal America deploys its penal power more extensively and intensively than any other country in the world. How could America, that storied land of liberty, be home to mass incarceration, frequent police killings, and racialized criminal justice?

In this book I insist there is nothing paradoxical about America's reliance upon a massive penal state. I argue that the liberalism characterizing modern American society is primarily an economic liberalism, dedicated to the free rein of corporate power and market forces rather than the dignity and flourishing of every individual. Since the collapse of the New Deal order in the 1970s, the nation's politics have been dominated by a tough-minded market fundamentalism that empowers corporations and the business class, renders workers insecure, holds individuals responsible for their fate, and pays little heed to the liberty interests of poor people, particularly if they are Black and accused of criminal conduct. In such a system, extensive penal control is a corollary of the nation's social relations—not a contradiction.

America, it has been said, is an idea as well as a nation. Animating that idea is a set of narratives—America as a land of plenty and the home of liberty, democracy, equal opportunity, and limited government—that provide Americans with a sense of identity and belonging.[2] Taken at face value, none of these conceptions would lead us to expect that the United States would develop the western world's largest prison system and its deadliest police. Nor would they suggest that the sources of this extraordinary regime of policing and punishment would be the distinctive political and economic arrangements that Americans are taught to think of as the envy of the world. But if we set aside these soothing narratives and foreground some salient facts of American history and social structure, a different picture emerges.

The United States is certainly one of the richest nations on earth, but as I show in the chapters that follow, it is also a strikingly unequal country: one of the most economically and racially unequal in the developed world. As we will see, the poorest Americans—above all poor Black people living in segregated neighborhoods, characterized by William Julius Wilson as "the truly disadvantaged"—live in conditions that resemble those in the developing world, while America's middle classes experience more insecurity and stress than working people elsewhere. And physical fear exacerbates economic insecurity, since gun crime and homicide occur in America at levels that are altogether unknown in other affluent nations.[3]

It is also true that for much of its history America was a world leader in expanding the franchise and subjecting government to democratic controls. The US Bill of Rights famously limited government's power to restrict individual liberty and provided Americans with freedom of speech and religion at a time when these were mostly absent elsewhere.[4] And by the middle of the nineteenth century, when European peoples remained disenfranchised, most American states had established something approaching universal suffrage for White adult males. But for most of that history, large sections of America's people have been neither free, nor equal, nor enfranchised. Black people, in particular, have experienced America not as a land of freedom but as a site of enslavement, state-supported segregation, and racial discrimination where even today they remain far from equal or fully enfranchised. The historical experience of Native Americans, Asian Americans, and other people of color has likewise been marked by discrimination, exclusion, and violence.

There have, of course, been potent countercurrents running throughout the nation's history, and popular movements for civil rights, racial equality, and a fuller democracy have achieved progressive victories such as Reconstruction, the New Deal and Great Society programs, civil rights advances, and the LGBTQ breakthroughs of recent decades. But America's welfare state and protections for working people have never been as extensive as those of other western nations. And the full multiracial democracy promised by the Civil

Rights and Voting Rights Acts of the 1960s has been repeatedly undermined in the decades since.

Antipathy toward government and a horror of state repression are two other tropes of American self-description that ought not to be overstated. It is true that in the early years of the Union, republican sensibilities and compromise with the slaveholding South shaped the design of the nation's political institutions in a way that limited the reach of the central state while empowering local government and private actors. And it remains the case today that Americans are mostly distrustful of government, expressing a great deal of skepticism about the ability of politicians to solve social problems. It is also true that America has a comparatively limited social state, a weak civil service, and an underdeveloped public sector. But the institutions of any state are complex and unevenly developed, and the repressive apparatus deployed by American government has always been powerful—even in the nineteenth century, when coercive functions were delegated to private actors or undertaken in partnership with them.[5] Actors with access to state power have not been slow to use it whenever their interests have been at stake. The considerable firepower of the American state has been repeatedly deployed to support powerful interests, most notably on the frontier against Native Americans, in the South to maintain slavery and Jim Crow, and elsewhere in efforts to crush labor union organizing and social protest. So it should be no surprise that when urban disorder and violent crime rates surged from the mid-1960s to the mid-1990s—producing homicide rates never before seen in the developed world—the reaction of many Americans was to approve an expansion of the government's power to punish. The creation of a massive penal state may contradict stories America tells about itself, but it is hardly the first illiberal episode in the nation's history.[6]

Viewed by these lights, the evident illiberalism of America's contemporary penal state is by no means anomalous. On the contrary: it is a social trait with deep roots in the nation's history, its economic structures, and its political institutions. If there is a paradox, or a tension between America's social arrangements and the fact of mass incarceration, it exists in the domain of ideology and national self-regard. And we know from the history of slavery and segregation that ideological dissonance of that sort can be tolerated for long periods of time.

Capitalism is always a socially disruptive force. And historically, it has been especially disruptive in the United States, where comparatively few restraints have been imposed on market processes and corporate power and where working people have enjoyed fewer protections than workers in other developed nations. But in American cities in the 1970s, 1980s, and early 1990s, these long-standing conditions were dramatically intensified by deindustrialization, by the retrenchment of federal urban policy, and by a resurgent "free market" capitalism that together caused new levels of social disorganization, disorder, and violence—problems that anemic welfare for the poor did little to counter.

In the face of this disorder, and against a background of deepening economic insecurity, a substantial part of the American electorate came to fear crime and violence—and the threat these posed to their property values— more than they feared the illiberal use of state power and the abuses that accompany it. The emergent result was a new kind of social contract between Americans and their government: a "law and order" covenant in which voters consented to tough-on-crime policies promising public safety through harsh policing and extensive penal control. For thirty years, American voters and their representatives repeatedly embraced such policies, even as they gave rise to a penal state—a law and order Leviathan—of world-historic proportions.

In the Bible's Book of Job, "Leviathan" was the name of a fearsome sea monster, but its modern usage was given to us by the English philosopher Thomas Hobbes, who used the term to describe the modern state: a figure of enormous power to which "no power on earth can be compared." In Hobbes's famous account, Leviathan was established by the terms of a social contract in which the populace—in order to escape a chronically insecure "state of nature" in which life is "solitary, poor, nasty, brutish and short"—agrees to submit to Leviathan's gargantuan power in exchange for protection from one another.[7] I invoke the metaphor here to convey three distinguishing features of America's penal state: its monstrous, extraordinary nature; its grounding in popular fear of violence and disorder; and its authorization by the American electorate.

America's penal Leviathan emerged not from a Hobbesian state of nature but from a peculiarly American state of insecurity caused by the political economy of late twentieth-century US capitalism and the violent disorder to which that political economy gave rise. And it emerged not in a single momentous agreement but instead over the course of three decades, in one election after another, as fear for personal safety and property values generated popular demands that government take aggressive steps to control crime and secure public safety.[8] And rather than protect all from each, as in the Hobbesian social contract, America's penal state provided protection to some groups and some places while oppressing and excluding others. This was the repressive, racialized regime that the Black Lives Matter protests of summer 2020 forced upon the attention of the American public and, for a brief time, made to seem intolerable.

This book traces the structural sources of the economic insecurity, social disorder, and extraordinary violence that characterized America in the last quarter of the twentieth century. It explains how these distinctive structures and problems led, over time, to a profoundly illiberal politics of policing and punishment and to the formation of a penal state so monstrous that it has no equivalent in the developed world. It does so by viewing the United States in a *comparative* light, since only a comparative perspective can point up the extraordinary nature of America's penal state and the extraordinary features of America's social structure that explain it.[9]

The argument I set out in this book is a comparative, structural one. It explains America's peculiar penal state by showing that it is grounded in, and indirectly caused by, the structures of America's political economy—a set of structures that, like the penal state, is highly unusual in comparative terms.

I argue that because of that political economy, American criminal justice operates against a background of social dislocation, impoverishment, and gun violence to a degree unknown in other developed nations. In contrast to more conventional comparative accounts, I argue that it is not racism, nor religion, nor punitive culture that sets America's penal state apart—though each of these accentuates its repressive, discriminatory characteristics. What sets it apart is the socioeconomic context and material conditions in which America's criminal legal system operates. These material conditions are long-standing, as is their outlier status relative to those found in other developed nations. But the restructuring of political economy that occurred after the 1960s served to deepen social dislocation and lethal violence, while limiting the extent to which government could deploy positive means to remedy them. It was in these circumstances, and from these causes, that America's law and order Leviathan first emerged.

1

Challenging Leviathan

POLICING AND PUNISHMENT are fundamental institutions in modern society and so are rarely up for debate in any deep or far-reaching way. But in the summer of 2020, the legitimacy of America's criminal legal system was challenged in a critique that went to the root of the institutions. That challenge was all the more impactful because it occurred in the middle of a historic plague year, when government efforts to control the spread of COVID-19 disrupted social and economic life, putting millions of people out of work and giving rise, simultaneously, to widespread insecurity and to a vague optimism that the crisis might create the possibility of real structural change.[1]

In late May and June of that year, following a shocking, widely publicized episode of police violence, a wave of demonstrations brought America's criminal legal system to the forefront of public attention and, momentarily at least, persuaded a great many Americans that such a system was simply intolerable. In cities around the nation, millions of people marched beneath the banner "Black Lives Matter," pressing for a radical transformation of policing and punishment and an end to racial oppression. Millions more watched at home as, night after night, protesters assembled to demand that authorities "defund the police," "end mass incarceration," and dismantle a criminal legal system they insisted was deeply imbued with anti-Black racism.[2]

That radical moment was especially striking because for much of the previous fifty years, a very different politics had prevailed: a law and order politics focused not on the problem of excessive policing and punishment but on precisely the opposite: the perceived need for aggressive policing, severe punishment, and extensive control to protect against dangerous predators, unsafe streets, and violent crime. That earlier politics had given America proactive policing, hard-charging prosecution, mass incarceration, and the world's most extensive system of penal control. And surprising as the protests made it seem, it had, until relatively recently, enjoyed decades of broad bipartisan support and little organized opposition.[3]

For anyone following the news, there had been no end of police violence and excessive punishment in the period before 2020.[4] And in the years immediately preceding, opposition to mass incarceration and the penal state—which had long been a concern of activist and advocacy groups, public interest lawyers, progressives, civil liberties organizations, and so on—had begun to attract more mainstream political support, as violent and property crime rates continued to decline and the public grew less fearful.[5] But the event that caused this opposition to catch fire was the killing of George Floyd—a forty-six-year-old Black man murdered by a police officer in Minneapolis following his arrest for the passing of a counterfeit $20 bill. Though Mr. Floyd was unarmed, subdued, and lying prone on the ground, Officer Derek Chauvin knelt on his neck for more than eight minutes until he died from lack of oxygen. Captured on a teenage girl's cellphone video and uploaded onto social media, the scene was soon being viewed by millions around the world. Street protests ensued, first in Minneapolis and eventually, massively, everywhere.[6]

In the days that followed, this singular event took on a more universal meaning. Mr. Floyd's image became a quasi-religious icon, his face painted on city streets and protest banners. On social media and in popular culture, his murder became a meme: a rapidly circulating symbol standing for the problem of police violence and the oppression of Black people. An incident that began as a low-level police arrest came to symbolize all that was wrong with America's penal state.[7]

Isolated, alternately anxious and frustrated, and confined to their homes by COVID lockdowns, many Americans longed for a chance to be outside and reconnect with others.[8] And because they had been released from the demands of work and school, millions who in normal times would have been unavailable and indifferent were now willing and able to join the protests.[9] Organizers responded to the moment by doing everything they could to maximize participation; the brilliant simplicity of the mantra "Black Lives Matter" enabled people of all backgrounds to come together and demand fundamental change.[10] Seemingly overnight, a problem that had persisted for decades without attracting much popular attention became a matter of urgent public concern. Mainstream journalists discovered that police killings occur much more frequently in the United States than in any comparable nation—and that America's rate of imprisonment massively exceeds those of every other country. They also learned there was no national government agency charged with keeping a tally of how many such deaths occurred. Because only things that count get counted, this too implied a disparagement of Black people's lives. For much of that summer, these were the stories that dominated the headlines.

News reports made clear the anger and despair with which many activists and demonstrators regarded the criminal legal system and the possibility of reforming it. So reviled was the penal state in that moment that the truly radical idea of *abolishing* the police and the prison came to seem morally compelling and urgently relevant. Rather than being dismissed as utopian fantasy, "abolition" was presented as a serious moral imperative: the only appropriate response to an intolerable system.[11] In that radical moment, the audaciousness of the idea made it appealing to journalists and commentators, causing it to burst into public discourse. Before long, abolition and the related idea of "defunding" were being discussed in liberal parts of the mainstream media and given serious consideration by editors, journalists, and political representatives.[12]

Supporters of "abolition" took a familiar progressive trope—the idea that crime should be traced to its root causes and dealt with at a deeper societal level—applied it to policing and punishment, and gave it a new urgency. America's policing problems were not, its advocates claimed, the fault of "bad apples" or rogue officers: the police were acting as they were supposed to act—as a force to manage the poor and protect ruling class property.[13] Similarly, it was "no accident" that America's jails and prisons imposed racial controls while generating commercial profits: that was the point of the prison-industrial complex.[14] Nor was it anomalous that places like Ferguson, Missouri, extracted millions of dollars from justice-involved individuals and their families: local policing was not an arm of justice but instead a form of state predation targeting the poor.[15] These egregious penal state arrangements were, the radicals insisted, dictated by the underlying structures of American society—by corporate capitalism, neoliberalism, and White supremacy. And these problems would be alleviated only when their root causes were eliminated.[16] The radical critique took a familiar liberal idea and pushed it to its logical conclusion.

For those swept up in the movement, the summer of 2020 promised to mark a turning point: a moment when the injustices that activists and advocacy groups had long protested—police violence; stop-and-frisk searches; "no knock" warrants; fees and fines; cash bail; racialized law enforcement, mass incarceration, the "New Jim Crow"—were at last making an impact on the consciences of a broader public. In that moment, it seemed possible that America's penal state might yield to the demand for fundamental change.

In that same moment, critics of America's political economy also had reason to hope that government responses to the pandemic might bring deep and lasting change to that larger domain. Those with a sense of history knew that progressive structural change rarely occurs, but when it does, it is most often in the wake of some major disruptive event, such as a war, a revolution, or an economic catastrophe. And by March 2020 Congress had already enacted the first of a remarkable series of government measures designed to prop up the economy and support working people.[17] By 2021, barely a year into the pandemic, the federal government had abandoned the hands-off logic of neoliberalism and pumped trillions of dollars into the economy to boost demand, preserve jobs, and patch together a pop-up European-style welfare state that provided income support, child-care allowances, health care, protections against eviction, student loan forgiveness, and free vaccines to all Americans. Amidst a years-long public health catastrophe, there appeared to be glimpses of a manifesting future in which the iniquities of America's penal state and political economy would be remedied once and for all.

But the moment of radical hope soon passed. The masses who took to the streets during the summer months did not stay around for fall and winter. The protests and large crowds became less frequent. By the end of 2020, challenges to the penal state had become more muted—on the streets and in the media.[18] Similarly, the European-style welfare measures hastily assembled at the height of the pandemic were, one by one, dismantled in the years immediately following.[19] As so often before, federal support and welfare provision were viewed not as citizenship entitlements but as emergency measures to be discarded once the crisis was over. The structures of the nation's political economy—and the social forces empowering them—had flexed in response to the emergency. But they forcefully reasserted themselves as soon as that moment had passed. The point of the Keynesian-style intervention had been to preserve American capitalism, not to transform it.

In retrospect, this reversal appears inevitable, in the penal sphere as well as the wider political economy. An extraordinary moment of that kind was always going to be difficult to sustain over the longer term. America's "free market" capitalism is, as everyone knows, stoutly defended, but so too is the penal state, even if the events of summer 2020 made it appear open to radical change. Continual mass mobilization over time requires an organizational infrastructure, a coherent leadership, a core membership, and a mass following—features BLM lacked in 2020.[20] And public attitudes that had been framed by George Floyd's killing were always liable to soften when that event was no longer in the news. But there were also deeper causes for the waning of radical energies—causes rooted in enduring structures rather than contingent events—and it will be helpful to point these out here.

For all its symbolic resonance, the Floyd case was not typical of the larger phenomenon it came to represent. Deadly encounters between police officers and civilians more often involve split-second decisions by officers who feel themselves or others to be in danger. And public opinion about such incidents is usually divided, making it difficult for prosecutors to persuade grand juries to indict the officers concerned. Officer Chauvin's conduct was, in that respect, extraordinary: not a momentary decision that might be second-guessed but a deliberate, prolonged assault resulting in the death of a helpless, unarmed man.[21] Chauvin's trial, which ended with jury verdicts of second- and third-degree murder and a twenty-two-year prison sentence, was also exceptional.[22] Police witnesses in such cases often cover up for one another. On this occasion, Minneapolis police testified against their fellow officer, insisting his behavior was outside the bounds of permitted police conduct and distancing themselves from his unlawful acts.

If the Floyd case was exceptional, so too was the historical conjuncture in which it occurred. For a decade and a half prior to these events, violent crime had been in steady decline and America's cities had become noticeably safer. This enhanced sense of safety relaxed the grip of crime fears on the American public. In 1994, 37 percent of Americans had identified crime as the nation's most important problem; by 2012 that number had fallen to 2 percent.[23]

During the high-crime decades of the 1980s and 1990s, when homicide, robbery, and crack cocaine dominated the evening news, American voters consistently embraced aggressive policing and harsh punishment, turning a blind eye to the injustices that followed in their train.[24] But when the crime threat receded, and with it the felt need for tough policies, attention began to turn to the penal state's pathologies.[25] Policies that had commanded widespread support in the 1990s—the War on Drugs, mass stop and frisk, "broken windows" policing, the all-purpose use of incarceration—were increasingly seen as ineffective, racially biased, and unconstitutional.[26] Prominent Republicans complained about exorbitant costs and urged that criminal justice be rolled back like any other overreaching government program.[27] State and local authorities pushed to trim correctional budgets. Progressive prosecutors were elected in big city districts, vowing to reduce mass incarceration and the harms it inflicted.[28] And following the high-profile deaths of Michael Brown and Eric Garner in 2014, police killings became, for a while, a recurring news topic.[29]

By the time of George Floyd's murder in late May 2020, a critique of America's penal state had been assembled. The public was primed to revise its views, and a movement seemed ready to take off.[30]

Yet within a year of the protests, law and order politics had made a forceful return. What explains this rapid reversal?

The answer, I want to suggest, is the constraining effect of social and economic structures, together with settled patterns of public opinion and political alignment that support them. Most Americans abhor overt racism and brutal behavior by officials, so it was understandable that graphic depictions of police violence against Black victims shocked people into action, especially at a time when millions were laid off from work and school by the COVID pandemic.[31] But most Americans, most of the time, are broadly supportive of law enforcement. And in normal times, American public opinion, particularly White working-class opinion, defaults to pro-police positions, a preference that is well understood by centrist and conservative politicians.[32]

Unless they are poor people of color, most Americans' life chances are not adversely affected by police violence or over-incarceration.[33] But they *are* affected by crime—and middle-class, home-owning voters become alarmed and vocal whenever rising crime rates appear to jeopardize their safety, their neighborhoods, or their property values. In late 2020, when reports began to appear of sharp increases in robberies, shootings, and homicides, right-wing news outlets downplayed pandemic disruptions as the likely explanation and insisted that crime was rising because of lawless protestors and because Democratic mayors and "woke" city councils were hamstringing police and undermining their authority.[34]

Before long, President Donald Trump was tweeting out law and order messages; counterdemonstrators were proclaiming "*Blue* Lives Matter"; signs appeared on suburban lawns urging neighbors to "Support Our Local Police"; and electorates were voting to recall progressive prosecutors. Meanwhile, on the streets, protests were being met by aggressive police responses, leading to mass arrests and widespread allegations of police brutality.[35] BLM demonstrators were also attacked by right-wing groups; on one occasion, three protesters were shot, two fatally, by a teenager armed with an AR-15 style rifle.[36] In the course of 2020, homicide rates spiked by 30 percent—the highest single-year increase in more than a century—and gun purchases surged, with Americans buying almost 60 million firearms during the pandemic years.[37] If the immediate aftermath of George Floyd's killing had suggested a nation united in protest, it wasn't long before the familiar deep divisions reappeared.[38]

So the radical moment passed. And measured by electoral outcomes, legislative achievements, or public attitudes, the challenge to America's penal state has had few victories in the years since then. Several years on from the death of George Floyd, little has changed in the basic character of America's criminal legal system. "Defund the police" is widely regarded as an electoral liability. "Abolition" has returned to the activist margins of local politics. The prison population in 2022 was higher than the prior year. Police killings were higher in 2023 than in any year since systematic counts began. In 2024, Donald Trump regained the presidency, having run on a platform that stated, "There is no higher priority than quickly restoring law and order and public safety in America."[39]

In the longer term, however, electoral success and legislative victories are not the only indicators of political change. And if we look closely, we can see that the events of 2020 brought important shifts in public consciousness, in the crime-control discourse, and in the politics of policing and punishment. The entry into the mainstream of radical ideas such as "defunding the police" and "ending mass incarceration" and "abolishing the prison" has expanded the field of action and the range of possibilities, establishing new horizons for reform, even if these horizons remain quite distant.[40] Similarly, that government action could so swiftly protect working families, fund broader healthcare, and reduce child poverty by half provided an instructive example of what can be done if the political will is present—a lesson that will surely feature in future debates. Journalists and academics have assimilated these ideas, as has a generation of young people and political activists on the left of the Democratic Party. So even though they remain highly controversial, the presence of these ideas structures political debate in a way that is altogether new.

The events surrounding George Floyd's death reset the debate about America's penal state. The social movement that gathered pace in the wake of that event foregrounded racial injustice, overly aggressive policing, and mass incarceration in a way that will not soon be forgotten. But the widely felt need for more effective crime control has not disappeared, and the background sensibility of the American public remains decidedly conservative on these issues.[41] Above all, the United States continues to be a society marked by extraordinarily high rates of lethal violence—the surge of gun crime and gun sales during the pandemic being a sharp reminder that the recent improvements in urban safety were always a precarious achievement. And, of course, these "safety" levels were only ever relative: America's homicide rates in the 2010s may have been much lower than the peak years of the 1980s and mid-1990s, but they were still off-the-charts high when compared to other developed nations.[42]

This last, comparative, point, seems to me to be vital to understanding the whole problem. As the sociologist Eric Klinenberg points out, the COVID-19 pandemic was a global event, but America's reactions were in many respects exceptional. Other countries "experienced a spike in generalized anxiety when the pandemic started. Their lockdowns were extensive. Their social gatherings were restricted. Their borders were sealed. Their offices were closed. Yet no other society experienced a record increase in homicides. None saw a surge in fatal car accidents. And of course, none had skyrocketing gun sales either."[43]

The pandemic years did not transform America into a progressive, liberal society, newly merciful toward lawbreakers. They did not lastingly alter the social and economic foundations of the nation's law and order Leviathan. But they did produce a shift in the balance of political forces to the point where progressive reforms to police and prisons—and to the nation's welfare state and political economy—stand an improved chance of winning support among an otherwise conservative electorate, at least in the longer term, as today's young voters reach political maturity.[44]

It is in this political conjuncture that I situate the following reflections on America's extraordinary penal state, its structural causes, and its political prospects.

2

Toward a Structural Explanation

CRIMINAL LAW enforcement is always and everywhere prone to excess and injustice. But Americans, above all poor Black Americans, are subject to altogether exceptional levels of police violence, incarceration, and penal control—levels that exist nowhere else in the developed world. This monstrous penal state demands explanation, not because it contradicts the nation's fundamental liberalism but because, as a comparative matter, it is so clearly extraordinary.

In what follows, I offer a structural explanation of this extraordinary law and order Leviathan, tracing the structural arrangements and historical processes that created it and keep it in place, describing how these political and economic structures differ from those of other nations, and indicating how the macro-structures of political economy interact with community-level processes of social ordering and informal social control to shape street-level practices of crime, policing, and punishment.[1] At the end of my analysis, I consider the prospects for radical change, taking account of the constraints these structures impose but also the scope for variation they allow.

This theory describes how the structural sources of America's extraordinary penal state flowed from America's political economy along three distinct causal pathways. It was structural shifts in America's political economy in the 1960s and 1970s that triggered an upsurge of social disorganization and criminal violence, leading to demands for governmental action. It was the structure of America's political economy and the limitations of local state capacity that ensured that the response to these disruptions was a massive rollout of penal control and highly aggressive forms of policing and punishment rather than social or economic investments. And it was America's racialized political economy that sustained segregation, limited solidarity, and enabled public indifference toward the millions of people caught up in the penal state. Each of these causal pathways involves multiple processes and mechanisms, with interacting conditions, causal chains, and historical contingencies. And the framework highlights the interactions that take place between the macro-level forces of political economy and the community-level processes of social organization, social control, and criminal justice policy. Rather than a tight theoretical argument, this account offers a broad explanatory framework, linking a series of sensitizing concepts—drawn from comparative social policy, the sociology of punishment, urban sociology, and the sociology of violence—with a specific historical account. As an explanatory framework it is, in principle, generalizable, provided it is adapted and respecified to fit the historical and institutional context to which it is applied.

In developing this theory, I take seriously the "root cause" analyses and radical proposals that recent developments have put on the agenda, but I approach these proposals from the standpoint of a comparative and historical sociologist. This perspective sets aside the partisan left-versus-right debates about crime control—where the right deplores criminality and holds individuals fully culpable and the left decries criminal injustice and insists that social structures are to blame—in order to introduce a more encompassing structural framework within which these complex, vexing issues may be better understood.

In the course of my analysis, I discuss the extraordinary levels of lethal violence that are such a feature of American life, especially in its poorest communities—levels that, again, exist nowhere else in the developed world.[2] Criminal violence must form part of any explanation of America's penal state because, within the United States, high levels of criminal violence run in parallel with harsh policing and punishment and because increased levels of homicide, armed robbery, and gun crime were among the causes that precipitated the law and order politics of the 1980s and 1990s that led to today's massive penal state.[3]

I explain these linked phenomena—extraordinary levels of criminal violence combined with extraordinary levels of penal control—by showing that they are caused by specific historical processes operating within a specific social structure. My theory situates both phenomena within the context of America's racialized political economy—a distinctive set of structures and institutions that, as we will see, render America's poorest neighborhoods more disorderly, more violent, and more subject to penal control than those of any of the world's developed nations.[4]

Drawing on research findings from several social science disciplines, I show how America's political economy weakens the informal social controls of civil society; contributes to extraordinary levels of criminal violence; and predisposes government to deploy policing and punishment as its standard response.

That same political economy reinforces a pattern of racial division, social distance, and limited solidarity that allows White Americans, most of the time, to turn a blind eye to the harmful effects of aggressive policing and penal control.

American Political Development

High levels of criminal violence and a massive apparatus of penal control are two effects of a social structure characterized by high levels of inequality, widespread insecurity, deep racial divisions, and a weak welfare state. This social structure has a history. To bring the Southern slave states and Northern maritime interests into a single union and to enable westward expansion in the absence of a strong national government, the Framers of the eighteenth century forged a federal constitution that devolved power to the states, accorded rights to individuals (including the right to expropriate Indian land), and established antimajoritarian constraints entrenching these arrangements.[5]

During the nineteenth century, a weak central state and a rapidly expanding economy enabled the emergence of a hegemonic business class, which used its power to suppress organized labor and prevent the formation of a labor-based party, thereby setting America on a path of development that differed from most western nations, not least in minimizing the impact of socialism, social democracy, and institutions for the protection of working people.[6]

Over the course of the nation's history, this distinctive federal polity—in which a limited national government delegated public powers to private actors and municipalities—gave rise to political arrangements that are highly unusual in comparative terms.[7] From the beginning to the present day, the US Constitution has allocated responsibility for policing and prosecution to local authorities, resulting in a criminal legal system more radically decentralized than that of any other nation and, consequently, lending the state a comparatively limited level of capacity for dealing with the problem of crime. In the Jacksonian era, when electoral democracy was comparatively advanced but state bureaucracy underdeveloped, it led to the politicization of public functions, including criminal justice, that elsewhere are the preserve of civil servants. In the decades after the Civil War, when the governments of other nations had disarmed their populations and monopolized legitimate violence, it enabled the formation of an extraordinary gun culture in which private firearm possession was widespread and legally protected to a degree unknown elsewhere.[8]

In the middle years of the twentieth century, when other nations built strong social states that provided public goods and extensive social and economic protections, America opted for more market-oriented arrangements that left corporations in control, the social state relatively weak, and working people more exposed to market forces. Indeed, for much of the nation's history, particularly since the 1970s, America's political leaders, with the backing of the corporate class and substantial parts of the electorate, have empowered market forces and corporations while diminishing the social state—relying on racial divisions, anti-union laws, and periodic violence to weaken the labor movement and popular opposition. Finally, from the start of the union through the 1960s, America's political institutions sustained racial hierarchy by various means including constitutional rulings upholding segregation; Senate rules enabling a minority of Southern senators to block civil rights bills; and an insistence on "state's rights" and "local autonomy," enabling the continuation of localized racist practices.

The result is a nation that, despite its enormous wealth and its avowed commitment to liberal democracy, has some of the western world's highest levels of economic and racial inequality; tolerates widespread economic insecurity and deep poverty; permits gun ownership on a massive scale; and exhibits extraordinary levels of social disorder and lethal violence. Since the 1980s, it has also come to rely on an apparatus of penal control that has no equivalent in the developed world.

I argue that the fundamental causes of America's extraordinary penal state lie in the nation's ultraliberal political economy—a political economy that is also extraordinary when viewed in comparative perspective.[9] Relative to other affluent nations, America exhibits more inequality, more economic insecurity, more precarious and low-paid employment, fewer workers' rights and employment protections, and higher levels of poverty and material deprivation. And these material conditions result in a series of negative social indicators—child poverty, infant mortality, poverty in work, untreated mental illness, drug-related death, single-parent households, housing and health insecurity, high school noncompletion, and deaths from homicide—that are among the worst in the developed world.[10]

America's maximalist penal state is, in effect, a concomitant of its minimalist welfare state and results from the same structural arrangements and social forces.[11] But the relationship between the welfare state and the penal state is, as we will see, mediated by the social disorders that are a prominent feature of America's social landscape, disorders that are also directly linked to material conditions. As I show in detail, America's political economy negatively impacts the organization and functioning of poor communities and families, greatly increasing the probability of social disorganization, neighborhood disorder, and criminal violence. And given the nature of crime-control politics and the limits of local state capacity, these disorders lead to the ramping up of aggressive policing and penal control.

An underappreciated consequence of these comparative facts is that American policing, prosecution, and punishment operate in a socioeconomic context that is markedly different from other affluent nations. Particularly after the 1960s, when the New Deal order largely gave way to neoliberalism, this context was characterized by social disorganization and a breakdown of informal social controls in the inner-city neighborhoods and public housing projects where the poorest people live. In other nations—and in affluent American neighborhoods—informal social controls are the organic foundation of social order and the primary prophylactic against crime. In America's poor neighborhoods, especially in segregated inner-city neighborhoods where most residents are poor and Black, these informal controls atrophy for lack of support and resources. In such places, despite the best efforts of families and residents, the fundamental sources of order are often undermined by a political economy that exposes them to disruptive market forces while starving them of political and economic support.

The background cause of American criminal violence and penal state repression is thus a material one. Other affluent nations police and punish less harshly and more humanely, not because they are more civilized or have no tendency toward racism and vengefulness. They police and punish less harshly chiefly because they have economic arrangements, forms of political association, and welfare states that are more solidaristic, are more inclusive, and provide more support for poor individuals, families, and communities. These economic and social arrangements result in lower levels of disorder and violence and less demand for penal control. The American difference is, fundamentally, a matter of political economy.

There is by now a wealth of historical scholarship explaining the emergence of mass incarceration in the United States.[12] There is also a comparative literature documenting the outlier status of America's penal state relative to those of comparable nations as well as a comparative social policy literature documenting the outlier status of America's labor market arrangements and its welfare state. Taken as a whole, this research observes a strong correlation between high rates of violence and incarceration and low levels of equality and social provision.[13]

My theory builds on these bodies of scholarship, integrating their most important insights into a single explanatory framework. That framework draws out the implications of political economy for criminal violence and criminal justice decision-making; adds an account of the intermediating processes and indirect causal mechanisms that connect America's political economy to its penal state; highlights the importance of social control deficits, limited state capacity, and low levels of trust; and traces the effect of community disorganization and danger on the actions of criminal justice officials. Its central claim is that the United States is a comparative outlier—in policing and punishment, in criminal violence, and in social problems more generally—because, as compared to other developed nations, its economy is more unequal, its working people more insecure, its welfare state less adequate, and its poor neighborhoods more disorganized. That its gun ownership rates are the highest in the developed world amplifies these problems and renders them more deadly.

Compared to other developed nations, America's political economy exposes communities, families, and individuals to greater market-generated risks, and its welfare state provides them with fewer social protections—a situation that was greatly exacerbated by the economic and political restructuring that occurred after the deindustrialization of the 1960s and the decline of the New Deal order.[14] This risk exposure and its negative effects are especially detrimental in segregated neighborhoods where poor African Americans live in conditions of concentrated disadvantage. The result, from the late 1960s to the early 1990s, in cities across the country, was extraordinarily high levels of social disorganization and violent crime.

These problems did not prompt economic investment and social provision, as in the War on Poverty; or strict gun controls, as in nations such as Australia and Britain that experienced traumatic gun violence. Instead, they led, over time, to the widespread adoption of aggressive policing and harsh penal control: punitive responses that, as we will see, were overdetermined by a lack of local state capacity, by political resistance to redistribution, and by a culture largely indifferent to the suffering of justice-involved people, most of whom were poor and Black.

The Intertwining of Political Economy and Race

Political economy is at the core of this theory, but the theory does not understate the importance of race and racism in American crime, policing, and punishment. On the contrary: it insists that racial hierarchies, racial legacies, and racist assumptions are woven into the fabric of America's political economy and are routinely reproduced by its structures and processes.[15] That these assumptions are also woven into American culture, making the racial inequalities of political economy and the criminalization of young Black men seem somehow natural, serves to legitimize these arrangements and shield them from scrutiny.[16]

In the theoretical models of social science, "race," "economics," and "politics" are often conceived as discrete, independent variables that can be studied separately. But, in reality, they are interwoven dimensions of social processes and institutional arrangements that have been developed and reproduced over long stretches of historical time.[17] As a result, America's political economy gives rise to racially disparate outcomes across the whole social landscape: in wages and inherited wealth; in political representation; in access to education, jobs, housing, healthcare, and welfare benefits; in encounters with police, rates of incarceration, and subjection to penal control.

Racially disparate outcomes can result from deliberate discrimination by racist decision-makers and the crude interpersonal prejudice that still forms a subterranean current in parts of American culture, despite the antiracist progress of the last fifty years. But the main source of racial disparity today is the structural impact of an always-already-racialized political economy on the life chances of African Americans. This "structural" or "institutional" racism results from long-standing distributions of property and privilege, rather than the conduct of racist individuals. Structural racism affects America's political economy and penal state from one end to the other, which is why so many Black Americans are caught up in concentrated poverty, in violent crime, and in the criminal legal system.[18]

Structural explanations can seem overly abstract and deterministic, appearing to invoke anonymous, inexorable forces to explain the conduct of lawbreakers, penal agents, and politicians. So it is important to stress that the structures of political economy impact places and people in very tangible, observable ways—chiefly by controlling the flow of economic and political resources into communities and thereby determining the opportunities and life chances to which people in particular neighborhoods have access.

It is also important to stress that "political economy" is not a complete explanation of the structure of the penal state. Between the macro-structures of political economy and the micro-level activities of crime, policing, and punishment there are multiple community-level social and criminogenic processes that also play a role in determining outcomes.[19] The articulation of societal structures with these more localized arrangements and processes is a vital aspect of the theory and accounts for much of the variation we observe over time and space.

These "intermediating processes," as I will call them, include detrimental processes such as residential transience; housing stock deterioration; the withdrawal of capable guardians from public space; incivility and disorder; illegal economies; gang formation; cycles of violence; and so on, as well as positive, pro-social activities and interventions, whether by the state, the community, or local businesses that aim to counter these developments.[20] And while these community-level processes are conditioned by external structural forces, they also have their own dynamics and determinants—what Marxists would term a "relative autonomy"—which means that they do not always occur in the same way or produce the same results.

Acknowledging these intermediating processes means that the explanation of criminal conduct embedded in this theory need not rely on causal accounts that are implausibly economistic. Instead, as I discuss below, and as the leading sociological research has shown, it assumes that the impact of political economy on criminal violence is not direct and deterministic but rather runs through social disorganization and family functioning.[21]

Political economy shapes patterns of disorder, crime, policing, and punishment, but its impact on these practices is always mediated, never direct. The probability of high rates of crime and violence is greatly increased when adverse economic conditions converge with disorganized neighborhoods and form a soil in which criminogenic processes can take root and grow. And where criminal violence does become a problem, these same structures and organizational deficits increase the chances that the predominant policy response will be aggressive policing and harsh penal control. But the macro-level structures of political economy always leave room for interventions, variation, and change at the neighborhood or community level.

Penal Controls and Social Controls

Penal states—and the power they project through policing, punishment, and penal control—function in most developed nations as essential but relatively minor back-up mechanisms, supporting the positive controls of civil society and its social institutions.[22] In the routine course of social life, the conduct of individuals is steered toward norms of good order by a variety of means: by the self-controls and pro-social values young people internalize in the course of their upbringing; by the norms and law-abiding behaviors modeled by families, peers, neighbors; and by the prompts, incentives, rewards, and restraints that operate in schools, communities, workplaces, and social life more generally. The penal controls of the state—policing, surveillance, the punishment of criminal conduct—involve a different kind of control: more formal, more coercive, backed by force.[23] State controls of this kind are generally present, but they mostly stand in the background of social life and are activated only when mainstream institutions break down and fail to secure adequate levels of compliance.

When the state's penal controls are activated in well-regulated communities, they are enabled and reinforced by the community's informal social controls, that is to say by the norms, customs, and behavioral expectations held out by the group to its members. These routine restraints and cultural codes provide a thick, normatively legitimate platform upon which the more coercive controls of policing and punishment can operate. So, for example, Jonathan Simon has shown how parole officers in 1950s California succeeded in resettling clients because of the availability of employment, housing, and family support. When these social supports later diminished in the wake of deindustrialization, parole ceased to work toward social integration and became a straightforward mode of penal control. Similarly, police experts such as David Bayley have long insisted that effective policing depends not on the police alone but instead on the prior existence of neighborhood social controls and community cooperation.[24]

Only in the most disorganized neighborhoods, where routine social controls have broken down, will coercive sanctions be the primary means through which compliance is secured. In these circumstances, aggressive policing and harsh punishment may come to the forefront, controlling individuals and groups who have fallen through the cracks of regular socialization and social control.

There is an important lesson here to which I will frequently return. Crime control is, most of the time, a mainstream social achievement, routinely produced, rather than an effect of the state's policing and punishment. In that sense, the criminal justice system is to crime control what the welfare state is to people's welfare—which is to say, marginal, supplementary, and remedial. Most people, most of the time, have their welfare needs met by virtue of employment or family networks, with state welfare operating as a supplement or backstop rather than the primary provider. The same is true of crime control. Most people obey the law most of the time because of the values and self-controls they internalize during their upbringing and because families and institutions envelop them in webs of informal control and norms of pro-social conduct. The state's policing and punishment stand in the background as necessary supplements, but the informal controls of civil society do most of the work.

Viewed sociologically, the penal state is a governmental apparatus that forms a functioning component of the overall ordering and organization of society. But the primary sources of social order are the mainstream institutions and social settings in which people mostly spend their time and upon which they mostly depend for material and emotional support. Families, friends, schools, neighborhoods, labor markets, workplaces, and welfare states are, in the normal run of things, the basic sources of social control, socialization, and social integration. If most individuals comply, most of the time, with the normative demands of group life, it is because of these institutions, the norms they establish, the rewards they provide, the restraints they impose, and the self-controls they inculcate.

These processes are not, however, automatic. They depend on the existence of high-functioning, well-resourced institutions. Nor are they uniformly accomplished across time and space. As sociologist Philip Selznick puts it: "Socialization and social control are variably effective. They are implemented by real people subject to many limitations, distractions, and temptations, who may or may not take their responsibilities seriously, and may or may not be able to carry them out."[25]

In America, because weakly restrained market forces have a destabilizing, disorganizing effect on certain groups and certain places, mainstream processes of social control are often undermined to the point that they fail to establish orderly communities and regulate individuals effectively. This can lead to social disorganization, antisocial conduct, crime, and violence, all of which are seriously aggravated by the widespread (and, again, quite extraordinary) availability of guns.

In some places and in some periods, disorganized neighborhoods have combined with street gangs, open-air drug markets, and the presence of guns to give rise to extraordinary levels of armed robbery, shootings, and homicide. Violent disorder of this kind generates existential fear and urgent calls for improved public safety. When these processes unfolded in America's big cities between the mid-1960s and the mid-1990s, they triggered public demands and political processes that, over the course of several decades, resulted in the formation of today's extraordinary penal state.[26]

The Sources of Social Order

Classical social theory provides us with three fundamental accounts of the sources of social order. There is Rousseau's account, focused on shared rituals, shared values, and normative consensus. There is a Lockean theory highlighting how mutual self-interest and private property generate reciprocity and peaceful exchange. And there is a Hobbesian account that sees social order as the coercive achievement of a sovereign power, established by the collective agreement of fearful, insecure individuals who choose to submit to that overweening power in order to guarantee their own security.[27] As noted in the prologue, a massive penal state emerged in late twentieth-century America because, in large cities across the nation, a highly unequal and oppressive political economy undermined the possibility of order through common values and complementary interests, producing extraordinary levels of disorder, crime, and violence and leading to a Hobbesian embrace of law and order.

America's political economy has long generated high levels of inequality and widespread insecurity, above all for African American neighborhoods. In the last third of the twentieth century, these destabilizing effects were exacerbated by deindustrialization, the federal government's withdrawal of urban support, local fiscal constraints, and the concentration of worklessness and poverty in racially segregated neighborhoods.[28]

The result was widespread urban decline, social disorganization, and extraordinarily high levels of violence, which undermined the possibility of order through common values and complementary interests. Economically insecure, fearful of violent crime, and distrustful of each other, American electorates in the 1980s and 1990s voted time and again—in each of the fifty states and at all levels of government—for representatives offering aggressive policing and harsh penal control as paths to public safety. And in a piecemeal, additive process—that over time moved every state in the same, increasingly punitive direction—aggressive practices of policing, prosecution, and punishment were put in place. The de facto result, with its unmistakable echoes of Hobbes's political fable, was the embrace of a law and order covenant that, additively, piece by piece, authorized the formation of a monstrous penal state.

An American Bandwidth

The United States is a huge, diverse nation that varies by locality and changes over time. Policing and criminal punishment, being primarily local and state functions, are especially subject to variation, but political economy also varies across the United States, with investment opportunities, labor markets, and employment conditions differing in certain respects across regions and even between cities. Any attempt to describe this internal variation while simultaneously drawing international comparisons will tend to lose clarity, burying general claims beneath a surfeit of detail and complexity. So, in the analysis that follows I have chosen to focus on three large questions: What are the main features of America's penal state? How do these differ from those of comparable nations? And what are the likely causes of this American difference?

When describing differences between "America" and other nations, my comparisons are broadly drawn and mostly set aside issues of internal variation, the aim being to highlight the distinctive characteristics of the US system, not to dig deeply into the details of comparative penology. However, I return to the question of internal variation in the final chapter when I highlight the fact that the structural constraints imposed by the nation's political economy leave a certain amount of room for variation and therefore certain possibilities for change.

My central concern is with the extraordinary penal state that emerged in the late twentieth century, the high levels of violence that preceded it, and the shifts in political economy that brought these about. American violence and imprisonment rates were relatively high in the decades prior to the run-up of mass incarceration, just as America's political economy has long been an outlier among developed nations. As the political economy of a society changes, the broad bandwidth of penal variation is also reset. In the decades after the 1960s, as deindustrialization impacted American workers and New Deal politics gave way to neoliberalism, first the nation's homicide rates and later its incarceration rates spiked upward to levels never seen in the developed world. In the years between 1980 and the present, America's homicide rates, its incarceration rates, and its rates of police killings have varied over time and across states, but this variation has always been within a definite range. Even at their lowest, America's national rates of criminal violence, state punishment, and police killings have generally been significantly above the average for developed nations. And although US states vary considerably between themselves, even states with the lowest incarceration and homicide rates exhibit levels that are well above the European average.[29] The United States has exhibited significant levels of change over time and place, but comparatively speaking it is, and has long been, an international outlier in respect of homicidal violence, police killings, and the severity of state punishment.

Even the most solid social structures permit a degree of variation at the local level of policy and practice because these societal macro structures are articulated with community-level structures that possess a certain autonomy. As a result, social structures leave a specific amount of play in the joints, allowing variation within structurally defined limits, locally, and over time. It follows that patterns of crime and punishment in any society will be capable of some degree of change, independent of change in the larger structures of political economy. It also follows that when the political economy of a society changes, the broad bandwidth of penal variation will also be reset.

In the United States, variation within what I will call "the American bandwidth" is produced by differences in political economy across time and space; by local differences in demographics, politics, policies, and events; and by intermediating processes that mitigate or aggravate the effects of political economy on patterns of crime, policing, and punishment. Because these intermediate processes are relatively autonomous, with determinants and dynamics of their own, crime rates and crime trends cannot be simply read off from political economy; nor can criminal justice policies. The general connections between the political economy and the penal state are clear enough—as the comparative evidence demonstrates. But within the American bandwidth, they vary across time and place and are loosely rather than tightly coupled. Political economy impacts crime and its control, but it does so by acting through intermediating community-level processes that may be more or less criminogenic and more or less oriented around control. One policy-relevant consequence of this fact—to which I will return in the book's epilogue—is that local patterns of crime, policing, and punishment can be altered, within limits, *without* prior or accompanying changes in the structures of political economy.

Material Circumstances and Social Controls

Critics discussing America's extraordinary penal state point to racism and vengefulness and suggest that these reprehensible features of American society are the chief causes behind the buildup of penal control.[30] Explaining and blaming are thereby bundled in a causal account that also serves as a moral critique. But there is reason to doubt an explanatory account based solely on the American public's punitive sentiments. It is true that sections of the public express racist, vengeful attitudes toward the offenders they incarcerate.[31] But similar attitudes also exist in other nations. And although they generate racial disparities in these nations' incarceration rates—disparities that are sometimes more egregious than those of the United States—they do not give rise to monstrous penal states.[32] More significantly, by most measures, racist public attitudes declined in America during the decades the penal state was growing, making it seem unlikely that one was the major cause of the other.[33]

Racism undoubtedly plays a role in shaping policing and punishment in America and may explain much of the nation's penal excess and cruelty.[34] But what chiefly marks the United States off from other nations is not negative attitudes toward criminals, nor racist attitudes toward minorities. It is, I will argue, the socioeconomic circumstances in which these attitudes are brought to bear. Compared to other developed nations, America experiences high levels of lethal violence, set against a background of deep poverty and social disorganization, with few positive tools to deal with these problems due to limited state capacity at the local level.[35] What chiefly differentiates the United States are the materials conditions in which problems of crime control are embedded.

Politicians, policymakers, and control agents in American cities and suburbs behave differently than their equivalents in other nations not, or not simply, because they are more racist, or punitive, or inhumane. They behave differently because the decisions they make, and the actions they take, are shaped by material conditions and socioeconomic circumstances that are quite different from those of other developed nations.

In making this claim, I am pursuing an approach that generally refrains from dismissing the conduct of social agents as simply punitive, racist, or in bad faith. Instead, my analysis assumes that people—offenders, police, criminal justice officials, lawmakers, members of the public—generally respond, more or less rationally, to their material circumstances. It treats them as intelligent people with a basic understanding of the conditions in which they find themselves: as situated, rational actors who strive to pursue their interests as they understand them. This approach, I believe, opens the way to a better understanding of the interaction dynamics that shape the system. It also reinforces the conclusion that these agents are unlikely to alter their behavior unless and until these underlying circumstances are changed.

Of course, social action is shaped not by situations but by the actor's perception of the situation. And perceptions of the circumstances in which crime occurs are, no doubt, overlaid by ideologies and stereotypes that are interpreted using institutional scripts and approached in ways that may be unnecessarily risk-averse or aggressive. But in the end, circumstances make a difference. And the fact that material realities are so very different in the United States must be accorded an important place in any theory of America's extraordinary penal state.

As I argue below, America's dual epidemics of criminal violence and state punishment have their roots in the socioeconomic circumstances in which so many poor people live in America—conditions imposed by the larger structures of political economy and exacerbated by the ubiquity of guns. These conditions diminish the social control capacities of families and communities; increase pressures for offenders to engage in violence; and prompt officials to engage in aggressive penal control. It is not racist or punitive ideologies that make American penality exceptional: such ideologies exist, they reinforce the penal state and contribute to its cruelty and excess—but they are not its fundamental cause. The fundamental explanation of the American difference has to do with the dangerous, disorganized milieus in which so many poor Americans are obliged to live and the political economy that causes them.

Patterns of crime, public reactions to crime, the available means of control, and decisions about the use of control—all of these are grounded in, and shaped by, specific socioeconomic milieus. And these milieus are, in turn, structured by America's political economy, which is to say by political and economic decisions made by federal, state, and local government; by state and federal courts; and by private economic actors, such as banks, property developers, insurance companies, landlords, and retailers.

When conservatives condemn the conduct of offenders and residents in these communities—or when progressives criticize the way that police, prosecutors, and courts respond to that conduct—they tend to forget these conditions or else suppose that the actors in question are somehow responsible for them. But socioeconomic conditions always form the terrain in which crime and crime control are rooted and the unstated background against which decisions and choices are made. And these conditions are shaped by broader social structures that are largely beyond the control of local actors. That the material circumstances experienced by America's poorest communities are so different from comparable nations—being so much more disorganized, so much more disorderly, and so much more violent—is a consideration that must be central to the explanation of America's extraordinary penal state.

Structures and Actions

A theory that grounds the penal state in political economy is not a single-factor explanation. It is a structural account, in which a complex field of human action (the penal state and its practices) is explained by showing how it is patterned by a complex set of institutional arrangements and structural forces (the political economy). And as noted earlier, that political economy consists of three interconnected structures—America's political institutions, its economy, and its racial order. This peculiar political economy—and the structural transformations it underwent after the 1960s—explains why the nation exhibits such high rates of violent crime and why it responded by adopting an aggressive regime of policing and punishment.

But political economy is not the complete causal story. Intermediate community-level processes and local policy choices are also involved. These intermediating processes and policies are, as already noted, relatively autonomous—which is to say they are patterned by structural forces but not fully determined by them—and they produce their own localized effects.

In our daily lives, we do not see or feel "structures" or "structural forces"— the concept refers to a theoretical abstraction rather than a lived experience. So, if social structures sometimes operate like an iron cage, as Max Weber (or rather his translator, Talcott Parsons) famously observed, the bars of that cage are mostly invisible to the people they constrain.[36] The result is that people do not ordinarily think in terms of structures, and when they do, they often do so poorly—especially when they apply structural reasoning to questions of crime and criminal justice. People on the left tend to overstate the effects of structures, often espousing a form of economic determinism that denies individual agency, forgets there can be a variety of responses to even the most forceful of structural pressures, and imagines that most criminal offenses are committed out of economic necessity. People on the right make the opposite error. They flatly deny the effects of socioeconomic structures, insisting on a version of free-will voluntarism and individual responsibility that is as harshly blaming as it is sociologically untenable. By describing the concrete, observable processes and forms of action that link macro-structures to micro-outcomes, I aim to avoid these abstractions and provide a more detailed account of how large social structures are brought to bear on the dynamics of crime, policing, and punishment.

In the chapters that follow, I first describe America's penal state in comparative perspective (chapter 3) and then analyze the control imperative that runs like a thread through the American apparatus of policing and punishment (chapter 4). I next describe America's political economy, again in a comparative perspective, together with an account of the history of violence in America and the nation's peculiar gun culture (chapter 5). Thereafter, I argue that the structural impacts of political economy operate via three causal pathways to create an American penal state that is, on virtually every dimension, an international outlier. My account of the first pathway, set out in chapter 6, traces how America's political economy, in the wake of deindustrialization and the decline of the New Deal order, disorganized communities and families and gave rise to extraordinary levels of lethal violence. The second pathway is analyzed in chapter 7, which shows how institutional design and limitations of local state capacity—together with the political preferences these help create—made penal control a recurring policy choice. The third pathway is traced in chapter 8, which shows how economic stratification and racial segregation established social distance and divisions that limit cross-class, cross-race solidarity—all of which enabled public support for the penal state and indifference to the harms it inflicted. In the epilogue, I consider the implications of my comparative structural analysis for political action, highlighting the possibility of a politics that might challenge America's law and order Leviathan, even in the absence of any large-scale transformation of the nation's political economy.

3

America's Penal State

PROTESTERS IN 2020 depicted America's penal state as racist and oppressive. Comparative research makes clear that it is also quite extraordinary. Relative to other developed nations, America's criminal legal system is an outlier on virtually every dimension. In certain respects, it is altogether exceptional.[1] This chapter describes that extraordinary penal state, contrasting it to policing, prosecution, and punishment in other nations. Subsequent chapters explain it.

When I talk of "the penal state," I am referring to the legal and institutional arrangements, as well as the personnel and physical infrastructure, through which duly constituted government authorities exercise "penal power"—the general term I use to describe the power to police, to prosecute, to surveil, to punish, and to control.[2] This penal power takes a variety of forms: the power to stop and search, powers of arrest, the power to levy fines, powers of detention, the power to indict, sentencing power, disciplinary power, surveillance power, carceral power, and so on. Each involves the use of legal authority, backed by force, by an agent of the state against an individual who is suspected, indicted, or convicted of a criminal offense.

The run-up of mass incarceration and mass supervision, like the spread of aggressive forms of policing, prosecution, and penal control occurred in a thirty-year period beginning in the mid-1970s. American penal practices in the first half of the twentieth century appear to have been more severe than elsewhere, particularly in the South, where prison farms, convict labor, chain gangs, and lynchings were common.[3] From the 1920s to the 1970s, America's average rate of incarceration (including prisons and jails) was generally twice as high as comparable countries.[4] Thirty years later it had grown to a level seven times as high as the West European average, six times as high as Canada, and more than four times as high as Australia's.[5] The penal state's footprint was largest in 2007 and 2008, when the daily population of America's jails and prisons reached 2.3 million, with 5 million more offenders subject to probation and parole. My aim here is to describe the structures and processes that generated that historic outcome. In the years since then, these rates have seen steady, though modest, declines, so that in 2024, the figures are 1.9 million and 3.7 million, respectively.[6]

America's penal state is neither singular nor unified. On the contrary: it is an institutional domain that is tremendously complex, being composed of a federal system that includes the Department of Justice, the Federal Bureau of Investigation, and the Federal Bureau of Prisons; fifty state systems, each with its own penal code, state police, and prison institutions; and thousands of municipal, city, and county jurisdictions with their own police departments, prosecutors, and jails.

The term *mass incarceration* is also a simplification. Commentators talk of mass incarceration as if it were a unitary phenomenon, but America's local, state, and federal penal systems are complex assemblages of laws, policies, and practices, each of which has developed over time. And far from being the realization of some national plan or singular dynamic, the penal confinement of millions of Americans, a disproportionate number of them Black—which is what *mass incarceration* signifies—is the cumulative result of multiple contributing causes, operating at distinct governmental levels, prompted by different events and considerations, involving diverse political actors and coalitions, and enacted through thousands of laws, policies, and enforcement practices. *Mass incarceration* is a shorthand term referring to an aggregate outcome, not to a singular phenomenon.[7] America's law and order colossus is a composite creature, assembled, piece by piece, over a thirty-year period.

Differences between and within American jurisdictions are also highly significant.[8] Localism—one might say "ultra-localism"—is a defining feature of the US polity and ensures that policymakers and activists across the nation are faced with quite different circumstances and fields of action. But the striking thing about the period from 1975 to 2010 is the remarkable degree to which the fifty states and the federal system moved in the same direction, adopting broadly similar policies.[9] This common trajectory and shared policy regime make it possible to generalize about America's penal state and to compare America to other nations—as I will do here. But it is well to recall that claims pitched at this national level necessarily conceal local variation.

The penal state that took shape in America in the last quarter of the twentieth century was a truly extraordinary one, projecting penal control more comprehensively than any other developed nation.[10] As a result, by 2013, fully

45 percent of the American population had an immediate family member who had been incarcerated. For Black families, the number was 63 percent.[11] In this chapter, I set out a systematic description of America's penal state, highlighting its most distinctive features and placing them in comparative perspective. In the following chapter, I identify the penal control logic these features have in common and explain why American penality came to take this form.[12]

Policing

Policing is a complex function in any society, typically undertaken by a multiplicity of public and private agencies.[13] I focus here on the public police who form the front line of America's penal state, but even this institution operates at many governmental levels and engages in many kinds of activity.

The vast majority of sworn police officers work for municipal or county-level police departments, but there are also federal law enforcement agencies such as the FBI, the Drug Enforcement Administration, the US Marshals Service and so on, as well as state agencies, such as state troopers and state highway patrols. As for police activities, these range from quasi-military riot squads and armed crime-fighting units to highway patrols and traffic cops; from SWAT teams and rapid response tactical units to community police officers working with social service agencies. This multiplicity, together with the remarkable fact that there are more than fifteen thousand independent police departments in the nation, means that generalizations and comparative claims about American policing must be hung with many caveats.[14] Nevertheless, we can venture the following observations.

Since the 1980s, US police departments have become more aggressively "proactive," particularly in high-crime communities. This form of policing involves deploying officers to crime "hot spots"; using stop and frisk extensively; pulling over cars; and engaging more actively with the public—in contrast to the older, "reactive" approach where police saw their primary task as responding rapidly to 911 calls.[15] Incentivized by federal subsidies, enabled by new management techniques such as CompStat, and guided by new theories such as "broken windows" policing, American police in the 1980s and 1990s ramped up drug law enforcement, gave more attention to low-level "quality of life" offenses, escalated the use of stop and frisk, and increased arrest rates.[16]

American policing is unusual in several important respects. Policing in most nations is organized at a local level, but countries generally have national or regional authorities that fund, coordinate, and direct local law enforcement.

In the United States, by contrast, policing is organized, funded, and directed at the local level, being decentralized and devolved to an exceptional extent.[17] Police everywhere take steps to limit illegal drug use, but the American "War on Drugs" saw a level of enforcement and punishment that was altogether extraordinary. "Stop and search" is a standard practice of police forces everywhere and an important, albeit problematic, technique of crime control.[18] What is not standard is the use of stop and frisk on a mass basis, without reasonable cause, focused on young men in communities of color, but this was for several years the policy of police departments in large American cities. At its height this policy led to hundreds of thousands of on-the-street encounters each year—some 685,000 in New York City in 2011 and more than 714,000 in Chicago in 2014—before lawsuits and public criticism caused the policy to be scaled back.[19]

Police departments greatly expanded in these decades, adding thousands of new officers, often as a result of federal funding.[20] Police officers were increasingly posted in public schools and public housing, extending the penal state's reach and increasing the frequency of encounters with schoolkids and housing project residents.[21] These encounters led to increased arrests, to ever larger numbers of people with criminal records, and to the development of the "school-to-prison pipeline"—a process that transformed school disciplinary incidents into criminal charges and carceral sanctions for thousands of young people.

Compared to police in other affluent nations—many of which have more public police than the United States on a per capita basis—American police receive less training, are less well paid, and are recruited with fewer qualifications.[22] They are also routinely armed, and what little training they receive focuses mostly on preparing them to use deadly force and to avoid being shot or assaulted.[23] American police kill civilians—particularly Black civilians—at a rate that is many times higher than that of comparable nations.[24] As one expert put it: "About a thousand people are killed by the police each year in the United States, vastly more than in any country to which we would care to compare ourselves. This is true even after adjusting for population: the odds of getting killed by the police are roughly five times higher in the United States than, for example, in Canada, Australia, England, Italy, or Germany."[25]

US police officers are killed in the line of duty too, and at a much higher rate than in comparable nations. But the ratio of police killings to police deaths is exceptionally high. In other western nations around two civilians are killed for every police officer killed; in the United States the ratio is 20:1.[26] As for nonlethal force, we lack reliable comparative data, and the police forces of nations such as France are notoriously brutal.[27] But the comparatively high death rate from US police-civilian encounters where firearms were not involved suggests that brutal treatment may also be more frequent in America.[28]

"Revenue policing" is another feature of American policing that is increasingly prevalent and comparatively unusual. It refers to the deployment of police departments as fiscal arms of the local state, imposing fines and collecting monetary payments from offenders and their families.[29] In many American towns and cities, large numbers of poor people incur legal debt because of their involvement with criminal justice. This prompts people to avoid police for fear of being arrested for nonpayment, with the result that traffic stops and police-civilian encounters become fraught and conflictual. A video of Walter Scott being shot and killed as he ran from a police officer in Charleston in 2015 shows the kind of tragedy that can result. Scott, a fifty-year-old Black man, was in arrears for child support and had previously been jailed on contempt charges.[30]

Prosecution

Prosecutors are the most powerful actors in America's criminal legal system. Given the ubiquity of guilty pleas in the United States, it is now prosecutors and not judges who function as the de facto sentencers in most cases, making them responsible for much of the prison growth that occurred between 1975 and 2008.[31] Being political as well as legal actors, district attorneys have used their considerable discretion to align criminal penalties with public preferences, which, in the 1980s and 1990s, meant adopting an aggressive crime control posture. Like policing, prosecution expanded and became more aggressive in the 1990s and 2000s.[32] Empowered by tough-on-crime legislation that made numerous offenses punishable by mandatory minimums and by sentence enhancements that ratcheted up penalties for sexual, violent, weapon-related, and repeat offenses, prosecutors routinely piled on multiple charges and used the threat of severe sentences to extort guilty pleas or information.[33] Imprisonment-to-arrest ratios increased greatly as a result.[34] So did guilty pleas, which rose from 77 percent of cases in federal district court in 1980 to 95 percent in 2010—an expedited form of justice that is much less common in other nations.[35]

This prosecutorial conveyor belt, churning out massive numbers of guilty pleas, is a vital part of the machinery that enables and sustains mass incarceration. Because prosecutors control pretrial detention, they effectively determine the size of the jail population. And even without entering a guilty plea, tens of thousands of low-level defendants are subjected to burdensome controls, criminal marking, and reporting requirements, as Issa Kohler-Hausmann showed in a study of how prosecutors in New York City process misdemeanor defendants.[36]

In most nations, prosecutors are career civil servants who are not permitted political involvements. In the United States, by contrast, the district attorneys who head up local and state prosecution offices (there are twenty-three hundred of them in total) are mostly elected, and many go on to run for state governor or for a seat in the US Congress. Prosecutors' associations function as political lobbyists, and during the law and order decades they were among the interest groups lobbying for tougher penalties. More recently, these associations have opposed efforts to scale back drug law penalties and to eliminate sentence enhancements and mandatory sentences.[37]

In the last ten years or so, opposition to overcriminalization and mass incarceration has sparked a "progressive prosecutors" movement that has sought to elect district attorneys committed to limiting the use of incarceration, decriminalizing low-level drug possession, and increasing the use of "diversion" and alternatives to custody. These efforts succeeded in liberal districts in San Francisco, Oakland, Philadelphia, Baltimore, Los Angeles, and New York City—though several progressive prosecutors have since been de-selected or had their powers curtailed by more conservative state governors.[38]

Sentencing

Sentencing in American criminal courts became increasingly severe from 1980 onward and is, in most respects, much harsher than in comparable jurisdictions elsewhere.[39] Legislative developments such as mandatory sentences, statutory sentencing guidelines, and "truth in sentencing" laws functioned to reduce the judge's control of sentencing outcomes, even as it increased the power of the prosecutor. That judges at the state and local levels are mostly elected has meant that the judiciary has rarely acted as a brake on "tough on crime" trends or oppressive plea deals secured by prosecutors.[40]

American law permits certain penalties, such as the death penalty and life imprisonment without parole, that are prohibited in much of the developed world. In fact, capital punishment has been declining in the United States since 1998, although the death penalty is still on the books in half of the states and is actively used in a dozen of them.[41] Until recently, it appeared that the federal death penalty had been de facto abolished, since no one had been executed for almost twenty years. But in the final year of President Trump's 2017–2021 administration, thirteen people were put to death in rapid succession, constituting a gruesome confirmation of the theory that capital punishment is now a form of political display rather than a routine criminal justice practice.[42] The second Trump administration may well see a revival of this most controversial of sanctions and heighten still further the contrast between the United States and other western nations.

Sentences of life imprisonment and of life imprisonment without parole are routinely imposed in all fifty American states and in the federal system. In fact, there are currently two hundred thousand prisoners serving life sentences, two-thirds of them people of color, and fifty-five thousand of them without prospect of parole—meaning that they will spend the remainder of their lives in prison.[43] By contrast, nations such as Norway, Portugal, and Spain do not permit life sentences at all, let alone life without possibility of parole. And where life sentences are permitted in other nations, "life" usually means from ten to thirty years.[44] When mass murderer Anders Behring Breivik was convicted in Norway in 2012, he was sentenced to twenty-one years imprisonment—the maximum term under that country's law. Breivik, who had killed seventy-nine people and injured more than four hundred others, became eligible for parole after serving ten years of his sentence. As of now, he remains in custody, and he is unlikely to be released before the end of his sentence. But Norwegian law holds open the possibility of rehabilitation and insists on regular parole hearings even in the most heinous cases.[45]

Penalties for drug offending are higher in the United States than elsewhere and were very much higher when the War on Drugs was at its height in the 1980s and 1990s.[46] During these years, American authorities incarcerated people for drug-law violations at a rate that was higher than West European countries imprisoned people for all offenses combined.[47] Sentence enhancements—additional prison time imposed for repeat offending, weapons possession, violence, and sexual offending—are also exceptionally severe in the United States. In other countries, prior convictions typically increase sentences by marginal amounts. In America, repeat offending can double or triple the sentence.[48]

American courts impose sentences of imprisonment at a much higher rate than courts in other countries. In the United States in 2009, 73 percent of convicted felony offenders received prison sentences. National figures on the jailing of those convicted of misdemeanors are not available, but it is estimated that in the state of Minnesota, where data is available, 75 percent of those convicted of felonies or misdemeanors are sent to prison or jail.[49] In Germany, the equivalent figure in 2015 was between 5 and 6 percent, with 12 percent receiving a suspended prison sentence and the remainder being fined.[50] Across ten European countries, the rate at which convicted offenders are sentenced to imprisonment ranges from a low of 3 percent (Finland) to a high of 28 percent (the Netherlands).[51] Sentences of imprisonment—and time served in custody—are generally much longer in the United States than they are elsewhere.[52] According to the most recent American data, the average terms of imprisonment imposed on offenders by state courts were 91 months for violent offenses and 40 months for property offenses. By contrast, fewer than 2 percent of sentences in ten European nations were longer than 12 months.[53]

Incarceration

America's incarcerated population grew continuously from 1975 until 2008, giving rise to a comparatively and historically extreme rate of imprisonment that targeted whole groups of the population.[54] At its peak in 2008, more than 2.3 million people were in the nation's jails and prisons, and more than 10 million individuals passed through these institutions each year. At a per capita rate of 765 per 100,000, this level of incarceration was seven times as high as the Western European average and more than ten times as high as nations such as Norway, Sweden, Denmark, Germany, and the Netherlands.[55] The US rate was also seven times as high as that of Canada, its neighbor to the north, even though Canada's crime and violence rates had, like America's, increased steadily between the 1960s and the 1990s, albeit from a much lower base.[56]

With the emergence of mass incarceration, imprisonment changed from a rare event affecting individuals on the margins of society to a common characteristic of poor communities and a normal life course event for entire demographic groups. Young Black men were incarcerated on an unheard-of scale, with more than two-thirds of those without a high school degree being imprisoned at some point in their lives. In certain neighborhoods, there were "million-dollar blocks" where incarceration was so common that it cost more than $1 million per year to incarcerate residents from that block alone.[57] Incarceration was thereby transformed from a small background institution dealing with individual deviants to an organizing principle in the lives of poor people and their communities. And as the penal state grew, it became the basis for a multi-billion-dollar commercial industry—the "prison-industrial complex"—a factor that will surely obstruct efforts to decarcerate on any large scale.[58]

After 2008, America's incarceration rates stabilized and trended slightly downward, as declining crime rates reduced the throughput of cases, and concerns about fiscal costs and racial bias prompted a scaling back of drug-offense penalties and enforcement.[59] The Supreme Court's *Brown v. Plata* decision—ordering California to downsize its overcrowded prisons—together with efforts by several states to reduce prison spending, further reduced the national rate.[60] Larger reductions occurred during the pandemic years, as court systems closed and correctional authorities granted emergency releases to curb the spread of COVID-19 inside jails and prisons. The overall result is that America's incarceration rate has fallen from its 2008 peak of 765 per 100,000 to 608 per 100,000 in 2022. Even after these considerable reductions, America's imprisonment rate remains more than five times as high as that of Canada and the Western European average.[61]

There is an institutional division between prisons and jails in the United States that does not exist in other nations. In the American system, prisons are administered by state and federal authorities, housing convicted offenders serving a sentence of one year or longer. Jails are administered by cities and counties and mostly hold untried defendants (those who have been deemed a flight risk or a danger to the public and cannot afford cash bail) together with convicted misdemeanants serving sentences of up to twelve months as well as recently sentenced offenders awaiting transfer to state prison.

Jails

There are more than thirty-one hundred jails in the United States, ranging from tiny lockups holding a few detainees to large complexes such as Rikers Island in New York City, Cook County Jail in Chicago, and the Los Angeles County Jail System, which hold many thousands of inmates. The nation's aggregate jail population reached a peak of seven hundred thousand in 2008, with more than 10 million individuals passing through these institutions in the course of a year. Today, the daily population is around half a million.[62]

Detention prior to trial is more common in America than in other nations.[63] In most US jurisdictions, there is a system of cash bail, which means that defendants are detained in custody unless they post a monetary bond guaranteeing reappearance in court when their case is heard. Bail is typically set at a level in excess of what defendants have at their disposal, so most are obliged to borrow from bail bond firms—commercial businesses that charge fees and extend loans at extortionate costs in return for posting bail for a defendant. This for-profit bail bond system—another distinctive American institution—means that many unconvicted defendants must choose between spending time in jail or going into serious debt.[64]

Some of those held in jail have committed serious crimes and will be transferred to state prison following conviction and sentencing. But most are low-level offenders who cycle in and out of custody, more in need of social support and healthcare than criminal punishment. Mental illness is very common in this population, as is drug and alcohol addiction, physical ill health, unemployment, illiteracy, and homelessness.[65] In other affluent nations, people with these conditions are taken care of by healthcare and welfare agencies. In the United States, local jails are where they end up. And being funded by local taxation, these institutions rarely have the resources needed to deal with such problems.

Prisons

America's prisons are also numerous (there are 1,566 state prisons and 122 federal penitentiaries), diverse, and difficult to describe in general terms.[66] State corrections departments administer multiple institutions across different states and regions, and the varying levels of expenditure are a rough indicator of differences in the quality of prison regimes and the wages of prison staff.[67] Mississippi spends $18,000 per prisoner each year, the least of any state, while California spends more than $131,000 per prisoner.[68] Regionally, the lowest expenditure is by southern and southwestern states, whereas the highest is in California and the northeast.

Federal penitentiaries also exhibit considerable variation, ranging from minimum-security prison camps to tightly controlled "supermax" prisons such as ADX Florence in Colorado, reputed to be the most repressive in America. In the 1990s, as prison populations expanded, state funding declined, and Congress cut back programs in federal prisons, "cheap and mean" prison regimes—previously a feature of the south and the southwest—became standard across much of the nation.[69]

Instances of cruelty or neglect can be uncovered in prison systems everywhere, but conditions in America's prisons and jails are by most measures more severe than in those of other affluent nations. Comparative data suggests that American institutions exhibit more violence, more solitary confinement, less rehabilitative programming, and fewer staff, most of whom are less well trained.[70] In contrast to some European and most Nordic nations, where custodial regimes aim to provide conditions that bear close resemblance to life outside prison, the principle of "normalization" (which guarantees the right to vote, the right to a family life, and the right to healthcare at the normal social standard) plays virtually no role in America's prisons, which are more concerned to ensure that no incarcerated person enjoys conditions better than, or equivalent to, those experienced by the least well-off people outside prison—a principle the Victorians referred to as "less eligibility."[71]

That American prisons have, on average, relatively few officers per inmate also contributes to the poor quality of regimes and their administration. According to Bill Keller, "Staffing levels in Germany are about two employees (officers, counselors, medical personnel) for every three residents. In Norway, the ratio approaches one-to-one." In contrast, the Bureau of Justice Statistics reports that "state prisons in the US typically operate on a prisoner-staff ratio of five-to-one, and federal prisons more than ten-to-one."[72] American prisons are also less regulated—whether by courts, inspectors, or ombudsmen—than are the prisons of other nations, a feature that increases the likelihood of abuse and mismanagement.[73]

Low levels of provision continue when America's prisoners are released from custody, with most states and localities providing released inmates little more than a few dollars and perhaps bus fare.[74] In November 2020, hundreds of inmates were released from New Jersey prisons as an emergency measure to reduce the spread of COVID. The released men—many of them long-termers who had spent decades in prison, some of them physically and mentally impaired—were left on a winter street with no social services, no government ID, no housing, and no health care.[75] The welfare states of other affluent nations do not permit these levels of deprivation. When prisoners are released in Norway—to take a strikingly contrastive example—the Norwegian government guarantees offers of employment, education, suitable housing, medical services, addiction treatment, and debt counseling.[76] Such measures do not guarantee against recidivism, which is a problem for every system. But they do ensure that former prisoners are not forced to live in the kinds of disorganized, desperate circumstances that are the fate of so many in the United States.

Correctional Supervision

Like incarceration, correctional supervision—the surveillance and control of offenders "in the community"—is used more extensively and intensively in the United States than in any other nation. And like incarceration, supervision numbers surged continuously for several decades with the number of people on probation nearly tripling and parole numbers nearly quadrupling between 1980 and 2020.[77] At its peak in 2008, there were 5 million Americans on probation or parole, a per capita rate of supervision far greater than in any other nation and more than four times the average European rate.[78] The license conditions attaching to supervision orders in the United States are also more numerous and more onerous than elsewhere, making license revocation and incarceration that much more likely. Several states permit "lifetime probation"—a sentence that is unknown in Europe.[79]

In most developed nations, probation and parole are penal-welfare measures carried out by officers whose job is to support and resettle offenders, helping them access social services and find housing and employment.[80] For much of the twentieth century, that was true in America as well. But increasingly since the 1970s, probation and parole in the United States have become measures of penal control, undertaken by armed agents who are quick to return supervisees to prison if they test positive for banned substances or violate license conditions.[81] Instead of being alternatives to imprisonment, American-style probation and parole function as indirect "trip wire" routes *into* prison, with parole revocations in some states accounting for as many as a third of prison admissions.[82] And, in a shift that decreases costs while increasing control, supervision is increasingly imposed not by means of personal visits or office appointments but by electronic monitoring—a GPS monitor attached by means of a wrist or ankle bracelet—permitting round-the-clock surveillance.[83]

Collateral Consequences, Fees and Charges, and User-Pays Punishment

Another distinctive feature of America's penal state is the widespread use of "collateral consequences"—the imposition of disqualifications, ineligibilities, exclusions, banishment, deportation, and public criminal records—as a routine concomitant of criminal conviction.[84] Such restrictions—which are generally civil law measures that state legislators have added to criminal penalties—are more extensive, more onerous, and more enduring in the United States than elsewhere.[85] Their combined effect has been to disenfranchise massive numbers of former offenders; render them ineligible for welfare benefits such as affordable housing or student loans; bar them from specified occupations and residential areas; and mark some 79 million Americans with a criminal record that is publicly available and may continue in perpetuity.[86] Collateral consequences of some kind attach to crime convictions in most jurisdictions, but no other nation subjects former offenders to this degree of exclusion, discrimination, and control.

Finally, there is the distinctively American practice of imposing criminal justice fees and "user-pays" charges on offenders and their families, a collateral consequence of a distinctly commercial nature.[87] Most American states and localities now impose fees, charges, and processing costs on offenders and their families, burdening them with debt they can usually ill afford.[88] In some states, jail and prison inmates are charged a "pay-to-stay" fee for their time in custody. Probationers pay monthly supervision fees and are expected to meet the cost of drug tests. Defendants are charged legal fees for the processing of their cases. Individuals placed in diversion programs are charged for the privilege. Suspects who resist arrest are charged for the cost of the Tasers used to shock and subdue them.[89]

These fees, fines, and charges are, in effect, a criminal justice tax levied on offenders, the aim being to offset the system's costs and relieve the burden on local taxpayers. According to one estimate, "About 10 million Americans ... owe about $50 billion in debt due to criminal justice fines and fees in America today—and make nearly $40 billion in payments on their legal financial obligations each year."[90] Again, no other nation has such arrangements.

These, then, are the distinctive features of America's penal state, viewed in comparative perspective. It is, as we have seen, a complex assemblage of laws, powers, and practices operating at all levels of government: a composite creature that is massive in its reach and, quite often, shockingly cheap and shabby in its substance. The following chapter describes how these powers are deployed, the impacts they have had, and the control imperative that animates the whole apparatus.

4

The Control Imperative

AMERICA'S PENAL state is an extraordinary apparatus projecting penal power more extensively and intensively than that of any comparable nation. But how does that apparatus function? What logics underlie its operation? And why *these* specific logics and not others more in line with other nations?

To answer these questions, it is necessary to view the penal state through a social science lens rather than a legal one—a shift in perspective reminding us that, alongside the tasks of crime control and law enforcement, criminal legal systems everywhere also aim to govern the poor.[1] Policing and punishment certainly function to uphold the law, deter offending, and sanction offenders. But together with the labor market, social work, social services, and the welfare state more generally, penal states are involved in the management of poor people and the conditions in which they live. To capture this aspect of things, we have to set aside official rationales and view policing and punishment from the perspective of political economy.

Modern capitalism is, as Joseph Schumpeter observed, a system of creative destruction. But American capitalism, being relatively unrestrained, is more than usually creative and more than usually destructive.[2] The disruptive market forces characterizing America's political economy are, by comparison with other developed nations, very weakly restrained, thanks to the nation's employer-friendly labor markets and its market-friendly welfare state. The result is that working people's lives are more insecure, and the social organization of poor communities more precarious, than is true in other developed nations.

Deprived of economic resources and social supports—as urban communities increasingly were following the economic restructuring and the rightward shift of the 1970s—the social efficacy and control capacities of poor families and neighborhoods become attenuated, leading to disorder, crime, and violence. These problems attract the attention of penal state agencies and the imposition of coercive controls. In the 1980s and 1990s in poor neighborhoods across the United States, social order was increasingly maintained not by the spontaneous, informal controls of family, school, neighborhood, and workplace but instead by state controls of policing and punishment, the latter striving to compensate for the inadequacies of the former. To function as a substitute for the organic controls of civil society, America's criminal legal system developed a new logic of ever greater expansion and ever more intensive penal control. As it did so, the penal state moved from the margins of social life in America's poorest neighborhoods to somewhere nearer its core.

To trace how this shift occurred, we can begin by asking: who are the chief targets of America's penal state? And where does it project its power?

If penal officials faithfully enforced the law without bias or favor, the answer to this question would be "people who commit crimes or are reasonably suspected of having done so." But law enforcement is always targeted rather than uniformly distributed. It generally investigates "street crime" rather than the crimes of the powerful, poor neighborhoods rather than wealthy enclaves, and "known criminals" rather than a random selection of the population. Penal power is directed sharply downward, rarely troubling the wealthy or the well connected.

In the United States, Black people and the neighborhoods of concentrated disadvantage where so many of them live are disproportionately subject to police attention, experiencing more stops, more arrests, and more use of force by police officers than other ethnic groups.[3] Racial disparities in police killings, in highway stops, and in stop and frisk encounters have been repeatedly observed by research studies and documented in legal proceedings.[4] Black people are more likely than any other group to be shot and killed by the police. With respect to unarmed persons killed by the police, the disparity between Black and White people is greater still.[5] Between 2015 and January 2023, the rate of fatal police shootings among Black Americans stood at 5.9 per million per year; for White Americans it was 2.3 per million.[6]

Racial disparity is likewise a characteristic of American incarceration.[7] There is clear overrepresentation of people of color in jails and prisons and marked overrepresentation of Black people, who constitute 14 percent of America's population but more than 38 percent of those imprisoned. One in three Black men born in the 1970s will spend time in prison during their lifetime; that proportion rises to two out of three among those who did not complete high school.[8]

With respect to most offenses, and drug offenses in particular, this disparity is largely the result of racial bias and targeted enforcement, though with respect to crimes of violence, enforcement more nearly mirrors levels of crime involvement.[9] All else being equal, Black people are more likely to be stopped, more likely to be charged, more likely to be prosecuted, more likely to be sent to custody, and more likely to be given longer sentences than White people.[10] These impacts spill over into the families and communities of those immediately affected. In 2014, one in four women in America—and 44 percent of Black women—had a family member currently in prison. In the year 2000, some 2.1 million children had an incarcerated father.[11]

The racial complexion of America's prison and jail populations is striking and disturbing, but it ought not to obscure the economic class character of criminal justice in the United States. An overwhelming proportion of the penal state's clientele is undereducated, mentally or physically ill, and poor.[12] This is partly because America's penal state is decidedly unenergetic in its pursuit of corporate and white-collar offenders but mostly because street crimes are overwhelmingly committed by poor people.[13] Black people are much more likely than White people to be poor and to live in high-crime neighborhoods, so the disparate racial rates of incarceration are, in part, a function of class stratification.[14] That White high school dropouts are ten times more likely to be imprisoned than college-educated Blacks is a clear indication that social class, and not just race, is a causal factor.[15] The role of economics is also confirmed by the fact that incarceration rates for low-skilled workers—predominantly Blacks in the 1980s and 1990s and Whites in the twenty-first century—have risen as the demand for low-skilled labor has fallen in the US economy.[16]

Unlike other aspects of the American penal state, these disparate racial and class impacts are not unusual in comparative terms, even if their extent is extraordinary. Nations such as Canada, Britain, Australia, and Germany all exhibit levels of racial disparity in imprisonment greater than American levels.[17] So while racial disparity is a defining feature of mass incarceration in the United States—and anti-Black sentiment may explain some of its severity and extent—this is a characteristic it shares with other nations.

Impacts of the Penal State

The racial cast of America's penal state—which is well beyond anything that can be explained by differential crime involvement—is clearly a moral outrage. But what about the extraordinary size and reach of the system? Is that objectionable in itself? Might it somehow be justified?[18]

One normative rationale for America's penal state frequently voiced by conservatives is that aggressive policing and punishment are essential tools for curbing violent crime. Rates of homicide and armed robbery in the United States are, as we have seen, extraordinarily high relative to other developed nations, and conservatives insist that these rates necessitate an aggressive control response. Defenders of the penal state also point out that the decades when American policing, prosecution, and punishment were at their most aggressive—the 1990s and 2000s—coincided with significant declines in homicide, armed robbery, and most categories of crime. As Attorney General William Barr put it in 1992, "The experience of the last thirty years supports the common-sense notion that tough law enforcement works.... [T]here is less crime today than there would have been had we not substantially increased incarceration of criminals in the 1980s."[19] What should we make of these claims?

The evidence for a causal link between increased incarceration and decreased crime, or between aggressive policing and reductions in gun crime, is mixed and inconclusive. One or two influential writers insist that the growing power of the penal state and the incarceration of millions of offenders has had no impact on crime rates, which, they claim, declined for reasons unrelated to policing and punishment.[20] I regard this view as implausible. Others more reasonably estimate that between 10 and 25 percent of the crime drop is attributable to the deterrent and incapacitation effects of mass incarceration, and one expert has argued that improvements in policing effectiveness caused the large crime declines that occurred in New York City and other urban areas in the 1990s and 2000s.[21]

A massive penal state surely suppresses crime and violence to some extent—even if contact with the police or time in prison have criminogenic effects that offset this to a degree.[22] The incapacitation of millions of young men during their high-crime years is bound to have reduced offending, just as the pervasive use of "stop and frisk" in high-crime urban neighborhoods undoubtedly deterred the routine carrying of guns and, with it, the frequency with which casual altercations resulted in lethal violence. There were no doubt other causes at work—the retrofitting of situational crime prevention measures, perhaps, or the crime-suppressing activities of business and community groups—but it is implausible to think that the temporal association of a large decline in violent crime and the massive buildup of aggressive policing and punishment was mere coincidence.[23]

However, even if America's penal state did indeed contribute to a reduction in the nation's rates of crime and violence, this does not amount to a normative justification. There are several reasons for this. First, despite its extraordinary deployment of penal power, the United States *remains* much more violent than any other developed nation, and the states with the highest rates of incarceration also exhibit the highest rates of homicide and violent crime.[24] Moreover, there is a great deal of violent conduct behind bars that does not figure in the nation's crime statistics.[25] Aggressive policing, prosecution, and punishment may have curbed street crime and made cities safer, but they failed to make the United States anywhere near as safe as comparable countries. Second, in the 1990s and 2000s, New York City and New York State experienced steep declines in violent crime *and* a marked decline in jail and imprisonment rates, suggesting that reductions in violence can occur independently of increases in punishment and that America's penal state is evidently larger than it needs to be to control violence.[26] Third, an emerging body of evidence points to the crime-control efficacy of nonpenal interventions. The American neighborhoods where violence rates declined in the 1990s and 2000s turn out to be ones where community activists and business improvement districts took steps to improve public safety without resorting to harsh policing or incarceration.[27] So even if we grant America's massive penal state some efficacy in suppressing crime and violence, as I think we must, we are also obliged to ask: at what cost? And in the face of which alternatives?

Whatever crime-suppressing effects America's penal state has had, these were achieved on the backs of thousands of young Black men being harassed and humiliated on the streets where they live; millions of Americans languishing behind bars; and tens of millions whose justice-system involvements load them with debt, damage their health, bar them from legal employment, and exclude them from family life and political participation. Nor are these harms confined to individuals who have offended. The success of "stop and frisk" as a gun control tactic depends on convincing potential offenders that the police are omnipresent, "a message that is communicated largely by stopping enough people," the vast majority of whom are not guilty of any offense.[28] In other words, this policy depends on the harassment of masses of innocent individuals, most of whom will be poor people of color. The penal state's adverse effects also spill over to the children of offenders, their families, and the neighborhoods in which they reside.[29] They affect police-community relations and the political ties that connect individuals to the state, causing alienation from legal authority and a diminished form of citizenship.[30] People come to fear the police and distrust authorities. Residents become less willing to report crime, to provide witness testimony, or to cooperate with the police—which in turn causes crime to increase and clearance rates to decline. Homicide clearance rates fall to low levels—sometimes below 50 percent—in the worst affected communities, allowing offenders to kill with near impunity.[31] And as America has repeatedly witnessed, broken relations between communities and police can lead to serious disturbances and civic unrest.[32] In short, whatever crime-suppressing effects an aggressive penal state may achieve, the massive deployment of penal power detrimentally affects millions of justice-involved individuals, their families, and their communities, while worsening race relations and undermining social justice.

Phrased in social scientific terms, American policing and punishment are comparative outliers and deviations from the common standards of developed nations. Expressed more directly, in normative language, they are shockingly illiberal abuses of state power that unnecessarily inflict indignity, humiliation, and suffering on fellow Americans. That the homicide rates of American cities reached levels altogether unknown in other developed nations signals a failure of the first duty of the American state, which is to keep its citizens safe. That officials at all governmental levels opted for aggressive policing and penal controls in response to this problem is—or ought to be—a scandal in a nation that claims to be a liberal democracy.

However, in making these choices, American officials and policymakers were not faced with an open vista of possibility. On the contrary. As I show in the following chapters, American violence and the political responses that it engendered were overdetermined by structural arrangements. These structures—and the powerful interests supporting them—sharply constrained policy options and limited the extent to which American authorities could pursue the strategies favored by more social democratic nations.

A Control Imperative

America deploys penal power more than any other developed nation. It also deploys that power in a manner that is quite distinctive—a distinctiveness, I will argue, that provides the key to understanding the inherent logic of the American system.[33]

Writers have, with good reason, characterized the US system as harsh, degrading, cruel, and racist.[34] But none of these descriptors perfectly captures the American penal state's signature characteristic, which is, I will argue, the imposition of *penal control*—that is to say, the use of criminal law to impose coercive restraints on a person's freedom of movement and range of action.

If we consider the whole field of American criminal legal practices that emerged between 1975 and 2008, the imposition of penal controls on individuals deemed to threaten public safety is the principal logic and functional imperative that drives the whole apparatus.[35] By "penal control" I mean a specific mode of exercising penal power that aims not to exact retribution, or extract resources, or correct behavior—though these may be ancillary purposes—but instead to impose restrictions, restraints, and various forms of incapacitation that limit the freedom of movement and range of action of the person subject to them.[36]

Penal control is not punishment's only aim, nor its sole meaning: penal sanctions are intrinsically polysemic and are rarely reducible to a single function. And in other times and places, penal measures have emphasized other purposes, such as levying compensation, imposing afflictive injuries, or providing offenders with correctional assistance.[37] In America in the 1950s and 1960s, for example, many states passed expungement and rehabilitation laws erasing past convictions; early release was much more common; reimprisonment of parolees was less frequent; home leave and furlough programs commonly assisted with prisoner resettlement, and probation and parole emphasized social work rather than penal control.[38] But in contemporary America, penal control has become the essential, indispensable core of sanctions imposed by the state. Penal measures may exhibit secondary or tertiary aims—such as deterrence, cost control, or victim satisfaction—but these are rarely allowed to dilute the control functions that are, time and again, the primary aim of the sanction.

Take, for example, penal practices that have been characterized as "vengeful" or "degrading" or "cheap and mean."[39] On closer inspection, it becomes apparent that none of these practices involve any relaxation of penal control: the characterizations referring to their gratuitous cruelty, degradation, or cheapness typically describe the manner *by which penal controls are imposed*. Cheap and mean punishments (such as the "no frills" prison regimes of the 1990s) are the result of an underfunded penal state tasked by a tax-averse electorate with imposing extended penal controls at minimum cost. And harsh, vengeful sanctions (such as three-strikes laws, life imprisonment without parole, or the death penalty) are instances of punitive public sentiments being expressed in sanctions that combine penal control with penal degradation. The same might be said of criminal justice fees and charges or the exclusion of former felons from welfare benefits: these measures have rationales—vengeance, cost-saving, victim-satisfaction, deterrence, and so on—that go beyond the imposition of penal control. But all these measures operate in ways that neither diminish nor obstruct the control potential of the measures in question. They are all forms of penal control.

There is also a negative example—a practice that America's penal state *refrains* from adopting—that helps confirm the claim. In the sentencing patterns of most affluent nations, we see a reliance on the use of monetary penalties—above all, stand-alone fines—as the sentence of choice for all but the most serious offenses.[40] These fines have an obvious utility: they avoid the taint of imprisonment; they allow offenders to remain connected to their homes, their families, and their jobs; their administration is relatively cheap; and they generate revenues for the state. One would, therefore, have expected them to feature prominently in the sentencing practice of America's cost-conscious legal system. But in fact, *stand-alone* fines are rarely used by American sentencers, other than for traffic offenses and corporations, though fines are frequently imposed as an *add-on* to sentences of probation, jail, or imprisonment.[41] Given the concern to minimize public spending and the importance of the cash nexus in US society, one would have predicted that America's deployment of monetary sanctions would be at the top end of any international distribution. That the exact opposite is the case is revealing. If American courts use stand-alone fines so infrequently to deal with nontrivial offending, it is likely because, in the American context, fines lack the control aspect considered essential to penal measures.[42]

The leading characteristic of American criminal justice is not deterrence, nor retribution, nor rehabilitation. It is the imposition of penal control, a fundamental imperative that is firmly embedded in today's sentencing law and that underpins the whole culture of law enforcement. This stress on penal control and the extent of its deployment set America apart from other nations, such as Canada, Australia, or the countries of Western Europe. Sentencers in all these nations certainly impose penal controls. But they give a much larger place to stand-alone fines, suspended sentences, and penal-welfare measures in which coercive control is much less integral.[43]

The concern to maximize penal control also shapes American policing, with its proactive policies; its harassment of minority youth in the form of stop and frisk; its demand for instant compliance; its warrior style; and its extraordinarily high rates of civilian killings.[44] It shapes aggressive prosecution, with its routine overcharging, speedy extraction of guilty pleas, close monitoring of misdemeanants, and insistence on lengthy prison sentences for felony offenders. It shapes mass incarceration and mass supervision, together with the tangle of collateral consequences that ensnares millions of former felons in elaborate controls long after they have served their sentences. It even shapes sentencing legislation, much of which, since 1980, has been designed to constrain judicial and parole board discretion, lest lenient officials are inclined to relax controls on offenders or grant early release to incarcerated people.

Policing, prosecution, sentencing, incarceration, correctional supervision, collateral consequences—each of these is institutionally distinct, with its own specific history, values, and purposes. That each domain was, in the 1980s and 1990s, pulled into a shared project of maximizing penal control speaks to the power and extent of this undertaking.

As American penality came to revolve around penal control in the decades after 1980, the liberal values that previously shaped criminal justice were largely set aside. Proportionality had been a basic principle of sentencing, with the seriousness of the offense limiting the extent to which a lawbreaker could be punished. But there is nothing proportionate about the mandatory penalties now imposed on drug offenders or about the sentence enhancements that markedly increase penalties for repeat offending. Parsimony was once a basic consideration too, expressing a liberal belief that punishments in general—and incarceration in particular—have harmful effects and should be used sparingly. But there is nothing parsimonious about a situation in which most convicted offenders are incarcerated or about "truth in sentencing" laws that deny prisoners early release, even where they represent little risk to the public.

From the 1990s onward, cost considerations have also come to play an important role, pressuring penal agencies to impose controls in ways that minimize costs. America's penal state is massive, but it is also penny-pinching. The result is a system characterized by poorly paid and poorly trained police, prison, and probation officers; by austere conditions in jails and prisons; by the piling up of fees and charges on offenders and their families; and by the commercialization of criminal justice practices.

This predilection for penal control was not grounded in empirical research on offenders, their levels of dangerousness, or the threat they pose to the general public.[45] It was based on insistent demands for public safety; on cultural narratives stressing the violent propensities of young Black men; on the risk-averse decisions of penal state actors; and on the punitive public sensibilities that emerged in response to the violence and insecurity of America's large cities.[46] For significant parts of the American public, violent crime was an existential threat, and the people associated with that violence were viewed as fearsome public enemies. Political representatives took this as an instruction to enhance public safety by any means necessary.[47] The maximizing of penal control was the result.

Why the Stress on Penal Control?

Penal control is a vital tool in the armory of any justice system: every penal state deploys it.[48] But in other nations, there is more emphasis on sanctions that penalize offending without the imposition of close control—court-imposed fines, for example, or suspended sentences, or social work measures, all of which are used much more extensively elsewhere.[49] And when incarcerated persons are released into the community in other nations, they are supervised by staff (and sometimes social workers) who aid their resettlement, not by armed probation and parole officers primed to return them to prison. Why is American penality so singular in its commitment to penal control?

The reasons, no doubt, are several. Heightened perceptions of danger and otherness, a low regard for the liberty interests of poor people, and a bleak view of the reformability of offenders all likely overdetermine this outcome. But beyond these considerations, there is, I believe, a more fundamental cause. My hypothesis is that America's extraordinary resort to penal control stems not just from reactionary ideologies and punitive attitudes but also from certain social facts that shape the practical context in which crime control operates.

The social facts to which I refer are deficiencies of social integration, social solidarity, and social control that, in certain places and among certain groups, generate exceptional levels of disorder and violence. Given the extraordinary availability of guns in the United States, much of that violence is deadly—creating an existential threat well beyond that associated with crime in more peaceable nations.[50]

These "social control deficits," as I call them, are a consequence of America's political economy. Much more than in comparable nations, American-style capitalism generates widespread economic insecurity and social disorganization, and its welfare state for the poor does little to counter the criminogenic processes that result. My argument, which I substantiate in the chapters that follow, is that the fundamental cause of America's penal state—the cause that imparts to the system its size, its distinctive character, and its supporting ideologies—is a widespread problem of social disorganization, disorder, and violence brought about by America's transformed political economy in the decades after the 1960s.

How Social Systems Adapt

The formation of an aggressive penal state with a massive infrastructure of penal controls was the cumulative outcome of political action at the federal, state, and local level over a period of thirty years. Each of the thousands of legislative acts and executive decisions that contributed to this buildup was prompted by distinctive sets of circumstances and involved different political actors motivated by specific interests, incentives, and worldviews. It is therefore a remarkable fact that the great majority of the penal laws, policies, and practices that emerged during that period were organized around the singular imperative of imposing more effective and more long-lasting penal controls.

In his classic work *The Great Transformation*, Karl Polanyi argued that whenever a patterned outcome emerges from a diverse array of actions by differently situated actors with differing interests, the most likely explanation is that the actors are, whether they realize it or not, addressing a structural problem that simultaneously affects them all.[51] The historical example Polanyi presents is the vast array of social protection measures that was enacted by various authorities in late Victorian England in response to the widespread disruptions of industrialization and marketization. But we can see a similar pattern in late twentieth-century America with the sustained nationwide development of practices of penal control in response to widespread social control deficits and the resulting disorder and violence.

Sociologists refer to the process that Polanyi describes using the concept of a "functional adaptation."[52] The concept is somewhat abstract, in that it points to outcomes at the level of the social system rather than to the concrete motives of the actors whose day-to-day actions make the system function. But ultimately, it is based on empirical events and processes that can be observed and described.

In the present case, the actions and decisions that converged to create America's massive penal state were undertaken for tangible reasons having to do with public fears, popular demands, and a process of political representation that resulted in a politics of tough policing and enhanced penal control. Americans had long experienced elevated levels of violence, but between 1965 and 1994, homicide and armed robbery rates rose precipitously, as did perceptions of urban disorder, prompting public alarm and demands for protection. These political inputs gave rise, in some places, to a tough-on-crime policy response.[53] When this response proved popular with electorates and resonated with the political and racial agendas of neoconservative forces then in the ascendant, it was emulated by political actors at every level of government. If a "three strikes" law proved to be a vote winner in one election district, it wasn't long before it was being introduced everywhere. If "truth in sentencing" generated political support in one or two states, the federal government soon followed suit and introduced it everywhere. If "broken windows" and "zero tolerance" policing seemed to be succeeding in New York City, mayors and police chiefs across the country would adopt the formula and apply it in their jurisdictions. In time, a whole apparatus of aggressive policing, harsh sentencing, and penal control came to be invented, reproduced, and institutionalized by a host of political, professional, and commercial interests that formed around it.[54]

Social groups resort to penal control whenever more routine social controls prove inadequate to contain deviance and disorder. As already discussed, the work of socializing, integrating, and controlling individuals is primarily the task of parents, kin groups, neighbors, schools, workplaces, and communities. These primary institutions are embedded within a larger political economy (labor markets, housing markets, banks and commerce, and welfare state provision and the government policies that regulate them) that enables or obstructs them in their vital tasks. As I show in chapter 5, in the wake of economic and political transformations beginning in the 1960s, the capacities of primary institutions in America's poor neighborhoods were undermined by a changing political economy that deprived them of work, starved them of resources, and disrupted their functioning. The result was the widespread emergence of social control deficits that were deeper and more damaging than those of previous eras and much more pronounced than those of other affluent nations. Instead of supporting individuals and families and providing poor communities with the resources they need, America's market economy became a source of stress and disruption that America's welfare state did little to alleviate.

A low-wage labor market with precarious work and few employment protections resulted in insecurity and instability for working Americans, particularly for the two thirds of the labor force without a college degree and the 9 percent with no high school diploma. In the worst-hit neighborhoods, where work was scarce, the housing stock dilapidated, the schools underperforming, and the residents cut off from legitimate opportunities, worklessness became a chronic problem affecting successive generations of residents.[55] The result was social disorganization and family dysfunction, leading to low levels of social and self-control, widespread drug addiction, and high levels of crime and violence.

From 1960 to 1990, America's already high rate of homicide doubled, its property crime rate trebled, and the rate of violent crime almost quintupled.[56] Toward the end of the period, crack cocaine—highly addictive, affordable, and closely associated with violence—fueled these processes and became a focus of media coverage.[57] In the 1980s and 1990s, extraordinary levels of disorder and violence plagued the nation's cities, reaching epidemic proportions in places like New York, Chicago, Baltimore, and Washington, D.C.[58] As one writer put it, "If Washington D.C. had been an independent country" between 1988 and 1992, "it would have ranked among the top two or three of the most violent nations in the world."[59] The homicide rate in New York City in 1990 was more than ten times that of London.[60] America's homicide rate rose to around 10 per 100,000; no country in Europe exceeded 2 per 100,000, and most were less than half of that rate.[61] This was the context in which a law and order politics took off and an extraordinary apparatus of penal control was constructed.

The expansion of America's penal state was not a worked-out strategy or a deliberately undertaken project. There was no articulated philosophy; no plan to build mass incarceration; no explicit commitment to creating a vast web of penal controls. Instead, the penal Leviathan was a massive, makeshift adaptation, fabricated piece by piece by local actors whose resources and range of options were limited and who often operated in relative isolation.

The American Difference

For political and legal actors at the local, state, and federal levels, the fundamental principles and purposes of criminal justice are much the same in the United States as they are in other western nations. Public safety should be balanced against individual liberty; punishment should fit the crime and the individual's culpability; prison should be used only where necessary; first offenders can expect mercy; recidivists should be dealt with more severely; dangerous individuals must be contained; and considerations of deterrence, retribution, and public safety should shape sentencing. But somehow these familiar, internationally shared principles led, in late twentieth-century America, to results that were strikingly different from elsewhere.

My claim is that American officials apply these standard ideas and principles in a social context that is altogether exceptional compared to other developed nations, with the result that their decisions come out very differently—resulting in levels of police violence, sentencing severity, incarceration, and surveillance that are extraordinary. The fundamental explanation I will set out is that American criminal justice operates against a background of social dislocation, impoverishment, and gun violence largely unknown in other affluent nations. It is not criminological ideas or legal principles that set America's penal state apart, nor is it racism, religion, or punitive culture—though all of these play a part. What sets it apart is the socioeconomic context in which American criminal justice operates. The American difference is primarily a matter of material conditions.

Criminal justice authorities in other affluent nations do not typically carry out their duties amidst the severe impoverishment, social dislocation, and gun violence that are regularly encountered by American law enforcement.[62] The result is a stark contrast in how criminal justice operates. In these other nations, far fewer people are killed by police; far fewer offenders are sent to custody; many more are sanctioned by fines or suspended sentences; sentence lengths are much shorter; prison conditions are less harsh; open and minimum-security prisons are more common; home leaves and family visits are more routine; education and training programs are better developed; and re-entry provisions for released prisoners are more extensive.[63] Material conditions—and not just values and ideas—form the vital background against which penal practices take shape.

To make these contrastive points is not to idealize criminal justice elsewhere. The police and prisons of any nation are coercive institutions, directed primarily at the poor, deploying state power in difficult, hard-to-control circumstances. There is no nation where one cannot find evidence of the police or penal authorities operating in ways that invite criticism and moral opprobrium. British prisons are austere and overcrowded. French police are often brutal. Italian justice is notoriously slow. Aboriginal deaths in custody are an Australian scandal. Norwegian authorities may be less humane in their treatment of foreign nationals and their use of pretrial solitary confinement.[64] But these things are relative. And when rates and patterns are compared, the overall contrast between America and other nations could hardly be more striking.

Criminal justice authorities in other developed countries can assume that the primary institutions of civil society—family, school, work, community—are, for the most part, functioning effectively. They can assume that where these institutions fail, a publicly funded welfare state will provide income support and social services to relieve struggling families and treat needy individuals. In the United States, criminal justice officials in big cities and poor rural regions cannot depend on these institutions to function effectively. Neither can they assume that social services will take up the slack.

To understand why American penal state officials—and the lawmakers who empower them—choose to impose such harsh controls, we must understand the socio-economic landscape in which they operate. It is to this topic that we now turn.

5

America's Political Economy

America's penal state is rooted in, and shaped by, America's political economy. This chapter describes that political economy and its historical development, highlighting those characteristics that are unusual in comparative terms and causally connected to the nation's extraordinary levels of social disorder, violent crime, and penal control. Subsequent chapters trace the pathways and mechanisms that establish these connections.

A "political economy" is a system of economic action, together with the framework of laws, norms, and institutions within which that system is embedded. To study political economy is to investigate the interaction between government and business, tracing the political and legal processes through which economic phenomena—such as private property, corporate structures, production regimes, financial institutions, labor markets, and welfare programs—are constituted, regulated, and transformed.[1]

The structures of a political economy shape the flow of resources and the distribution of power. They strengthen or weaken corporations and labor unions; regulate the markets for finance, goods, labor, and property; enact employment protections and minimum wages; shape tax codes and patterns of public spending; lead to investment or disinvestment in cities and regions; and provide public goods, transfers, and benefits, all of which determine the economic fortunes of firms and industries and of individuals, families, and communities.[2] Political institutions play a fundamental role in these processes, so the structure and functioning of a nation's polity are of great economic significance. Viewed in comparative terms, America's political institutions are highly unusual in several respects. As I will show, these peculiarities give rise to economic, political, and social outcomes that have important implications for the penal state.

America's Peculiar Polity

State power in America is devolved and divided in ways that curtail federal authority and empower local governments to an extent that is unusual, even by the standards of federated nations. American cities and counties are responsible for policing, prosecution, jails, housing, education, and social welfare—functions that in other nations are undertaken by larger and better-funded regional or national governments.[3] The strict separation of powers, together with the world's most thoroughgoing system of judicial review, means that lawmaking and policy implementation in the United States encounter more veto points than in any other nation. These complex arrangements, together with antimajoritarian institutions such as the Senate and the Electoral College, make it difficult for Congress to enact and implement wide-ranging social policy, even when that policy commands popular support.[4] Penal legislation, by contrast, has been relatively easy to enact, especially during the law and order era, because there was little organized opposition to tough-on-crime policies.[5]

Compared to other nations, America's national government is limited in its capacity to project power at the state and local levels.[6] It is also limited in administrative capacity, with a civil service bureaucracy that is smaller, less professionalized, and more politicized than those of other rich nations.[7] The result is a distinctively American mode of governing that frequently relies on private market actors to carry out public functions. As we will see, this characteristic is apparent in the history of the nation's military, in its economic and industrial development, in the structure of its welfare state, and in the neoliberal policies that have predominated since the 1980s.

A corollary of these state characteristics is an unusually assertive and capable private sector, supported by a political class that has mostly been enthusiastically pro-business.[8] In the early nineteenth century, limitations of state capacity curtailed the ability of public authorities to undertake large economic projects or provide the infrastructure needed for a growing economy, so private actors were empowered to take up the slack.[9] And in contrast to post-feudal nations such as France, Germany, and Britain—where commercial classes struggled to overcome the residual powers of a landed aristocracy—American governments were from the beginning sympathetic to private enterprise and inclined to adopt a supportive, enabling role rather than be obstructive or directive.[10] The result is a business sector that is, by international standards, unusually powerful vis à vis the state and vis à vis organized labor and a public sector that is comparatively underfunded, poorly staffed, and held in low esteem. These arrangements are reinforced by the secular creed of "market fundamentalism" that has long been a powerful current in American thought and that became a kind of economic orthodoxy in the last quarter of the twentieth century.[11]

These developments help explain a second peculiarity of America's political economy, namely, the absence of a labor party and a powerful labor movement.[12] The historical strength of organized labor has been shown to be one of the best predictors of secure labor markets, comprehensive welfare states, and high levels of economic equality.[13] That America lacks a labor party—it is the only advanced nation without one—is likely a central cause of its comparative weakness in these respects.

America lacks a strong labor movement chiefly because American employers, aided by the state, succeeded in preventing the growth of workers' power. Throughout the nineteenth century, a nascent union movement—already roiled by religious, racial, ethnic, and political divisions—met with violent repression from employers who were backed by private police and government militias and supported by the courts.[14] In the face of this repression, union leaders resolved that any attempt to establish a political party would further damage the movement, and in 1894 the AFL voted decisively against such proposals.[15] Thereafter, American labor unions abandoned broader political ambitions and focused instead on securing workplace benefits for their members—a path that opened the way to "welfare capitalism" and America's distinctive style of employer-based welfare provision.[16]

A third feature of America's political economy is that it is thoroughly racialized. America's political institutions and economic arrangements were formed and have evolved in a context shaped by slavery, segregation, and White supremacy.[17] The result is that racial patterns are "always already there" in the design of political institutions, the legacies of inherited wealth and advantage, and the cultural tropes and social practices that disparage or disadvantage Black people.[18]

To describe America's political economy as "racialized" is to point to a structural characteristic rather than a pattern of interpersonal actions, which is why political economy continues to produce racially disparate outcomes even as racial prejudice declines.[19] American life today is chiefly shaped by the economic and political power of capital, corporations, finance, and private property. And the chief concern of economic actors who own, manage, and direct these powers is not racial domination but rather market share, company profit, and shareholder value. Because American institutions are so deeply marked by race and because the civil rights movement has not yet achieved reparations or a full measure of economic justice, the pursuit of otherwise race-neutral economic interests tends to reproduce inequality, exclusion, and segregation. Business as usual in the United States functions to disfavor African Americans.

The same is true of state and local government. Unlike Southern sheriffs and governors in the Jim Crow era, officials in the United States today are arguably motivated less by racial prejudice than by electoral calculations and the prospects of political advancement. It is not racial prejudice but rather the electoral power of White homeowners and "opportunity hoarding" of White working-class and suburban voters that prompts officials to configure tax, welfare, education, zoning, and housing policies in ways that sustain racial hierarchy.[20] Nevertheless, the result is the same, and local government in America remains a cornerstone of durable inequalities.[21]

In its income and wealth distributions, its access to real estate and labor markets, its provision of public goods, and its welfare laws and practices, American political economy is racialized through and through. The result is that, compared to White Americans, Black people are poorer, more unemployed, less well schooled and housed, more affected by social problems, more victimized by violent crime, and more targeted by the criminal legal system.[22]

Of course, America's political economy has features that are highly valued by certain groups in society and by many voters, which is why it is not more subject to political challenge. It provides market freedom for entrepreneurs, investors, banks, and corporations.[23] It ensures cheap labor for employers, cheap goods and services for consumers, and great wealth and low taxation for those who succeed in the marketplace. Its powerful dynamism rewards innovation, generating a high number of patents and high levels of research and development spending. It has comparatively high numbers of women in the workforce and in leadership positions; high rates of participation in further education; and high levels of retirement income as a percentage of earlier income.[24] It has more multi-millionaires and billionaires than any other nation and is, according to a recent report, "the world's undisputed leader in private wealth creation and accumulation."[25] These features are regarded as virtues by many Americans; they command the loyalty of sections of the electorate; and they attract large numbers of economic migrants, eager to share in the pursuit of prosperity. But however we choose to regard it, this is a political economy that gives rise to exceptional levels of violence and an extraordinary regime of penal control.

America's Economy Today

America's economic system is a capitalist one. But "capitalism" is an ideal type that exists in pure form only in economic textbooks. In the real world, capitalist economic action is always undertaken within a social context structured by specific legal rules, political institutions, and cultural norms, that is to say, within a specific political economy.

Comparative researchers disagree about how best to classify the different types of political economy, but they largely agree that America is, by international standards, an outlier, manifesting an extreme version of liberal market capitalism.[26] Viewed through a "varieties of capitalism" framework—the most influential classification scheme in the field—America is an extreme example of a "liberal market economy" located at one pole of a continuum that situates "coordinated market economies" at the opposite pole.[27] Liberal market economies are characterized by loosely regulated markets, minimal employment protections, weak labor unions, weak employer associations, and market-oriented welfare states. In these economies, firms and labor unions relate to one another via competitive market processes, with little in the way of cooperative arrangements, joint planning, or corporatist agreements.[28]

The welfare states of liberal market economies are chiefly designed to supplement and reinforce market processes rather than offer de-commodified alternatives such as free healthcare, education, housing, or childcare. Their role is to enable capitalist markets by managing their failures rather than redistribute wealth and income or promote solidarity. Cities and states also compete with one another, attracting investment and creating jobs by lowering taxes and employment protections or by restricting the ability of labor to organize. Production regimes in these economies are similarly market-based, meaning that producers rely on market processes to ensure their supply lines, labor supply, and technology, in contrast to coordinated market economies where government works with business and labor to plan investment, training, and education, thereby ensuring that growing industries have the capital and labor they need and young workers find employment at the end of their schooling or apprenticeships. Each of these "liberal market" characteristics is more pronounced in the United States than in economies with similar structures such as Canada, Australia, and the UK in a way that sets America off as "an outlier—in many respects a stark outlier."[29]

Comparative research on political economy studies variation between nations to discover which institutional arrangements are associated with higher levels of employment, growth, productivity, industrial militancy, and so on. For our purposes, however, the significance of America's outlier status lies in its extraordinary impact on social disorganization and the policies adopted to deal with it. I concentrate on two dimension of the US political economy, namely, its labor market and its welfare state, each of which is unusual in ways that bear directly on these issues.[30]

America's Labor Markets

Compared to other developed nations, America's labor markets are markedly business-friendly, with employment law and industrial relations policy doing little to offset the power imbalance between capital and labor.[31] Labor laws obstruct union organizing, prohibit closed shop workplaces, and allow employees to opt out of paying union dues. Federal employees and certain public sector workers are prohibited from taking industrial action, sympathy strikes are banned, and many workers are obliged to sign no-strike contracts. Legal restrictions like these, together with a history of violent repression by strike-breaking employers and internal conflicts born of racial and other divisions, have made for a labor movement that is weak by international standards.[32] The result has been low wages, poor working conditions, weak job security, and limited benefits for many American workers—all of which worsened after the 1960s, when manufacturing gave way to a service economy, union membership slid from 30 percent of the workforce to less than 10 percent, and the standard contract of employment gave way to more precarious forms of hiring. By 2007, the United States ranked second to last of thirty-four affluent nations in terms of union membership and had the highest proportion of workers in poorly paid jobs.[33]

Today, America's economy is largely service-based, with a split between high-skilled, well-compensated sectors of the knowledge economy (banking, finance, tech, the upper reaches of the legal and medical professions, etc.) and low-skilled, low-pay sectors, such as wholesale and retail trade, leisure and hospitality, domestic and care work, and guard labor.[34] For millions of American workers, zero-hour contracts, at-will employment, and gig work mean that their jobs provide little security, stability, or benefits. Unlike the unionized manufacturing jobs of the 1950s and 1960s, these do not pay wages that will feed a family and pay rent, let alone support a middle-class lifestyle.

At the end of 2023, some 43.2 million Americans had student loan debt totaling more than $1.6 trillion, and the average American carried nearly

$8,000 in credit card debt.[35] In-work poverty is widespread—affecting 8.6 percent of White workers and 14.3 percent of Black workers—and many people with jobs rely on food stamps, earned income tax credits, or multiple jobs to support themselves and their families.[36] As for the millions of working-age people who cannot find employment—and fully 34 percent of Black men aged 21 to 25 were outside the labor force in 2000—there is a depth of poverty and social exclusion in the United States that is unknown in other affluent nations.[37]

For those in work, employment in America comes with less security, fewer benefits, and fewer protections compared to workers in other rich nations. As a 2023 *Forbes* headline put it, "US Tops Rich Nations as Worst Place to Work."[38] At-will employment is legal in forty-nine states and in the District of Columbia, enabling businesses to dismiss workers with little or no justification.[39] Because of such laws, the United States ranks last out of thirty-eight OECD countries in terms of worker protections, including protections of equal pay for equal work; protections from sexual harassment; provision of disability, sick, and parental leave; and protection from chaotic scheduling.[40]

America's Welfare State

Capitalist economies, as already noted, are driven by processes of "creative destruction" that can destabilize and destroy established ways of life.[41] Industrial regions become rust belts, mining communities become ghost towns, and workers' hard-won skills rapidly become obsolete. If allowed to operate unchecked, market forces cause serious loss and privation to people who lack marketable skills or are too old, sick, or busy taking care of others to be in employment. To moderate these effects, modern societies have established welfare states that restrain market forces, insure against loss of income, and provide goods and services outside the marketplace.[42]

From the 1930s to the 1960s, a succession of mostly Democratic administrations in the United States did precisely this. They established Social Security, Medicare, and Medicaid. They guaranteed the right to join a union. They established an eight-hour workday and a minimum wage. They built on the nation's tradition of public schooling to create one of the world's first mass systems of secondary and higher education.[43] And they enacted a steeply progressive system of taxation. The result was an American-style welfare state, the core of which quickly became popular and has persisted to the present day.[44]

But at least since the 1940s, America's welfare state has generally been less comprehensive than those of other affluent nations. From 1980 until 2010 US public social expenditure ranked bottom or close to the bottom of eleven OECD countries as a percent of GDP.[45] And according to the Luxembourg Income Survey of 2000, which provides comparative data on income, labor, and demographic characteristics, its antipoverty effort was the weakest of the twenty-five nations included in the survey.[46] Lacking a powerful labor movement, America never developed the extensive employment protections, public goods, and social safety nets that workers in other nations enjoy. And following President Ronald Reagan's attacks on organized labor in the 1980s and President Bill Clinton's "welfare reforms" of the 1990s, workers' rights and welfare for the nonworking poor have become less adequate and more conditional, even as popular programs such as Social Security and Medicare have continued to expand.[47] Welfare for the nonworking poor, particularly for able-bodied, working-age men, is notably meager.

By comparison with other nations, America's welfare state is an outlier: less universalistic, less comprehensive, and less redistributive.[48] It is also steeply stratified, with well-paid employees and wealthier households benefiting most; and poor, unemployed, able-bodied males benefiting least.[49] For the rich and for high-skilled or unionized employees, it provides generous benefits in the form of tax allowances and tax-advantaged employment benefits.[50] Social Security provides decent benefits to retirees and their spouses and to disabled people, provided they made the requisite contributions during their working years. Medicare provides subsidized healthcare to seniors, and Medicaid provides a lesser form of coverage to low-income people.[51] Since the 1990s, the fastest-growing program has been the Earned Income Tax Credit, a government subsidy that lifts many low-paid wage earners out of poverty, thereby subsidizing employers and perpetuating the problem of low pay.

The distinguishing feature of America's welfare state is not what it provides but what it fails to provide. In contrast to other developed nations, the United States does not provide comprehensive and universal healthcare or healthcare insurance. It does not provide universal child allowances or universal subsidies for childcare. It does not provide paid parental leave. It does not provide free or affordable higher education. It does not provide much in the way of subsidized public transportation or public housing. It does not provide income support for unemployed working-age males who lack insurance. And, as noted above, it provides fewer employment protections for regular workers than virtually any developed nation.[52]

Single parents with dependent children may qualify for the Temporary Assistance for Needy Families program, and low-income households may receive food stamps, but benefits are low, vary by locality, and often come with work or training requirements. For people at the lowest end of the income distribution, America's welfare state does little to compensate for the instability and low wages that characterize its economy.

Together, these labor market and welfare state arrangements help make the United States one of the most unequal societies in the developed world. For all its wealth and power, America exhibits deeper poverty, more social disorganization, and worse social problems than any developed nation.[53]

Social Problems

Compared to other affluent nations, the United States exhibits higher-than-average levels of virtually every social problem. America's child poverty rates are among the highest in the developed world, with around 20 percent of children living in relative income poverty, compared to just over 13 percent on average across OECD countries. Measured from lowest to highest, the United States ranks close to the bottom—31st out of 34. Within America's population, Black children are three times more likely to be poor than White children.[54]

With respect to poverty in general, the United States in the late 1990s had one of the highest poverty rates of all countries participating in the Luxemburg Income Survey, both in relative and absolute measures.[55] Twenty years later, in 2019, America's poverty rate was still 17.8 percent, the highest percentage in the OECD. In that year, Canada's poverty rate was 12.4 percent, and most Western European nations were at or below 10 percent.[56] Again, the problem is worse for African Americans, for whom the poverty rate is twice as high as for Whites and for whom poverty tends to be spatially concentrated and persistent over time.[57]

Health outcomes are also worse in the United States, despite high total spending on healthcare. Across fifteen European nations, the average infant mortality rate is between 3 and 4 deaths per 1,000 live births. In the United States, the figure is 6 per 1,000; Black rates are, at 13 per 1,000, twice as high again.[58] America has the lowest life expectancy of all developed nations, an outcome that is worse still for Black Americans, who on average have a life expectancy that is five years lower that that of White Americans.[59] Adult male obesity is worse in the United States than in Europe; drug overdose death rates are higher than in any other high-income nation, and America has the highest rate of people with multiple chronic diseases.[60]

Homelessness rates are similarly high in the United States, as are rates of untreated mental illness, substance dependency, and drug-related deaths.[61] On an index of health and social problems, comparing twenty-three rich nations on multiple indicators, the United States had by far the worst overall score.[62]

Criminologists have shown that the link between economic disadvantage and violent crime flows chiefly through the family.[63] Research also shows that where families are economically stressed and deprived of support, their ability to socialize and supervise their children becomes impaired.[64] These difficulties of family functioning result in a close association between concentrated poverty, family formation, and high rates of violence—all of which were greatly exacerbated by the dramatic change in family structure that occurred in the 1970s, when the traditional family form collapsed, resulting in "a massive, class-biased decline in the number of children raised in two-parent families."[65]

According to political scientist Robert Putnam, the collapse of the two-parent family "hit the black community earliest and hardest, in part because that community was already clustered at the bottom of the economic hierarchy" but White families were by no means immune to these changes, and, especially in lower-class families, "childbearing became increasingly disconnected from marriage, and sexual partnerships became less durable."[66] This massive demographic change had serious implications for family functioning, which America's insecure, low-wage labor market and limited welfare state do little to alleviate. That both parents in two-parent households now tend to be wage-earners—a household characteristic more common in the United States than elsewhere—is also a source of stress.[67]

Particularly problematic is the tight link between poverty and single-parent, female-headed households that exists in the United States. In nations like Sweden, a solidaristic welfare state provides income support, subsidized housing, free healthcare, and free childcare, making single-parent households much less impoverished than they would otherwise be, but in America, single parenthood is closely associated with poverty and child detriment.[68] As *The New York Times* recently reported, "In the US, families headed by single mothers are five times more likely to live in poverty than married-couple families. Children in single-mother homes are less likely to graduate from high school or earn a college degree [and] are more likely to become single parents themselves."[69] Given this association, it is especially problematic that America has the world's highest rate of children living in single-parent households. Some 30 percent of American children today live with a single parent or no parent at all, while for Black children, the proportion is 62 percent.[70] Among the twenty-one nations that have complete statistics, America also has the highest rate of teenage pregnancies, though this rate has recently been decreasing.[71]

The US record of social failure is truly remarkable, but it is well attested and of long standing. Its primary casualties are the urban poor, particularly Black families living in segregated, multiply disadvantaged neighborhoods where ill health, food and housing insecurity, high school noncompletion, poverty, and crime and violence are often endemic.[72] But White Americans, who form a majority of the nation's poor, are also badly affected. Between 1990 and 2018, increased economic insecurity for working people, poor social services, and prescription drug addiction produced falls in the life expectancy of Americans without a college degree—a phenomenon rarely seen outside of wartime or pandemics.[73]

Perhaps the most disturbing of America's social problems is lethal violence. For much of the last century, and still today, the United States has exhibited rates of homicide that are altogether exceptional for a developed, affluent nation. And these rates were at their highest in the 1980s and 1990s, when the penal state expanded at its fastest pace.[74]

With respect to lethal violence, the United States is not just at the high end of the distribution: on any comparative chart of developed nations, it is an extreme outlier.[75] America's homicide rate was, for most of the twentieth century, markedly above that of comparable nations. It increased sharply in the mid-1960s, reaching its modern peak in 1980. Later in that decade it dipped and then rose again, reaching an annual toll of 10 homicides per 100,000 people in 1994, when more than 23,000 Americans were murdered. Between 1994 and 2018, the homicide rate fell more or less continuously, bottoming out at 5 per 100,000 before climbing again during the pandemic years.

Even at its lowest, America's homicide rate was markedly above those of comparable nations. In the 1980s and 1990s, it was five times as high as Canada's and more than ten times as high as the Western European average.[76] Much of America's murder count is the result of firearm homicides, the rate of which is around twenty-five times higher than that of other high-income countries. But America's non-firearm rate was also high, being 2.6 times higher than in the other countries.[77]

Homicide rates are shockingly high among African Americans. In 2019, the rate for this group was 15.5 per 100,000, making homicide the leading cause of death among Black, non-Hispanic males in the age groups 1–19 and 20–44.[78] Black Americans are six times more likely to die from homicide than their White compatriots. But White Americans are also killed (and kill each other) at a higher rate than the populations of other Western nations.[79] Murder rates are especially high in America's majority-Black cities. In 2017 four such cities—St. Louis, Baltimore, New Orleans, and Detroit—were listed among the top fifty most violent in the world. No other cities in the Global North were on that list.[80]

What this overview of the comparative data has shown is that, for all its wealth and prosperity, the United States exhibits some of the most serious social problems in the developed world. Franklin D. Roosevelt's New Deal, as extended by Lyndon Johnson's Great Society programs, greatly reduced the insecurity and immiseration to which working people are exposed. Senior citizens, in particular, benefited from them, which is why the elderly no longer constitute a large fraction of America's poor.[81] But America's welfare state has never provided the levels of social provision and economic protection that the peoples of other developed nations have enjoyed. Above all, it has failed to remedy the problems that plague the poorest Americans, the most egregious of which is a homicide rate altogether unknown in other affluent nations. As we will see, these problems have had definite implications for America's penal state.

Deindustrialization and Neoliberalism

The social democratic phase of American political development was a relatively brief one, lasting just over thirty years. From the mid-1970s, American economic policy increasingly reverted to free-market liberalism, albeit in a new "neoliberal" form.[82] The last great project of postwar social democracy—Johnson's 1964 "War on Poverty"—rapidly came to be regarded as a failure because it coincided with a wave of urban riots and violent crime; because critics judged it against unrealistic expectations; and because many White voters resented policies designed to help poor Blacks.[83] When deindustrialization, automation, and rising foreign competition led to a massive loss of manufacturing jobs in urban centers, the old New Deal remedies were no longer viewed as politically or economically viable. The result was devastating for unskilled workers, initially mostly for Black men but later for White workers too.[84] According to Clegg and Usmani, in 1960 "about 19.8 percent of unskilled, black men between the ages of eighteen and fifty, and living in cities, were neither in a job nor in school. By 1970, 21.3 percent were. And by 2010, a full 52 percent of these men were neither employed nor in school."[85]

The New Deal coalition collapsed in the 1970s, along with the Keynesian policy assumptions that had sustained it.[86] Falling productivity, budget deficits run up by the Vietnam War, runaway inflation, and high unemployment disrupted the deindustrializing economy, while political developments eroded the Democrats' congressional dominance. Johnson's landmark legislation—the Civil Rights Act, the Voting Rights Act, and the Fair Housing Act—marked the high point of New Deal liberalism. But it also marked the beginning of its end. A conservative reaction to civil rights, and especially to Johnson's effort to combat Black poverty, broke apart the Democratic Party coalition, prompting a realignment that enabled Republicans to build a neoliberalized economy and to alter how it is governed.[87]

American politics shifted sharply rightward—starting with Richard Nixon's "New Federalism," continuing with Jimmy Carter's prioritizing of inflation control over full employment, and culminating in Reagan's attacks on organized labor and the welfare state.[88] In a single generation, American policy abandoned the modest social democracy of the New Deal and embraced the free-market fundamentalism, corporate empowerment, globalization, and financialization that we have come to call "neoliberalism." What ensued was a fifty-year period marked by union decline, wage stagnation, shifts in the tax burden from rich to poor, dismantled safety nets, a run-up of household debt, a reduced federal workforce, increased insecurity, increased inequality, and deepening poverty.[89]

Urban neighborhoods were especially badly hit, prompting a spiral of decline in many of the nation's large cities.[90] Businesses and landlords disinvested, and middle-class families moved to the suburbs, causing the local tax base to collapse and, with it, the funding needed for social services. But rather than provide support and public investment, state and federal governments reduced funding for municipalities and for urban policy. By the mid-1980s, poor neighborhoods in America's large cities were experiencing chronic worklessness, dire social problems, and record levels of violent crime.[91]

In the social democratic 1930s and again in the 1960s, upsurges in social problems and violent crime prompted federal government investment and efforts to address economic and racial injustice.[92] In the neoliberal 1980s, an increase in social problems produced right-wing outrage and a reactionary discourse portraying welfare "dependency" and violent crime as expressions of the "moral poverty" of poor Black people.[93] Blending law and order themes with tax-cutting promises, these ideas proved wildly popular with large parts of the electorate and were soon embraced by Democrats as well as Republicans. In the mid-1990s, President Bill Clinton, a Democrat, signed two major pieces of legislation into law: one dismantled the federal social safety net; the other accelerated construction of a massive penal state.[94] It would be hard to conjure up a more precise encapsulation of the political zeitgeist.

A Note on Violence

By the standards of modern affluent nations, the United States is a remarkably violent place. In 2020, one in seven Americans—some 47 million people—lived within a quarter mile of a place where a gun killing occurred that year: in many cases, not just one killing but two or three.[95] Homicide has a high prevalence, but it is unevenly distributed and, in places, highly concentrated. About half of these homicides occurred in neighborhoods where just 6 percent of Americans live, which is to say, in the poorest, most segregated communities.[96]

High levels of concentrated violence are an effect of political economy insofar as market forces disorganize poor communities, disrupt processes of social control, and set criminogenic processes in train, a process I describe in the next chapter. But this extraordinary violence also derives from the long history of legally tolerated violence that formed an essential element of slavery, of Jim Crow, and of the violent appropriation of American Indian land. The private use of violence was a taken-for-granted entitlement of frontier settlers, slave owners, plantation overseers, lynch mobs, and Southern Whites more generally.[97] And because public policing rarely extended to Black neighborhoods before the 1960s, this lack of state protection gave rise to habits of violent self-defense and retaliation in poor Black communities.[98] In no other developed nation did interpersonal violence form such a core part of institutional arrangements and daily life over such long periods of time. To appreciate why Americans are so prone to lethal violence today, we must recall these historical experiences and their likely effect on popular culture. More concretely, we should consider their role in shaping the peculiar place of guns in contemporary America.

The ubiquity of guns in the United States today is truly extraordinary. There are estimated to be some 400 million in circulation—more guns than people—and roughly 40 percent of Americans live in households owning one or more firearms.[99] Some twenty million AR-15 assault rifles are in circulation, contributing to the frequency and lethality of mass shooting events—another of the nation's exceptional features. Equally extraordinary is the permissive legal regime regarding firearm possession.[100] And while high rates of gun possession do not automatically lead to high levels of gun crime, in America they are a major contributor.

The process of state building in most Western nations in the nineteenth century involved the establishment of powerful militaries and police forces; the placing of the means of violence under state control; and the close regulation of private access to firearms. And during the twentieth century, several nations responded to mass shooting events by imposing additional controls on the possession of guns, sometimes banning them altogether.[101] The result is that today, the twenty-seven member states of the European Union have an average gun ownership rate of 5 percent—less than one sixth that of the United States.[102]

Gun ownership in most developed nations is rare and strictly controlled, and owners report that their guns are for sport or for hunting. In the United States, by contrast, gun possession is common, controls are comparatively weak, and most firearm owners keep guns for self-protection. The means of violence are widely distributed among private citizens, many of whom forcefully assert their right to bear arms and express strong support for the principle of armed self-defense.[103]

The right of individual Americans to bear arms dates to the founding of the republic, although this right was never unqualified. Legal controls also date from the founding era and were, at times, quite restrictive. Slaves and free Blacks were everywhere prohibited from possessing firearms. And in the early years of the republic, state and county authorities inspected privately owned guns to ensure that the local militias would be adequately armed. Throughout the nineteenth century, frontier towns imposed strict controls, requiring visitors to relinquish their arms on arrival, with harsh penalties for noncompliance.[104] After the Civil War, vigilante groups and southern authorities forcibly disarmed Black people. During Prohibition in the 1920s and 1930s, state and federal authorities banned machine guns and sawn-off shotguns. Americans' access to guns was never unrestricted.

Despite this, the dominant current running through American history is the right of private citizens to bear arms—a right that is legally codified, not just in the much-disputed Second Amendment of the US Constitution but also in the constitutions of some forty-four states. From the Civil War onward, Americans have been more extensively armed than the populations of any other developed nation: a situation that US governments have generally permitted and encouraged. In the 1980s and 1990s and again in the early 2020s, when rates of homicide and armed robbery increased, gun ownership rates trended upward and legal restrictions were relaxed.[105] In America, more gun violence leads to more guns.

A distinctive feature of the American state, as we have seen, is that it frequently outsources public functions to private and quasi-public organizations—and these functions have sometimes included policing and the systematic use of violence.[106] Instead of creating state monopolies and exercising these functions itself, the American way has been for the national state to devolve power to lower levels of government and share it with private actors such as slave owners and plantation overseers, settlers on the frontier, corporations with private guard forces, vigilance committees, ethnic militias, gun clubs, and private individuals.[107] None of this renders the American state "weak" necessarily—weakness or strength depends on how well this complex infrastructure is coordinated and how effectively it achieves its objectives. But it does make it distinctive. Instead of claiming a monopoly of legitimate violence—a feature that, since Max Weber, has been thought of as an essential state characteristic—the US state has historically overseen, as Jonathan Obert puts it, "multiple, fragmented, and often contradictory forms of organized violence" that "overlap and co-exist while still providing effective governance."[108]

The origins of these unusual arrangements lie in the revolutionary break with colonial Britain and the republican ideas that shaped the founding of the nation. Distrust of remote government, fear of tyranny and powerful standing armies, civic virtue ideals, a commitment to popular self-government, a refusal to allow British authorities to restrain the encroachment of settlers into native lands—all of these conceptions shaped the design of the republic's institutions.[109] And instead of the imperial model of a powerful center and a weak periphery, the Founders established radical forms of localism and popular participation. These commitments underlay the young nation's reliance on local militias rather than a standing army or a National Guard. They also informed the idea that bearing arms was, for the individual citizen, a civic duty, supportive of government.[110] Militias were supposed to bind together the people, the local state, and the national government—making sovereignty compatible with popular rule and empowering "the people" while avoiding state bureaucracy.[111] Such was the republican theory. In practice, local militias were rarely up to the task. When the War of 1812 exposed their weaknesses, their role in the nation's defense began its long decline.[112]

Republican ideals depicted the carrying of arms as a virtue, but aspects of American life made it a necessity. Above all, the South's slave economy depended on violence to retain its labor force, and Southerners haunted by fear of a bloody slave revolt like the one in Saint-Domingue took care to arm themselves and maintain tight controls. Firearms were also a fact of life on the frontier and wherever settlers engaged with indigenous people.[113]

Historians debate the extent of gun possession in the eighteenth century and antebellum America, but the Civil War was undoubtedly a turning point in this respect.[114] The armies of the North and South issued weapons to millions of Americans and trained them in their use. And the arming of the population carried over into peacetime, because at war's end many veterans of the conflict were permitted to return home with their weapons.[115] In the decades immediately thereafter, an American gun manufacturing industry emerged, supplying cheap, reliable weapons to private customers and soon giving rise to widespread handgun ownership. As one historian puts it, "By the mid-1870s, guns were everywhere in American life."[116]

In the early twentieth century, thanks to the mass advertising campaigns of companies like Colt and Winchester, handguns became cultural icons, and myths began to circulate depicting gun-carrying as a noble part of the nation's character and frontier heritage.[117] Then, as now, the spread of guns was accompanied by the spread of gun violence. In 1932, a published research paper calculated that US homicide rates were 10 times higher than those of Japan; 17 times higher than England; and 47 times higher than Switzerland.[118]

The political institutions that enabled gun ownership to spread in this fashion continue to shape law and policy up to the present. Until the Efficiency in Militia Act of 1903, the nation's defenses relied on private and public-private organizations—ethnic militias, gun clubs, vigilante committees, municipal police forces, private detective agencies, and state militias—to supplement the small force maintained by the federal government.[119] Local policing and security were devolved to slave patrols, watch committees, and the "law and order leagues" that businessmen and community leaders formed to maintain public order, an activity that included repressing labor organizing and breaking strikes.[120] As Jason Kaufman observes, "Eventually, the difficulties of this situation led to the formation of uniformed state police, the expansion of federal forces and reserves, and the rationalization of the National Guard, but only after lasting legacies of private gun ownership and resistance to government authority were well entrenched."[121]

The peculiar relationship of Americans to guns and lethal violence has deep institutional and historical roots, having emerged as a direct outcome of the nation's unusual process of state formation. And so long as Americans continue to distrust their government and fear each other, that destructive heritage is unlikely to be dismantled. Nevertheless, America's modern gun culture would seem to be a peculiar historical legacy rather than any kind of functional requirement of America's political economy. Reducing its grip on the nation is thus a political and legal task rather than an economic one.

6

Political Economy and Social Disorder

AMERICA'S POLITICAL economy is associated with high levels of social disorder and criminal violence. But how should we understand this relationship? What is it about America's political and economic institutions, particularly its labor market and welfare state, that helps produce these exceptionally high rates? And what changes in that political economy caused these social problems to surge in American cities from the mid-1960s onward?

As noted earlier, the explanation has two parts. First, I show how America's distinctive political economy destabilizes poor neighborhoods, disrupting the normal functioning of families and communities, a disruption that increased in the decades after the 1960s.[1] Second, I explain how criminogenic processes take root in socially disorganized neighborhoods, leading to elevated rates of violence and eventually to increased levels of policing and punishment, particularly in America's poorest, most disadvantaged, neighborhoods.

Capitalist markets bring competitive pressures and disruptive change to bear on everyone, and where social groups or residential areas are mostly composed of weak market actors, these disruptive effects can be especially pronounced. But capitalist processes are always undertaken within specific political economies that can counteract and moderate these effects, so we need to focus on the specific institutional framework in which market forces operate. What we find is that in America's highly competitive, lightly regulated economy, labor markets generate more insecurity for more working people than do those of comparable nations, and America's employment laws and welfare state provide fewer protections. Levels of social disorganization and neighborhood disorder are correspondingly high, especially for Blacks living in segregated, multiply deprived neighborhoods.

In the 1970s and 1980s, structural transformations in America's economy imposed new stresses on working people and city governments. Instead of mitigating the adverse impacts of this economic restructuring, government policy exacerbated them. Under Nixon and Reagan, the federal government largely abandoned efforts to combat Black unemployment, segregation, and social exclusion, simultaneously shifting social policy funding to a block grant system that imposed fewer controls on how funds were spent by states and municipalities.[2] A vital economic support that had helped sustain vulnerable communities was thereby withdrawn, leaving poor communities to fend for themselves.

Cash-starved municipalities reduced public spending, cutting back on public transportation, schools, public housing, and social services. Cities relaxed enforcement of city codes and maintenance of residential housing units, leading to deterioration of the housing stock. Neighborhoods fell into ruin, and housing projects in cities such as New York and Chicago became burned-out, abandoned ghettos.[3] In the worst-hit areas, public housing became "a federally funded, physically permanent institution for the isolation of black families by race and class."[4]

The decline of inner cities brought out-migration, the concentration of poverty, and family disruption. Middle-class families, White and Black, fled poor neighborhoods, leaving the remaining residents uniformly poor, deprived of positive role models, and cut off from social networks that might help them obtain jobs and other resources. Worklessness led to economic distress, but it also caused loss of status and self-respect, declining marriage rates, and increased problems of family and neighborhood functioning. It increased high school nonattendance and noncompletion. And for unsupervised teenagers and unattached young adults, it increased criminal opportunities and the comparative returns of the illegal enterprise.[5]

As the institutions of work, family, and neighborhood came under stress, social problems and criminal violence increased. In declining areas of large cities, drug use increased, drug gangs proliferated, street robberies became endemic, and murder rates among young Black men reached levels never before seen in the developed world.[6] In the nation's capital, the homicide rate reached an astonishing 78 per 100,000.[7]

Poverty is often described as a "root cause" of crime, but the relationship is complex. Similarly, the causal mechanisms linking political economy to poverty, social disorganization, and violent crime are attenuated and probabilistic, involving intermediate variables and indirect effects. The structures of political economy do not "determine" crime rates in any direct or mechanical fashion:

there is no one-to-one correspondence or lockstep pattern of change. Instead, these phenomena are linked by intermediating processes consisting of disruptive, disorganizing processes that undermine neighborhood organization, family structure, and local culture as well as criminogenic processes that give rise to illegal markets, criminal gangs, the spread of guns, and spirals of violence. These processes, which are localized and contingent, are the proximate causes of criminal conduct. But they are made more or less likely by larger political economic forces that emanate from elsewhere.

Economic Stress and Social Disorganization

Economic hardship undermines neighborhood stability as well as family formation and functioning. Where men are detached from the labor market or earn low wages in insecure jobs, it puts pressure on family life, making marriage less likely and increasing the likelihood of separation, divorce, single-parent households, and births to unmarried women.[8] Worklessness and poverty, unstable households and family breakdown, population turnover and social problems are circumstances that result in weak social ties between residents, low participation in communal activities, and a lack of trust—a state of affairs encapsulated in the concept of "social disorganization" that describes a community's inability to act collectively in its own interests.[9]

Political economy patterns the distribution of economic and political resources. When investment, wages, rents, and welfare benefits—together with schools, day care centers, housing, parks, libraries, social services, and political influence—flow into neighborhoods, this expands employment, wealth, social capital, and opportunities. Steady economic flows, reliable social services, and effective political support create stable neighborhoods, fostering social organization and enabling effective social control.

But where there is a dearth of decent work, sparse public or private investment, and little in the way of social services or welfare support, decay and disorganization can set in. Residents who can, move away. Investment dries up. Banks, supermarkets, and retail outlets disappear. The housing stock deteriorates, producing empty lots, boarded-up buildings, and apartment blocks in dire need of repair. Neighborhood schools decline and become less safe. Dismal employment prospects make high school seem pointless, leading to high rates of noncompletion. Jobless men are less marriageable, so family formation is disrupted. More children are raised in impoverished, single-parent households.

Short of time and lacking resources, parents in these circumstances are less able to care for and supervise their children. Teenagers and young men spend more time on the streets. Public drinking and drug use, littering and graffiti, begging and verbal harassment of women become more common, making public space unattractive and unsafe.[10] Law-abiding residents withdraw and no longer act as capable guardians exerting informal controls. The disappearance of businesses and visitors also means fewer eyes on the streets, more distrust and suspicion, less capacity for self-regulation. A downward spiral sets in.

Of course, residential areas vary in their reaction to economic and political pressures.[11] Neighborhoods have an inherent structure, an organizational and associational life that gives the area a collective character that persists even as residents come and go.[12] Variation in these structures means that not every neighborhood—not even every poor minority neighborhood—becomes disorganized under the impact of economic privation. Depending on background levels of trust and solidarity, some neighborhoods succeed in undertaking collective action—mobilizing residents, supervising kids, accessing resources, securing political support, and so on—while others fail.[13]

Stable, well-organized neighborhoods with high levels of collective efficacy prove resilient in face of economic pressure. Such places withstand disasters or the challenge of rising unemployment and poverty without becoming disorderly.[14] Neighborhoods with low levels of trust and cohesion, on the other hand, are much more prone to disorder.[15] Vulnerability is greater where there are fewer organizations such as churches or tenant groups; fewer amenities such as banks, supermarkets, and retailers; higher levels of residential turnover; more single-occupancy dwellings; more single-parent families; and more households dependent on welfare. Racially segregated neighborhoods with concentrated poverty are the most vulnerable of all.[16] Such neighborhoods are not simply a fact of life or an inevitable product of the housing market. They are shaped by the laws and policies of federal, state, and local government; by choices made by banks, insurance companies, landlords, and investors; and by decisions made by the courts. Which is to say, they are a product of the nation's political economy.

As sociologists Doug Massey and Nancy Denton point out, "Middle-class households—whether they are black, Mexican, Italian, Jewish, or Polish—always try to escape the poor."[17] So when explicit segregation was made illegal in the 1960s, and it became possible for middle-class Blacks to move to the suburbs, many did, increasing concentrated poverty in the inner-city areas they left behind.[18] Being poor in an economically mixed neighborhood is different than being poor where everyone else is also poor. Concentrated poverty means fewer possibilities of local jobs; less exposure to people in mainstream institutions; and less access to eligible marriage partners.[19] When emergencies occur, it means fewer neighbors with spare assets to provide support.

People everywhere derive welfare and support from three sources: from employment; from family, friends, and neighbors; and from the state. In America's inner-city neighborhoods, in the decades after deindustrialization, all three of these sources dried up. Deprived of support from work, family, and government, residents became more likely to participate in the illegal economy or join criminal gangs.[20] All this took place in a period when large-scale political and cultural changes were undermining institutional authority and established patterns of life.[21]

Social Disorganization and Criminogenic Processes

Researchers have known for some time that forms of political economy are correlated with levels of crime and disorder, and multiple studies provide cross-national data demonstrating this association.[22] What was not clear until recently was exactly how these structural effects occurred. But recent work on informal social control, neighborhood effects, and collective efficacy has identified the mediating processes that link one to the other, while explaining the close association between poverty, racial segregation, and social dislocation.[23]

These studies begin from the theoretical premise that interpersonal violence is a product of social and economic structures mediated by patterns of informal social control and enacted in specific social situations by at-risk individuals. Violence is viewed as a patterned social phenomenon, and those most prone to—and victimized by—criminal violence are disproportionately drawn from highly disadvantaged neighborhoods and families.[24] Of course, poverty and unemployment do not invariably lead to crime and violence: most poor people overcome adversity to live decent, law-abiding lives, and antisocial behaviors are plentiful among the rich.[25] But concentrated poverty and social exclusion undermine collective efficacy and reduce the effectiveness of families, schools, labor markets, and communities, resulting in social control deficits that make crime and violence more likely. Similarly, worklessness and poverty make the emergence of illegal markets for drugs, gambling, and sex more likely, and violence is frequently a corollary of such markets.[26]

To recognize that many poor minority neighborhoods exhibit very high rates of violence is neither to blame their residents nor to suggest a causal link between race and violence. As Thomas Abt points out, violent crime is no more inherently "Black" than financial crime is inherently "White."[27] It is, instead, to call attention to a social problem disproportionately experienced by Black communities and rooted in America's distinctive political economy.

It is also to point to a cause of America's penal state and its disparate racial impact. Rather than disconnect mass incarceration from criminal violence—as some scholars insist on doing—we need to consider these phenomena together and show how each of them is grounded in America's racialized political economy.[28]

Economic distress, social disorganization, and cultural alienation form a soil in which criminogenic processes more easily take root.[29] Macro-structural pressures can combine with local circumstances to create concentrated poverty, communal disorder, and family disruption, which in turn make violence more likely.[30] Economic distress sometimes leads directly to crime, for example where homelessness, untreated mental illness, drug addiction, and domestic abuse motivate various forms of "survival crime." But causal processes are more often indirect. The fundamental elements underlying criminal involvement are motivation, control, and opportunity, and each of these is affected by economic hardship, which can motivate the use of deviant means to achieve conventional goals, put young men on the streets instead of in school or at work, and reduce social controls as public spaces lose their capable guardians.[31]

The most powerful criminological explanation for high levels of violence in socially disorganized communities points to the weakness of informal social controls, socialization, and social integration.[32] Where urban areas become socially disorganized, parents, neighbors, and communities are prevented from carrying out the essential tasks of socializing, integrating, and controlling young people.[33] As we have seen, the creation and reproduction of social order depends on the capacity of mainstream social institutions—families, schools, workplaces, communities, legal authorities, and political systems—to socialize, integrate, and control individuals. In well-organized neighborhoods, where informal social controls are an unobtrusive background feature of social life, high levels of participation and collective efficacy lead to low levels of violence.[34] But when an area is disorganized and social controls are sparse, youth go unsupervised, incivilities and disorderly conduct go unchecked, and public spaces become uninviting and dangerous. In such circumstances, deviance, crime, and violence become much more likely.

Economic exclusion and social control deficits cause young people to become detached from the integrative processes of the normal life course—from parental supervision, school attendance, paid employment, marriage, family, and so on. The result is an increased supply of individuals with a limited stake in conformity, weakly developed pro-social values, and poor impulse control, spending time together in settings where there are few responsible guardians and plentiful opportunities for crime.

The interaction of economic circumstance, social disorganization, and criminal violence is theorized in a classic 1995 article by Sampson and Wilson that argued that family disruption is the key mechanism connecting economic disadvantage with violent crime. In a later article reassessing the evidence, Sampson, Wilson, and Katz note that when patterns of violence become established in a neighborhood, cultural codes emerge to normalize and valorize its use, representing violence as source of respect, a means to respond to implied slights, and a sign of power. Once such codes emerge, they form "cognitive landscapes" in which crime, disorder, and violence become an anticipated dimension of daily life, making it more likely that young men will join a gang—or buy a gun—to defend against the threats posed by others.[35]

Conservatives often insist that offenders are rational, free-willed adults who freely choose to break the law and should be punished accordingly. But each of us begins life as an infant and grows into adolescence and adulthood as a result of developmental processes that unfold in specific environments at specific historical moments. In the course of this developmental process, we are each shaped by the particular psycho-social dynamics of family life, peer networks, neighborhood, school, and the social and historical environment of our formative years. Habits, attitudes, and cognitive capacities are shaped by these experiences, as are the strategies, techniques, and survival skills developed to deal with them.[36]

When violence figures prominently in childhood experience—as it so frequently does for people growing up in America's poorest neighborhoods—its effects can be powerful and long-lasting. Childhood exposure to violence—as victim, perpetrator, witness, schoolmate, or neighbor—produces cognitive, emotional, and behavioral consequences, one of which is an increased probability that violence will be a part of one's own behavioral repertoire.[37]

The institutions of work—the workplace, the employer, the labor market—also bring social controls to bear upon individuals and play a role in their socialization. People in full-time employment are busy much of the time. They become disciplined by the work process. They have positive incentives to stay out of trouble. They earn an income with which to meet their obligations. And they enjoy the status and self-respect of someone who works for a living. When work is absent or intermittent or when it is poorly paid, low-status, or degrading, these positive controls diminish. The chronic worklessness affecting many American neighborhoods and families thus has all kinds of negative ramifications.[38]

The absence of legitimate employment makes crime more attractive. When people get into debt, fall behind with rent, or have trouble paying bills, illegal conduct becomes more tempting. In neighborhoods where many people are commonly in this situation, illegal opportunities become more available and come to seem less culpable. Social norms emerge that skirt the law and normalize deviance. Activities such as theft, trafficking in stolen goods, benefits fraud, illegal drugs, and prostitution come to be portrayed as "hustles" that people need to get by. Deviance is normalized in a way that weakens social and psychological restraints.[39]

Where illegal markets for vice and drugs get established, gangs and criminal subcultures form around these activities, and violence—"the default contract enforcement mechanism in markets for illegal goods"—becomes a means of enforcing transactions and protecting illegal assets.[40] In such settings, violence becomes an effective means to get things done, a preemptive defense, and an essential tool of illegal business. As Sampson and Wilson write, "youngsters are more likely to see violence as a way of life in inner-city ghetto neighborhoods. They are more likely to witness violent acts, to be taught to be violent by exhortation, and to have role models who do not adequately control their own violent impulse or restrain their own anger." And because firearms are, in such contexts, readily available, "adolescent experiments with macho behavior often have deadly consequences."[41]

Once established, patterns of violence tend to persist, as more individuals join gangs or acquire guns to defend themselves and cycles of retaliatory violence take hold.[42] If the police response is an overly aggressive one, police-community relations become strained, leading to low levels of reporting and the reluctance of witnesses to assist police. The result is low clearance rates, which signal to intending offenders they are unlikely to be caught. A negative feedback loop is thereby set up, increasing the likelihood that individuals offend with impunity, while generating a fearful climate that leads onlookers to hurry past altercations rather than intervene.[43] Lower levels of social control and higher rates of criminal violence are the inevitable result.

Complex Causation

I have argued that the macro-structures of political economy exert causal effects on rates of street-level violence by virtue of intermediating sociological and criminogenic processes. I have also argued that the exceptionally high levels of violence and social disorder that characterized the United States throughout the twentieth century, and especially from the 1960s to the 1990s, resulted from America's ultraliberal political economy and the transformations it underwent.

Stated in these stark terms, my thesis might easily be misinterpreted or too quickly identified with familiar positions in the field, so let me stress some points of clarification.

I want to distance myself, first, from economistic theories that assume that criminal acts are driven by economic necessity. As well as overlooking the offending behavior of well-heeled corporate actors and white-collar criminals, such theories simplify the causal processes that lead to involvement in street crime. Although it is true that most convicted offenders are poor, it is a mistake to assume that their offenses are generally acquisitive crimes motivated by material need. As Robert Crutchfield notes, "While the image of the desperate yet heroic Jean Valjean may capture the romantic imagination ... a more accurate stereotype may be the teenager who mugs a schoolmate to steal his expensive athletic shoes."[44] There are, it is true, "crimes of survival": destitute mothers steal to feed their families; homeless people trespass to find a place to sleep; runaways engage in prostitution; welfare recipients shoplift when food stamps run out. But such crimes are not the main business of any prosecutor's office, nor are they the ones that land offenders in prison for lengthy periods.[45] Even though offenders' lives are often economically precarious, most offenses are not survival crimes.

Poverty is associated with higher rates of crime and violence, but the causation is complex. Adverse economic conditions—unemployment, absence of welfare benefits, poor housing, food insecurity, deep poverty—do not lead directly or inexorably to crime, and most poor people live law-abiding lives. Still less do these conditions directly give rise to violence. Poverty and deprivation describe social contexts in which criminogenic processes take hold, but they are rarely operative causes in themselves. Temptation, the example set by criminal associates, weak impulse control, relaxed inhibitions, poor calculation, addictions, trauma, absence of situational controls—these are all elements that often enter the criminal equation. The criminogenic processes that generate violence in disorganized neighborhoods are mostly the result of weak social and self-controls and an adverse balance between legitimate and illegitimate opportunity structures: not material deprivation as such.

Nor does the theory presented here imply any kind of structural determinism. My explanation of America's high rates of violence identifies a set of structural causes that produce crime outcomes indirectly and probabilistically, depending on the intermediating action of social processes and criminogenic forces. To talk in this way of structural causes and criminal outcomes is not to imagine irresistible external pressures that drive people to steal or engage in violence. Social structures are established patterns of action and institutionalized ways of doing things that shape the distribution of resources and the thinking and actions of large numbers of people. These structures, which are supported by powerful interest groups, enable and prevent action of various kinds; create or close off opportunities; and incentivize and disincentivize various kinds of conduct. Their durability ensures that the hierarchies and distributions that make up the status quo today will be there again tomorrow. In the United States, with its racialized, ultraliberal market economy, one effect of structural arrangements is the creation of racially segregated, multiply disadvantaged neighborhoods marked by inadequate resources, crumbling infrastructure, and scarce amenities. These neighborhoods, in which the poorest Americans are obliged to live, experience levels of deprivation and exclusion that are unknown in other affluent nations. Social milieus of this kind increase the probability that disorder and violence will result.

The impacts of social structures and institutions are altered as one moves from macro-level social arrangements to micro-level actions. Structural effects are countered, deflected, or amplified by other structural or institutional forces; they are modified by intermediating processes that operate between macro- and micro-structures; and they are altered again by on-the-ground actors who align themselves with, or set themselves against, the patterns of action these structures put in place.

As a matter of causation, the processes that generate specific offenses and rates of criminal violence are not the macro structures of political economy but instead the intermediating processes made more likely by the political economy's effects. These consist of contingent sociological processes (e.g., neighborhood decline and disorganization, residential turnover); situational circumstances (e.g., the presence or absence of effective guardians, the presence or absence of handguns); and the actions of groups and individuals in these situations (e.g., the decision to join a gang, to buy a gun, to stay in school). The emergence of antisocial norms, of illegal markets, of gangs, and of organized crime networks, are fateful developments that, once established, take on lives of their own. The structural causation of rates of crime and violence is a complex process, involving intermediate causal processes, contingencies, and time lags. There is no simple top-down determinism.

America's political economy makes social disorganization and criminal violence more probable, and more deadly, than in comparable nations. But these phenomena are neither inevitable nor uniform in their distribution. Social disorder, social problems, and criminal violence accompany social disadvantage, not as an inevitable effect but as an increased probability. Sociological and criminogenic processes are varied, multiple, and complex. And they operate probabilistically, not with an iron-law determinism. Abandoned neighborhoods, underserved communities, and unsupported families are at higher risk of being caught up in these processes, but there is nothing inevitable about their fate. Some poor neighborhoods remain safe and orderly.[46] Most poor people stay out of trouble. Many people who offend in their teens go on to live law-abiding adult lives.

America's extraordinary rates of criminal violence are not directly determined by America's political economy but are instead an indirect outcome of these economic structures, operating through a series of relatively autonomous sociological and criminogenic processes that, together with local conditions, events, and contingencies, give rise to distinctive patterns of individual action. Which is why levels of violence and social disorder vary from place to place and why local community initiatives and policy choices can make a difference to these outcomes.

A structural account of American violence does not imply a denial of individual agency nor any questioning of the concept of personal responsibility. In presenting a structural explanation, I make no claims about the responsibility of individual offenders for their criminal acts, which is a complex question, quite distinct from the one addressed here. Instead, I aim to show how community-level effects (such as social disorganization or rates of violence) are produced by structural conditions and processes. A structural account explains why a specific residential area or demographic group has elevated rates of violence; how these change over time; and why US rates are so much higher than those of comparable nations. It does not explain why specific individuals get involved in crime, nor does it imply that individual offenders are somehow "determined" in their behavior or not responsible for their actions.

Finally, it is important to clarify how this argument bears upon the plight of poor families, especially poor African American families. To discuss the links between social disorganization, family formation, social control deficits, and violent crime is to risk appearing to blame poor families for the social problems experienced by their communities.[47] But assigning blame to poor families or poor communities is no part of the argument I am making here. On the contrary, I agree with Messner and Rosenfeld when they write, "Any discussion of the role of the family in the black community must acknowledge its durability and vitality in the face of persistent structural disadvantage."[48] Instead, I want simply to insist on an obvious fact of life: families in such circumstances face severe disadvantages in their struggle to lead law-abiding lives and do the hard work of socializing, integrating, and controlling their children.

When single parents are deprived of adequate income and social service support—as is so often the case in the United States—it reduces their capacity to socialize and supervise their children, making neglect and maltreatment more likely.[49] Families play a large role in shaping the child's cognitive capacities, value orientation, and capacity for impulse control, so these difficulties can have major consequences for child development, which in turn shapes the probability of criminal involvement.[50] But other institutions also contribute, for example by shaping the opportunity structures that young people encounter and providing them with economic incentives, cultural norms, and social controls. And generous welfare states in other nations do a great deal to limit the detrimental effects that can flow from family difficulties. When a neighborhood is starved of political and economic resources, the result is failing schools, limited employment, spatial segregation, cultural exclusion, harsh policing, poor health, and background violence. In these circumstances, the children of stressed families are more liable to drift into criminal involvements.

Structural conditions and community-level processes explain why violent crime is higher among Blacks than among Whites. Elevated levels of violent crime among poor Black males are an effect of socioeconomic circumstances—not an effect of race.[51] Blacks reside in the most segregated, disadvantaged, and decaying neighborhoods, and it is these ecological differences that explain their higher rates of violent crime. Middle-class Blacks who live in more affluent, more organized neighborhoods have much lower rates of violence. Blacks with a college degree have the same rates of violence as middle-class Whites. And Whites who live in similarly deprived, disorganized neighborhoods exhibit violence rates that are as high as Blacks, though so pronounced is the racial character of concentrated poverty in the United States that is it rare to find White families in such circumstances.[52]

Crime and violence accompany social disadvantage not as inexorable effects but as increased probabilities. Individuals make choices, but, as Karl Marx observed, not in conditions of their own choosing.[53] My analysis is not a story about special kinds of people, with special kinds of criminal propensity: whatever separates Americans from the people of other nations, or Black Americans from White Americans, it is certainly not that. It is a story of how, as compared to other developed nations, America's political economy exposes neighborhoods and people to more severe economic pressures and more deadly criminogenic processes.

In the next chapter, I explain why America's reaction to this disorder and violence took the form of aggressive penal control and not the more positive social policy strategies that many African-American communities wanted and most affluent nations embrace.

7

Political Institutions and Crime Control

AMERICA'S POLITICAL economy is associated with high levels of social disorder and criminal violence because of the socially disruptive and criminogenic processes it sets in motion. That same political economy has implications for crime control. Scholars have long known that, because of America's distinctive political institutions, its criminal justice system is more directly exposed to political forces than those of other democratic nations. I will argue that American criminal justice is also more affected by socioeconomic forces in ways that press toward a greater deployment of penal control.

The impact of America's polity on the character of law enforcement is, in the first instance, a story of institutional design. American-style federalism, localism, elected justice officials, weak bureaucracies, and a limited welfare state all affect the character of criminal justice administration and crime control policies, not least because limitations of local state capacity restrict the range of actions American authorities can take to combat crime. But I want to suggest that there is also a second, less visible way in which political economy influences American law enforcement—this has to do with the impact that social disorganization and physical danger have on policing and punishment.

Criminal justice officials everywhere make rapid decisions when dealing with suspects, defendants, and prisoners. Is the suspect armed? Will they resist arrest? Is the offender a danger to others? Should they be placed in custody? This decision-making is, we know, shaped by legal guidelines, criminological knowledge, and professional experience as well as by risk tolerance and time pressures.[1] But other considerations also play a part. When police make snap judgments about the demeanor of a suspect; when prosecutors assess whether a defendant will show up in court and stay out of trouble; when sentencers and parole boards determine whether an offender is a danger to the public—these decisions are shaped by background facts concerning the circumstances in which suspects, defendants, and offenders live and the ways these circumstances are assumed to influence criminal behavior.[2] Though rarely acknowledged, these background facts are vitally important; they vary from place to place; and they have varying implications for action. In the United States, where so many justice-involved people live chaotic lives in disorderly, dangerous, gun-laden neighborhoods, they incline officials to act in ways that minimize risk—to themselves, to system processes, and to the public. That is to say: they prompt officials to impose penal controls. Officials in other nations, operating against different backgrounds, behave differently.

In what follows, I first outline the familiar ways in which America's political arrangements influence criminal justice practice. I then consider more novel questions of state capacity and how they restrict the scope of local governmental action. Finally, I describe the distinctive socioeconomic background against which American crime control operates and speculate about how it bears upon the decisions of penal state agents.

America's Polity and Its Penal State

America's criminal legal system is structured by the larger US polity, of which it forms a part; by America's labor market, which it supports; and by its interaction with the American welfare state, which it supplements. Like the larger American state, it combines federal, state, and local jurisdictions in a complex structure of powers and practices.

Responsibility for criminal justice is distributed across multiple levels of government, as in other federal nations, but, as we have seen, America's polity allocates an exceptional degree of authority to local jurisdictions.[3] In contrast to most other nations, including federated ones, America's cities, towns, and counties have primary responsibility for policing as well as for running municipal courts and local jails. American criminal justice is, as a consequence, hyper-local.

It is also peculiarly political. In most western nations, prosecutors and judges are career civil servants who are appointed in a nonpolitical process, enjoy security of tenure, and form part of a powerful state bureaucracy.[4] Their primary loyalty is to the law and the legal system rather than to a political party, an electorate, or a sponsor, and norms of bureaucratic authority and institutional autonomy shield them to some extent from popular sentiment and media headlines.[5] In America, by contrast, district attorneys and state attorneys general, municipal and state judges, and local sheriffs are mostly elected officials subject to popular recall.[6] Chiefs of police are hired and fired by mayors and municipal councils, so they too are embedded in local politics. Rank-and-file police officers, correctional officers, and assistant district attorneys belong to unions that are politically active and often quite powerful. The result is that electoral politics impact American criminal justice more directly and extensively than in other liberal democracies.[7]

A corollary of politicization is the comparative weakness of America's criminal justice bureaucracy. Like the public sector more generally, much of America's criminal legal system is under-resourced, with lower levels of professionalism, lower levels of autonomy, and more reliance on the private sector than is typical in other developed nations. This is especially true of criminal defense: public defender offices are chronically underfunded, and most defendants are obliged to rely on badly paid court-appointed attorneys with huge caseloads.[8]

Being mostly small and under-resourced, America's police and penal agencies are more open to political influence, malfeasance, and incompetence. Departments of corrections are headed by patronage appointees who rely on political favor. Parole boards are composed of politically appointed placemen with limited expertise, making them overly responsive to public opinion and risk-averse in their decisions.[9] Penal state functions are often subcontracted to private agencies and enterprises, or carried out in partnership with them, mixing public service with private profit.

All of this is quite distinctive in comparative terms, and some of the penal state's distinctive practices can be directly traced to these institutional arrangements.

That American criminal justice officials are elected is certainly consequential. Research shows that the conduct of officials is responsive to electoral discipline, with election cycles affecting the pace of police hiring, rates of prosecution and charge dropping, conviction rates, sentencing patterns, and the likelihood of capital indictments.[10] Given that public opinion has mostly favored tough-on-crime policies, being "responsive" has meant growing the penal state.

Or consider the spread of criminal justice functions across multiple levels of government. From the viewpoint of local officials, sentences of imprisonment, which are paid for by the state, are effectively cost-free, while sentences of jail or probation are a drain on municipal revenues.[11] These same federalist arrangements help explain America's reliance on imprisonment rather than policing, the former being cheaper and funded by the state and the latter more expensive and funded by municipalities. Compared to other nations, America spends much more on prisons and somewhat less on police, especially in its southern states.[12] In each case, choosing the more punitive option makes economic and political sense to the decision-makers.

Localism and Policing

Policing in the United States is a local government function. The result is that, compared with other affluent nations, police departments are mostly small, lacking in resources, and underprofessionalized.

Comparative research shows police training in the United States to be quite minimal relative to other affluent nations. And that training is mostly focused on the use of force, with new officers being taught to be alert to the slightest hint of danger and ready to draw their weapons in self-defense.[13] These poorly trained police are nevertheless heavily armed, generally carrying sidearms as well as Tasers and batons. Even the smallest departments are loaded up with military armaments and equipment, thanks to the federal funds that flowed during the War on Drugs and to offloading by the military following wars in Afghanistan and Iraq.[14]

Some larger departments such as the New York Police Department— usually in response to public outcries and court orders—have improved training, use-of-force guidelines, and reporting requirements with respect to "weapons drawn" incidents. Shootings, fatal and nonfatal, have been significantly reduced as a result.[15] But such reforms require resources, leadership, and effective management, which are not generally available. This is likely why the smallest police departments have the highest rates of police killings, with officers in Wyoming and New Mexico killing civilians at ten times the rate of their colleagues in Connecticut.[16] It also helps explain why police-involved civilian deaths are so much higher in the United States than in other developed nations.

Police accountability is also underdeveloped in America as compared to other developed nations.[17] Civilian review boards exist in many jurisdictions but are mostly toothless. Legal liability is also attenuated because prosecutors and grand juries are reluctant to indict; federal courts rarely become involved; and legal doctrines such as the "split-second" rule (which instructs judges and juries not to second-guess a police officer's split-second decisions) and "qualified immunity" (which shields officers from personal liability for constitutional violations) ensure that few officers are ever sued or indicted and fewer still convicted.[18]

Local government is where Americans address their crime complaints, but these authorities have limited resources with which to deal with them. Social and economic policy responses—which are more expensive than policing and punishment, and more controversial—are mostly beyond their reach. Large-scale efforts to deal with urban problems and the "roots" of crime would require extensive federal funding and support, but since the 1960s this has not been forthcoming.[19]

In a localized tax economy, municipalities with predominantly poor residents have low tax bases, while wealthier localities have more means at their disposal. Housing, schools, social services, and other amenities reflect these inequalities, resulting in a divide between affluent, high-amenity neighborhoods and areas blighted by social disorder and criminal violence. Poor districts with the worst crime levels generally have the lowest tax base and the fewest resources to deal with their problems.[20]

In cities that combine rich and poor districts, local politics limits the provision of social services to the areas they are most needed. Homeowner voters dominate local elections, so their (White, suburban) interests tend to shape urban policy.[21] City governments are pressured to deal with inner-city crime but are discouraged from doing so by means of social investment, because taxpayers in wealthier suburbs are unwilling to pay for aid to poorer center cities.[22] Lacking the power, resources, and political will to build public safety by strengthening communities, local governments adopt the means at their disposal. The result is a crime control policy in which police, jails, and prisons are favored but minimally funded; where "cheap and mean" regimes are standard; and where revenue policing subsidizes local budgets by extracting fees, fines, and charges from justice-involved residents.

"Cheap and Mean"

The United States incarcerates more people per capita than any comparable nation. Such evidence as we have strongly suggests that, compared with nations such as Canada, Germany, or the Netherlands, its prisons and jails also provide poorer conditions and lower levels of amenity.[23] One explanation for this difference points to the principle of "less eligibility"—a hallmark of prison administration everywhere—which insists that the inmates of prisons and jails ought never to receive better treatment than the poorest non-offenders on the outside.

The condition of the poor thus sets a ceiling for the conditions of the incarcerated, and because wages and welfare provision in America are mean—leaving America's poor much worse off than the poor of comparable nations—the treatment of people in America's jails and prisons has tended to be meaner still.[24]

A second explanation points to the difficulties that state and local governments experience when demands for punitive policies are accompanied by resistance to raising taxes. The problem these authorities face is, as Marie Gottschalk puts it, "How do you engineer a massive and expensive expansion of the penal system while at the same time spearheading a vehemently anti-tax, anti-government movement?"[25] This was the situation in America in the 1990s when politicians faced urgent demands for public safety, together with stiff resistance to increased taxation, and again in the mid-2000s, when a fiscal crisis drastically reduced local government funds. In both cases, legislators proceeded to outsource, to privatize, and to monetize criminal justice. They reduced costs by contracting functions out to private agencies, by imposing "user fees" on offenders and their families, and by embracing "revenue policing." And they pared back nonsecurity spending in jails and prisons, which increasingly became harsh, low-amenity institutions prone to overcrowding and high levels of neglect. The "cheap and mean" approach long characterizing penal policy in the South and Southwest thereby spread out to the rest of the nation.[26]

"Cheap and mean" regimes emerged when a rapidly expanding penal state combined with underfunded local government, neoliberal politics, and public animosity toward offenders. The same circumstances opened new vistas for private enterprise. Cash-strapped governments turned to commercial companies to build prisons, provide prison and probation services, and buy up criminal justice debt—thereby relieving public authorities of expensive tasks and providing opportunities for private-sector profit making.[27] Like the American state more generally, the penal state became a kind of franchise, in which public functions were carried out by private, for-profit agencies—generally with detrimental consequences for the quality of criminal justice.

America's criminal legal system has become a domain in which for-profit firms and state agents extract cash from defendants, probationers, prisoners, parolees, and their families. What in other nations is a tax-funded public function has, in America, become an occasion for predatory practices that extort the poor and profit from their punishment: a welfare state turned upside down. That this occurred in late twentieth-century America no doubt reflects the influence of market fundamentalism and the neoliberal remaking of the state. But it also reflects the design of the American polity and its consequences for law enforcement.

State Capacity

Penal control is the standard response of American authorities to problems of crime and disorder. Social control deficits in underserved communities make this a functional response, with the penal controls of the state substituting for the weakened social controls of civil society. But how did this policy regime come to be formulated and generalized?

We know from historical studies that, from the late 1960s onward, American communities urged authorities to do more to control violent crime and move drug dealers off their streets. Sections of the public strongly favored public health measures, rehabilitation, and restitution, and community leaders frequently called for "root cause" solutions involving social prevention, welfare provision, and healthcare. But in the event, what these neighborhoods received was aggressive policing and harsh penal control.[28] Why was this?

One obvious reason is the widespread skepticism that exists in the United States about the efficacy of government social programs, a skepticism that is, in a classic self-fulfilling prophecy, reinforced by the poor performance of underfunded government agencies. Skepticism is especially powerful with respect to social programs that aim to assist poor African Americans—the supposed failures of the War on Poverty being cited as proof that such initiatives do not work.[29]

Welfare policy, it is said, simply backfires, making the problem worse. At the same time, there is a widespread assumption that, when it comes to crime control, penal control *does* work. To many Americans, policing and punishment appear as immediate, inexpensive, morally appropriate, and emotionally satisfying policy responses that give offenders the hard treatment they deserve. By contrast, social policy interventions are seen to be more costly, to operate on a longer time scale, to be uncertain in their crime-control impact, and to reward criminal conduct rather than discourage it.

These considerations—reinforced by Republican opposition to social spending; popular hostility toward offenders and people on welfare; and political institutions that provide numerous opportunities to veto controversial legislation—ensure that American governments rarely enact preventative social investments to deal with crime.[30] That this is a settled disposition creates the effect of path dependency, meaning that any effort to mount a substantial social intervention requires novel forms of expertise, personnel, and agencies as well as a willingness to engage in long-term investment and institution-building. In contrast, the familiar, ready-made resort to police, prosecution, and imprisonment makes penal control the path of least resistance.[31]

There is also, however, an important structural explanation that is insufficiently appreciated—namely, that social approaches to crime control run up against the limits of state capacity, leaving American officials less able to adopt social measures than are their counterparts in other affluent nations.

State capacity is the institutionalized ability of a state to exercise its powers and ensure the implementation of its decisions throughout its territories, an ability that derives from the size and strength of a state's bureaucracy, its relations with other social actors, and its spatial and societal reach.[32] As one writer puts it, "high capacity states are . . . better equipped to establish a monopoly of violence, enforce contracts, control their populace, regulate institutions, extract resources, and provide public goods." Low-capacity states, by contrast, have limited control over territories and populations and frequently fail in their efforts to shape conduct and determine outcomes.[33] When New York City received federal funds to expand the NYPD by almost ten thousand officers in the 1990s, it thereby grew its policing capacity. That the early 1990s was the point at which NYC's crime rate began to fall suggests that this expanded capacity—together with improved techniques of management, accountability, and data-tracking—may have helped secure governmental ends.[34]

State capacity is not a one-dimensional characteristic. It is a complex variable that must be viewed in relation to specific agencies and specific policy goals. States may be capable of enacting and implementing certain policy initiatives but not others. Or they may be able to deal with a particular problem in one way but not in others.

My hypothesis is that considerations of state capacity—and not just policy preferences—led American legislators at the federal, state, and local levels to enact measures of penal control rather than pro-social measures such as crime prevention, social services, or economic investment. In other words, the differences in crime control policy that mark the United States off from other nations were caused by structural constraints and not simply by political choices. That public safety is the responsibility of the smallest and least well-funded unit of government accounts for part of this structural difference. The character of America's welfare state accounts for the rest.

American authorities have less capacity for remedial social action because America has a welfare state for the poor and the marginal that is less expansive, and less enabling, relative to the welfare states of other developed nations. And that welfare state—or at least the sectors of it addressed to the nonworking poor—was scaled back in the 1980s and 1990s.[35]

Welfare states are generally thought of as systems for tax-and-spend redistribution, but they also involve large-scale expansions of state capacity—infrastructures of positive state power—through which governments affect the fates of families and firms and the conduct of individuals. The character of a nation's welfare state thus has consequences for state power and the effectiveness of government.

In the welfare states of other rich democracies, there are governmental agencies, employees, and funding streams, the task of which is to ensure that households, schools, and communities are supported; social exclusion is combatted; affordable housing are made available; job-training and placement are provided; and employment is made secure. Highly developed welfare states provide diffuse, extensive, front-end forms of social crime prevention, furnishing support for families, schools, local employment, leisure facilities, social services, and so on, all of which improve social integration and informal social control at the same time as they enhance welfare. And when deviance or disorder do occur, there are social services, public health agencies, community agencies, and professional caseworkers ready to deal with problems of homelessness, mental illness, drug addiction, prisoner reentry, and the needs of crime victims.[36]

The social infrastructure of American government is, by comparison, less extensive and less well-resourced. City governments, in particular, lack the power to undertake elaborate or costly social initiatives at scale, with the result that urban problems cannot be effectively addressed in the absence of substantial state or federal assistance.[37] America's welfare state is less well endowed with the kinds of soft power—universal social provision, trained social work personnel, social service infrastructure, a capacity for coordinating care and control, and available expertise and resources—that other nations use to deal with crime and disorders. It consequently lacks social reach and effectiveness.

When American politicians, policymakers, and judicial actors face urgent demands to respond to criminal violence, they have fewer options at their disposal, and those they have are mostly repressive. Consequently, American criminal justice agencies are charged with tasks that other nations allocate to their social services. Jails are America's biggest mental health facilities, a role for which they are singularly ill suited.[38] America's police are expected to manage problems such as drug addiction, homelessness, mental illness, and school discipline in addition to the work of law enforcement. As Dallas Police Chief David Brown complained: "We're asking cops to do too much in this country. We are. Every societal failure, we put it on the cops to solve."[39] And when social service programs are provided in poor neighborhoods, they are often run through criminal justice agencies simply because that is where funding becomes available.[40]

Highly developed welfare states shape penal policy ideologically by inserting welfarist conceptions, aims, and values into the practice of criminal justice. But they also shape it substantively by providing an operational infrastructure and an array of soft controls. American authorities, poorly equipped in these vital respects, turn to policing and punishment.

Disorganization, Danger, and Decision-Making

We have seen why American authorities default to a penal control regime. But why are these penal controls so aggressive? Compared to other developed nations, American police more readily draw and fire their weapons; prosecutors are more inclined to remand suspects in custody and press for severe sentences; judges send a much higher proportion of offenders to prison for much longer terms; and parole boards are less likely to grant early release. How are we to explain these differences?

My hypothesis is that what makes America's criminal legal system different from other nations in these respects is the exceptional socioeconomic background against which America's penal state operates. American criminal justice actors think and act differently because the social milieus where many offenders live are, in fact, more disorganized, more violent, and more gun-laden than is the case elsewhere and because their perceptions of these areas are laden with stereotypes born of racism and social distance.

The conduct of American police and criminal justice officials is profoundly affected by the fact that so many of the neighborhoods in which they work are disorderly and dangerous, with high levels of gun crime and lethal violence. Because these socially disorganized settings lack the usual informal controls of family, employment, and community, penal state agents are unable to build on a solid platform of already-existing normative constraints. Nor can they leverage the disciplines of family or work or reputation to aid them in their efforts. Penal controls must be made to work all by themselves, unsupported by a functioning background social order. Consequently, they are ramped up and made more severe than would otherwise be the case.

America's police officers are known for their aggressive, "warrior-style" demeanor, and they kill civilians at a much higher rate than the police of any comparable nation. I want to suggest that an important part of the explanation for this has to do with the social milieus in which police officers carry out their duties.[41]

Law enforcement in the United States frequently operates in disorganized, dangerous, gun-laden environments, more like Brazilian favelas than British housing schemes or European public housing. The result is that police officers are often afraid for their lives.[42] This background danger is a prominent theme in American police culture, which insists that each time officers begin a shift, they are "putting their lives on the line" and that they should make it their first concern to go home alive at the end of the day. It is also a leading theme in police training. Police recruits are taught to fear for their lives at all times, especially when engaging in risky encounters such as "stop and frisk," traffic stops, and domestic violence call-outs.[43] By contrast, in the relatively gun-free nations of Europe, "[p]olice have much less reason to fear civilians in Europe, and civilians there don't have to worry about how they can demonstrate that they are not carrying a gun."[44]

American police are frequent victims of homicide. Between 2000 and 2021 some 1,166 were feloniously killed in the line of duty, with 73 such deaths occurring in 2021, a level of danger that is "vastly greater in the United States than in other developed nations."[45] For every police death by shooting, there are four times as many occasions on which police officers are shot at—which is to say, "assaulted with deadly force." A further 40,000 American officers are assaulted each year by unarmed civilians, with 12,000 of these resulting in reported injuries.[46] Braga and Cook report that "[r]oughly 10% of all [American] police officers are assaulted per year" adding that "[w]hen fatal and non-fatal assaults are combined, police experience the highest rate of violent victimization in the workplace."[47]

Gun possession is exceptionally widespread in the United States. That police officers are also armed means that at least one loaded gun is present in every encounter. In some 10 percent of line-of-duty homicides, officers are shot with their own guns. More than in any other developed nation, American police officers have reason to fear they may be killed while doing their job.[48]

These background facts affect how American police officers conduct themselves. In other dangerous occupations, deaths and injuries occur because of carelessness, human error, or lack of training and experience. Police officers have accidents too—particularly in high-speed chases—but they mostly face death and serious injury because of violent acts on the part of others. Being careful in these situations means being in control. If American police officers routinely take charge of a situation, demanding total compliance from civilians, it is because they are trained to "treat every individual they interact with as an armed threat and every situation as a deadly encounter in the making."[49] Michael Sierra-Arévalo reports that in police academy classes across the United States, trainee officers are made to watch a dashcam video from 1998 in which Deputy Kyle Dinkheller is shot and killed by the White driver of a pickup truck in the course of a routine traffic stop, the lesson being that "any seemingly routine interaction can snap to lethal violence, and that everyone is a potential assailant." One instructor told Sierra-Arevalo that the curriculum is designed to teach recruits that "Everybody wants to kill you."[50]

Police-involved killings—civilians killed by police and officers killed by civilians—are much more prevalent in the United States than in other developed countries.[51] The background presence of firearms is a big part of this story, but so too is what O'Flaherty and Sethi call "the fear hypothesis." As these authors point out, a climate of fear "amplifies violence by increasing the incentive to kill preemptively."[52] Police kill for fear of being killed, much in the way that gang members kill when they believe they will be killed if they don't act accordingly. And though these fears are frequently exaggerated and shaped by misleading stereotypes, they are not without a rational basis. The likelihood of a suspect being armed and dangerous may be low, but the probability is very much greater than in comparable nations. And when low-probability events can have disastrous consequences, the rational response is to proceed with extreme caution or else resort to preemptive action.

Perceptions of danger are always prone to exaggeration. Studies show the extent to which US police training emphasizes and exaggerates "the danger imperative."[53] And an exaggerated sense of danger leads, in turn, to unwarranted, preemptive violence, generally against groups that are negatively stereotyped. As Rosa Brooks writes "When you start with the belief that you're in constant danger, you're more likely to perceive situations as threatening. You'll shout and jump at a girl for reaching into her handbag in her own living room. You'll stop and frisk people who look at you funny and put their hands in their pockets. And maybe, eventually, you'll shoot and kill a driver who's reaching for his wallet, or a child playing with a toy gun."[54] But relative to other developed nations, many of the neighborhoods where American police are deployed are, in fact, dangerous, with rates of gun possession, gun crime, and homicide that are off-the-charts high in comparison. As Boston's police commissioner remarked, "We have so many guns that deadly force, to us, is always there."[55] Having guns in the background of every encounter conditions how

American police officers comport themselves and how they view on-the-street encounters.[56] Improved training and accountability could, no doubt, reduce the frequency of police killings, as the NYPD experience indicates. And progress in ending racist attitudes and perceptions could reduce the extent to which Black Americans are overrepresented in the number of civilians killed.[57] But until there is a major reduction in gun crime and homicides, it is unlikely that American police violence will approach the much lower levels of otherwise similar countries such as Canada, the UK, or Australia.

The disorganized, dangerous character of America's poorest neighborhoods also influences other aspects of criminal justice decision-making. In her study of misdemeanor justice in New York City, Issa Kohler-Hausmann showed that the issue determining how prosecutors and judges deal with their cases chiefly concerns the nature of the person before them: "Is this defendant a manageable person?" As she notes, most misdemeanant defendants are "people hauled in from disorderly places," leading court actors to presume that "almost anyone brought into misdemeanorland is in need of some level of social control."[58]

When prosecutors and judges know that offenders lead chaotic lives, lacking stable homes, jobs, and income, it is hardly surprising that they choose to send so many of them to jail—the United States has a rate of pretrial detention much higher than comparable nations—or subject them to marking and monitoring.[59] Officials in other nations release most defendants awaiting trial and impose fines or suspended sentences in a majority of adjudicated cases, because they feel confident that these offenders pose no danger to the public. And they rely on the background availability of free public services to treat mental illnesses or addictions, to provide housing support and essential social services, and to limit the extent to which offending individuals are socially excluded. American prosecutors and sentencers operate against a very different social background.[60]

Sentencers in European jurisdictions utilize stand-alone fines as a standard penalty for low- and mid-level criminal offenses. In the United States, criminal courts rarely use them, other than for traffic violations or corporate crime cases. As noted previously, this might seem puzzling, given the importance of the cash nexus in American society and the paucity of resources in local court systems. But when we consider that many defendants in the United States are too impoverished to pay and regarded as too dangerous or disorderly to be merely fined without imposition of further controls, the puzzle disappears.

The same is true of probation and parole. In many European nations, these are social work measures intended to rehabilitate or resettle offenders. In the United States, they are ambulant forms of penal control, undertaken by armed officers who consign their clients to custody at the first sign of noncompliance. Probation and parole officers in America are judged by how well they prevent reoffending, their chief concern being public safety, not client well-being.[61]

As compared to other nations, prisons and jails in the United States exhibit high levels of security, extensive use of solitary confinement, few amenities, and high background levels of violence. And the primary role of prison staff is that of ensuring security rather than encouraging rehabilitation. Again, the perceived dangerousness of the people in prison explains an essential part of the control regime.[62]

Compared to other affluent nations, the social background against which American criminal justice operates is an exceptional one that produces far-reaching effects. American officials decide the fates of suspects, defendants, and offenders under conditions of uncertainty, with scant information and limited time. They do so against a background of social disorganization and lethal violence that is objectively worse than that of any other affluent nation. And they do so in the full awareness that any perceived leniency in their treatment of offenders may affect their political careers—and in the case of police and prison officers, their physical safety—while aggressive choices will usually be met with approval. In these circumstances it should not surprise us that their conduct is so aggressively control-oriented.

The peculiar character of America's political institutions, together with economic constraints and limitations of local and welfare state capacity, shape the nation's crime control in distinctive and sometimes exceptional ways, making for a more localized, more politicized, more penal, and less welfarist form of criminal justice than exists in other nations. But as a comparative matter, what chiefly distinguishes crime control in the United States is the socioeconomic context in which it operates.

In no other developed nation do police and criminal justice officials work against a social background that is so frequently disorganized, so extensively armed, and so lethally dangerous. This danger is acknowledged by America's courts, which have shown a marked reluctance to hold police officers responsible for using force against civilians or to restrain the discretionary use of penal power.[63] It is recognized by that large part of the American public that supports "getting dangerous criminals off the streets." And it is acknowledged by American legislators when they enact extraordinarily aggressive regimes of policing and punishment and justify them in the name of public safety.

8

Social Sources of Indifference

IN THE AFTERMATH of George Floyd's death in 2020, American policing and punishment were subjected to intense criticism and scrutiny. Massive nationwide protests caused long-standing problems of police violence, mass incarceration, and racist law enforcement to break through into media headlines and become a focus of public concern. Within days there appeared to be broad agreement that the criminal legal system in its current form was intolerable, and commentators of all stripes urged the need for radical reform. Listening to this chorus of critics, experts, and journalists talk about the "broken system" and its scandalous characteristics, it was hard to understand how it could have been ignored for so long.

But ignored it had been. For decades previously, much of the American public supported the widespread use of aggressive policing and harsh punishment, paying little heed to the social and racial harms involved—or to the complaints of poor Black communities that they were being overpoliced and underprotected. Electoral majorities voted time and again for candidates promising to increase criminal sentences, empower the police, and enhance penal controls.[1] Reports of police killings, racial profiling, and the routine harassment of young Black men did little to disturb these law and order commitments. Voters raised little objection to the emerging regime of mass incarceration that consigned millions of Americans to penal segregation and second-class citizenship. They looked on as penal control reached a level never previously seen in any democracy. They embraced policies that lightened their tax burdens by shifting costs onto offenders and their families. And they and their representatives did so without offering up any explanations or excuses.

Millions of Americans, mostly people of color, segregated in harsh penal confinement. Police killings at levels seen nowhere else in the developed world. Predatory justice extorting revenue from offenders and their families.

Collateral consequences excluding millions of ex-offenders from mainstream society. Death penalties and whole life sentences imposed long after their abolition elsewhere. The persistence of these peculiarly American phenomena raises a question that is as much moral as it is sociological: how could such a monstrous penal state be tolerated by majorities of Americans and their political representatives?[2]

Are Americans more hard-hearted than the peoples of other nations when it comes to crime control and the treatment of offenders? Are they more vengeful and more cruel? Perhaps. But the hypothesis I present here is a different one. My conjecture is that this widespread indifference to the fate of so many fellow Americans was enabled by social relations that are a concomitant of America's political economy. Segregation and social distance, racial fears and hostilities, low levels of trust and cross-class solidarity—all traceable to America's racialized political economy—are, I will suggest, among the fundamental reasons why sections of the American public and their political representatives were able to tolerate such a monstrous penal state for so long.

Cruelty and indifference, like mercy and compassion, are socially structured emotions. We are inclined to feel sympathy for people who suffer unjustly, through no fault of their own, if they resemble ourselves. If, for example, they are members of our kin, our community, or our ethnic and religious groups; if they are people with whom we regularly interact; or if they are people whose fate is tied up with our own.[3] But we tend to be indifferent, or even hostile, toward groups that appear "other" or alien; who compete with us for resources; who threaten our interests; or who have (we suspect) brought harm upon themselves. Such people are often foreigners—enemy nations, trade competitors, geopolitical rivals, and so on—but sometimes these "others" are our fellow citizens, people who live alongside us in the same towns and cities.

What is remarkable about the United States is the extent to which poor people—particularly poor Black people—are set apart from the rest of society and viewed negatively. And it is these social divisions, I want to suggest, that have made it possible for most Americans to ignore the excesses and injustices of the penal state.

That the penal state's ill treatment of millions of fellow Americans could long remain a matter of public indifference is testimony to the weakness of cross-class and cross-racial solidarity in the United States—a weakness exacerbated by the de facto economic, educational, and residential segregation that so deeply divides the nation. Indeed, when we consider these deep and abiding divisions, the stigmatized form of segregation we call "mass incarceration" looks less like a distinctive phenomenon and more like the end point of an exclusionary, segregationist logic that runs like a thread through the entire society.

In liberal democratic societies, where liberty and equality are valued and public opinion matters, massive penal control on the scale seen in the United States is neither normal nor unproblematic. Outside of emergency or wartime conditions, it is likely to be tolerated only where there is widespread hostility or indifference to those being controlled; where the affected groups lack both power and functional value; and where the costs of control are narrowly targeted and its perceived benefits widely shared. In the United States at the end of the twentieth century, each of these preconditions appears to have been met.

I will develop this hypothesis in a moment, but first let me note the other causes that also play a role.

Visibility and Acceptability

Public indifference in the face of penal injustice is enabled by the low visibility that characterizes much of the criminal legal system. Modern jails and prisons, in particular, operate in relative obscurity, away from the public gaze. They put masses of people behind the scenes of social life, ensuring that they are neither seen nor heard much of the time.[4] And because the impact of mass incarceration is spatially concentrated, with poor Black neighborhoods most affected, the daily lives of White, well-to-do Americans are rarely directly impacted.[5]

Police misconduct, too, is largely invisible outside of inner-city neighborhoods. Police harassment, brutality, and shootings have long been everyday occurrences in America, but before the advent of cellphone cameras and social media, such events rarely captured the attention of a wider public. Had it not been for the teenager who videoed George Floyd's murder, the American public might have believed the statement that was issued by the Minneapolis police department immediately following the incident. Titled "Man Dies after Medical Incident during Police Interaction," the statement noted that Floyd, who "appeared to be under the influence," had "physically resisted" and that police officers "noted he appeared to be suffering medical distress" and "called for an ambulance."[6] In countless instances in the past, an official statement of this kind would have been the last word on the subject.

As for "collateral consequences" (the myriad civil disabilities that flow from a conviction), these were largely unknown, even within the legal community, until researchers showed that felon disfranchisement laws had tipped the result of the 2000 presidential election.[7] Debilitating fees, fines, and charges were, likewise, being routinely imposed on offenders for years before the 2015 Ferguson Report drew attention to the practice in the wake of the fatal police shooting of Michael Brown in Ferguson, Missouri.[8]

Even when these practices *were* made visible, the public often lacked ready-to-hand metrics with which to judge them. There was until recently no reliable count of police-involved killings of civilians, nor any sense of how US rates compared with other nations. International comparisons have shown the United States to be incarcerating at extraordinarily high rates, but such data rarely reached the general public, and when it did, it made little impact. Americans are used to thinking that things are different in the United States. It wasn't until the incarcerated population reached two million; video recordings of police killings appeared; protesters took to the streets; and the media foregrounded the story that the public began to take notice. Before that point, most Americans had little sense of how altogether extraordinary their penal state had become.

But even had they known, electoral majorities would likely not have called for change in the high-crime decades of the 1980s and 1990s. Aggressive policing, prosecution, and punishment were widely viewed as necessary responses to violence and social disorder in a period when crime was at the forefront of public attention.[9] Voters consented to these policies because they considered them necessary and believed that they worked.

And they were not altogether mistaken in this belief. Though the issue remains controversial, most experts believe that aggressive policing and mass incarceration—combined with the retrofitting of crime prevention and the emergence of community action—succeeded in reducing violent crime in the 1990s and 2000s, thereby benefiting masses of people, not least the residents of large cities and high-crime communities.[10] But it is also well understood that these policies imposed very serious social harms, above all on young Black men and communities of color.[11] And we can't know for certain whether a much less aggressive, much less punitive response might have contained criminal violence equally well. The example of New York, where jail and imprisonment rates were drastically reduced and mass stop and frisk was practically abolished, without interrupting the state's crime decline, strongly suggests that it might.

The issue that concerns us here is not whether aggressive penal controls produced crime-reduction benefits but whether the human costs involved were conscionable. Because these costs were so very high and so disproportionately suffered by poor Black people, one might have expected a radical reconsideration of policy. That the practices continued for decades, relatively undisturbed, suggests that for much of the American public, penal excess and racial bias were no bar to the pursuance of policies otherwise viewed as effective.[12] In the decades before 2020, there had been no shortage of activist protests, research reports, and investigative journalism documenting the harms of aggressive policing, mass incarceration, and racialized criminal justice. Why did so many people simply turn a blind eye?

The hypothesis I offer here is that majorities of American voters feared violent crime and unsafe streets more than they cared about those caught up in the penal state.[13] High levels of lethal violence powerfully shape public attitudes. When street robberies become a common occurrence; when homicide reports dominate the evening news; when everyone knows someone who has been mugged, or shot, or threatened, crime becomes a pressing concern. When violence ceases to be an aberrational event and becomes an existential threat and when it threatens to affect everyone and not just the residents of the poorest neighborhoods, public attitudes harden. People demand protection and look to strong government to provide it. Liberal values of freedom, equality, and due process are displaced by demands for protection and public safety; fear of violent others becomes more salient than fear of state power. Public identification with victims ("us") prompts antipathy toward offenders ("them"). That the groups caught up in the carceral state—poor, lower-class people, many of them Black—were anyway held in low regard and blamed for the disorders plaguing America's cities only strengthened this indifference.[14] As public opinion expert Justin Pickett bluntly remarks: "The reason we were free to get so harsh is, nobody cared about Blacks."[15]

In America's high-crime years, any feeling of empathy for the millions of people being stopped and searched, locked behind bars, or excluded from jobs and benefits was likely overtaken by a sense of relief that dangerous groups were being closely controlled. Police officers were regarded by many not as agents of an oppressive state, infringing the rights of innocent minority individuals, but as hard-working men and women doing the vital, hazardous job of keeping the public safe. They received unwavering support from most Americans, much of the time, because an aggressive penal state was viewed as much-needed protection against the depredations of dangerous criminals. These attitudes explain why police brutality, which repeatedly triggered riots in Black communities, was largely ignored as an issue by working-class and middle-class Whites.[16] Through their iterative political choices, American voters signed on, in effect, to a law and order covenant authorizing the buildup of a massive, racialized criminal legal system—a penal Leviathan. And they did so because they had been persuaded that the control of whole groups of lower-class, predominantly Black people was vital to their safety.

Race and the Limits of Solidarity

The racial division between White and Black people is the deepest fault line in America's social landscape. And racism undoubtedly explains some of the antipathy and indifference many Americans feel toward those caught up in the penal state. Support for the police, support for harsh punishment, and anti-Black attitudes have been shown to be closely associated.[17] That a majority of people caught up in the penal state are Black or Latino enables people holding such attitudes to regard police and prisons as essential institutions for the containment of dangerous classes and to oppose efforts to scale them back.[18]

Anti-Black sentiment leads to indifference about aggressive policing, excessive punishment, and racial bias in law enforcement. It also makes White voters less likely to support crime prevention policies that involve economic investment in poor communities. Such was the fate of the War on Poverty—America's last great attempt to tackle the roots of poverty and crime in Black neighborhoods—which was depicted by conservatives as an unacceptable transfer from White taxpayers to Black welfare claimants, rioters, and criminals.[19]

Racism is, no doubt, a source of public indifference toward the injustices and excesses of the penal state.[20] But racism, for all its specificity and historical roots, can be seen as a special case of a broader and more basic social fact: the low levels of trust and social solidarity that characterize American society. And when we attend to that social fact, it becomes easier to explain why Americans tolerate a penal state that aggressively targets poor people of *all* ethnicities.[21]

America's criminal legal system is heavily racialized, with Black suspects and offenders experiencing the worst of its excess and injustice. But it also metes out harsh treatment to millions of White, Hispanic, Native American, and Asian suspects and offenders—and this too was tolerated for decades without serious demur. Blacks are heavily overrepresented in the criminal legal system, but in 2022 fully 31 percent of state and federal prisoners and almost 50 percent of local jail populations identified as White.[22] Black victims, particularly unarmed Black victims, are overrepresented in police killings; but Whites form the majority of those who die at the hands of the police. Blacks are overrepresented on death row, but the majority of those put to death in

America in the modern era have been White. To tolerate America's penal state is therefore to tolerate a massive imposition of penal control on White people as well as on African Americans—to an extent that can hardly be dismissed as the "collateral damage" of a racist project.[23] Social distance and strained group relations in America go well beyond the fact of anti-Black hostility, even if that is their leading edge and most visible manifestation. Polling research shows the number of Americans who say most others can be trusted is below the international median and well below the expected level for such a prosperous nation.[24] My hypothesis is that these strained relations supply a fundamental condition without which America's monstrous penal state would not have been possible.

When Americans allow lawbreakers to be harshly treated—to be brusquely frisked, locked behind bars, consigned to a lifetime of second-class citizenship, or even put to death—they treat them not as fellow Americans deserving of dignity, rights, and respect but as inferior, alien others. The concept of an "underclass" that suffused right-wing policy discourse in the 1990s vividly expressed this "othering": crystallizing in a single term the identification of poor Black people with idleness, welfare dependency, drug use, and criminal violence.[25] Americans were taught to view this "underclass" with fear and resentment. They were repeatedly told about the extent of "welfare dependency" and the need for welfare reform. They read about chronic drug use and lethal violence in poor Black neighborhoods. They saw TV and magazine images of poor people living in disorderly, dangerous conditions. They heard such people described as "superpredators" and "crackheads" and as public enemies in the "war on crime."[26]

Once a group is labeled in this way, it becomes easier to withhold sympathy for their plight. Consequently, young Black men rarely became an object of public concern, despite the fact that they were, and are, the group most likely to be harassed by police, incarcerated by the state, or fall victim to homicide.[27]

City and suburban residents avoid neighborhoods associated with crime and disorder, increasing the social distance that marks their relations with such places. As social distance increases, stereotypes become more powerful, characterizing poor Black people as dangerous "others" rather than fellow Americans going through hard times. Under such conditions, the mass incarceration of Black men came to be viewed "as an unsurprising occurrence . . . not a shocking condition that demands immediate redress."[28]

Criminal legal systems everywhere mobilize ethical judgments about the people who are subjected to penal control. In America, these ethical judgments devalue justice-involved people and set their liberty interests at zero, reflecting a pattern of social relations that sets rich apart from poor and Black apart from White. In such circumstances, stereotypes prevail, variation and complexity are ignored, and whole groups come to be characterized by the conduct of their worst-behaving members. Instead of evoking feelings of empathy and compassion, the residents of high-crime neighborhoods are regarded as alien and threatening. Rather than being seen as deserving of financial support or social services, poor young Black males are viewed as obvious candidates for penal control. Social distance sets Americans apart. Segregation produces ignorance and stereotyping. Mass incarceration is what results.

Criminal offenders in any society are regarded as proper subjects for condemnation and punishment. People who commit serious violence are everywhere viewed as despicable and dangerous and are punished to the full extent of the law. But in liberal democracies outside the United States, penal law is much less harsh, penal conditions much less severe, and offenders are treated with greater humanity. As Émile Durkheim observed long ago, in modern liberal societies the passionate urge to wreak vengeance upon wrongdoers is countered by solidaristic identification with individual offenders, who, despite their crimes, remain human beings deserving of dignity and respect.[29] The striking thing about America's penal state is the degree to which this residual solidarity and inter-human identification so often appear absent.

The most startling example of a lack of solidarity between punished and punisher is the death penalty—a sanction that expresses a total absence of fellow feeling and that is used in the United States and nowhere else in the Western world. But the tendency to view offenders as disposable, dangerous others rather than erring citizens who remain fellow Americans is visible in other American practices such as high rates of police violence; mass incarceration; and life without possibility of parole. It is, in fact, a condition of existence for America's monstrous penal state.

Solidarity

The excesses and injustices of America's criminal legal system are tolerated and condoned because many Americans feel little solidarity with the people caught up in its controls. But what exactly is "solidarity"? And why is it so attenuated in contemporary America with respect to the racial and socioeconomic groups that are the chief targets of the penal state?

Solidarity is a characteristic of social relations, consisting of "bonds of mutual obligation and linked fate" together with feelings of attachment, trust, loyalty, and fellowship.[30] Émile Durkheim describes it as the bonds that unite men one with another and with the groups of which they form a part—a set of ties that gives order and cohesion to the group and a sense of belonging to the individual.[31]

Solidarity is a contingent rather than an essential characteristic. It varies within and across groups and within and between countries.[32] It can emerge spontaneously in small, tight-knit groups such as families, churches, neighborhoods, or military combat units where there are established norms of mutuality and concern for the common welfare. In larger associations, it must be actively constructed through practices of reciprocity and the development of shared values and mutual interests. It is more easily built where people regularly interact and share a life in common. It is more difficult to create where people are strangers to one another or where they lack common values, norms, and routines.

People in close solidaristic relations may feel an emotional connection, a sense of love and belonging, which can encourage them to make sacrifices for each other. But in larger groups, solidarity is more often based on reciprocity and mutually reinforcing self-interest rather than virtue or self-sacrifice. It depends not on altruism but on arranging things so that it becomes rational for individuals to behave in solidaristic ways—as, for example, where people facing common hazards engage in risk pooling to incentivize mutual assistance.[33] Solidarity has a practical, relational character that can be built and sustained by repeated interactions and involvements over time. In its broader forms, it can be a product of institutional design and need not depend on deep emotional connection or some preexisting cultural belonging.[34]

Solidarity can be created by institutions that establish and encourage shared membership, mutual interests, and a parity of esteem: institutions such as churches, colleges, social movements, labor unions, professional associations, and community organizations.[35] At a societal level where tens or even hundreds of millions of strangers are involved, it is possible to design institutions that build solidarity by actively affirming shared values, observing common rituals, and establishing practices of risk pooling and mutual aid. These practices constitute people as members of ongoing collective projects and routinely remind them of their shared fate. Practices of democratic citizenship such as voting, jury service, national service, and patriotism; Social Security and Medicare; participation in Labor, Memorial, and Independence Day parades are all real-world examples of institutions that function this way.

When people of different ethnicities and socioeconomic classes live together in integrated, mixed-income neighborhoods; when their children attend the same public schools; when they belong to the same labor unions, churches, neighborhood cooperatives, or cross-class civic organizations; when they share public goods and amenities; when they use the same public transportation; when they undertake national service or fight alongside one another; when they have common membership in universalistic welfare state institutions; and when political leaders stress values that unite the whole city, state, or nation, it becomes possible to build solidarity at the societal level, even with heterogenous populations that might otherwise be disunited.[36]

But solidarity can also be blocked or simply fail to emerge. High levels of inequality; "culture war" value conflicts; zero-sum competition over scarce resources; polarized politics; and social media bubbles—all of these deepen social divisions and destroy fellow feeling.[37] Above all, solidarity is negated by segregation, by "othering," and by the fostering of social divisions that emphasize incompatible difference, distrust, and mutual animosity.

Solidarity in the United States

The United States is a huge, pluralistic, diverse nation with state and civil society institutions operating at different levels, scales, and locales. Some of these institutions are impressively solidaristic. America has traditionally had a strong civil society characterized by tight-knit ethnic and religious groups, an ethos of self-help, generous philanthropic giving, and a practice of rallying together in times of crisis.[38] These characteristics emerged in colonial America and on the frontier, when the absence of developed state institutions and public provision threw pioneer and settler communities back on their own devices, eventually making a republican virtue out of this necessity. Early nineteenth-century visitors, Alexis de Tocqueville among them, were famously impressed by the young nation's self-reliant, self-governing communities, and these have formed part of America's national iconography ever since.

Today, in small communities around the country, one still sees high levels of solidarity expressed in the extent of volunteering, churchgoing, community activities, charity, and the provision of mutual aid. And it has become a cliché of American journalism that the reporting of any disaster always hastens to describe how the trauma will be worked through and healed by displays of community resilience, solidarity, and mutual support. Community solidarity is, we might say, a trope of American self-understanding.

But real and impressive as they are, these examples of communal solidarity have always existed alongside deep fault lines and major social divisions. Hostility and mutual suspicion mark relations between religious groups, between North and South, between immigrants and nativist Americans, between coastal liberals and heartland conservatives, between rich and poor, and above all between Black and White.[39] The pattern and depth of these social divisions has changed over time, sometimes becoming more fluid as immigrant groups assimilated and religious identities became less central to public life; sometimes being subject to powerful challenge as when slavery and racial segregation were effectively countered by abolitionist and civil rights movements. But many of the fault lines that divided America in the past remain powerfully present today. And while high levels of in-group solidarity are exhibited by some groups, relations between rich and poor and between Black and White are more often marked by distrust, social distance, and de facto segregation.[40] America's poor live different lives. The education, housing, healthcare, nutrition, access to services, and physical security they experience are not those enjoyed by middle-class Americans, let alone by the superrich. This is especially the case when these poor people are Black, as they disproportionately are.[41] Relative rates of racial and economic inequality suggest that America's social divisions are deeper than those of comparable nations. So do measures of trust.[42] And if we take rates of child poverty to be the most reliable overall measure of social solidarity—as political scientist Bo Rothstein has proposed—then the United States ranks as the least solidaristic nation in the developed world.[43]

De Facto Segregation

Segregation is the antithesis of solidarity. So it matters for these purposes that America is today a highly segregated society, both racially and economically.[44] Segregation is a corollary of antipathy, inequality, and estrangement, and it functions to deepen the social divisions that produced it in the first place. Segregation fosters ignorance, prejudice, reliance on stereotypes, mutual hostility, and indifference about the fate of others.[45] The more segregation, the less solidarity and the less mutual trust. Trust levels tend to be higher in prosperous nations than in poor ones. But "the share of Americans who say they do not trust other people in their neighbourhood is now roughly double what you would expect based on US socio-economic development."[46] According to Kevin Vallier, social trust in the United States declined from the early 1970s, when half of Americans said most people can be trusted, to 31.5 percent in 2018.

By contrast, 67 percent of people in Sweden report that they can trust others, 54 percent in Australia, and 42 percent in Germany.[47]

Until the middle of the twentieth century, racial segregation was encoded in American law and custom, ensuring that neighborhoods, schools, public amenities, and transportation were divided by race and that facilities reserved for Black Americans were generally inferior. Segregation of that kind is now illegal. But in much of America today, poor people, particularly poor Black people, live in neighborhoods that are, as a matter of fact, economically and racially segregated.[48] The residents of these neighborhoods have little contact with middle-class or wealthy people. They work low-wage jobs; send their children to under-resourced, often dilapidated public schools; use poorly funded public transit; shop in low-end retail stores; bank with extortionate same-day lenders; and rely on fast-food eateries that better-off people avoid. Rich and poor live separate lives in most societies, but in the United States poverty is deeper, more extensive, and more concentrated, and a greater distance separates America's poor from other Americans.[49]

Racial segregation was made illegal by the Fair Housing Act of 1968. And "redlining"—the practice of refusing to lend for mortgages in minority neighborhoods—was also outlawed. But the legacies of these arrangements, most notably the huge wealth gap between White and Black families and the concentration of poor Black families in de facto segregated neighborhoods, continue into the present. Of the Black families currently living in neighborhoods that are "majority Black and among the poorest quarter of all American neighborhoods," more than 70 percent "were raised by parents who also lived in a ghetto a generation earlier," meaning that poverty and social exclusion continue to be transmitted from generation to generation.[50] These forms of segregation are reproduced at the local level by exclusionary zoning laws that restrict the building of multifamily dwelling houses, thereby keeping poorer people out of prosperous neighborhoods. *Brown v. Board of Education* may have declared school segregation unconstitutional, but the racial segregation of schools is worse today than it was in 1954.[51]

America's most profound solidarity deficits flow from slavery, Jim Crow, and its long history of racial domination. But social division is also a consequence of American-style capitalism. America's political economy generates exceptionally high levels of inequality and extols a meritocratic culture stressing individual achievement and depicting economic success and failure in moralistic terms.[52] When poverty is viewed, in this way, as a moral failure for which individuals are themselves responsible—or when crime is viewed entirely as an individual choice—it reduces the inclination of others to provide aid or offer mercy.[53] If American culture has been prone to demonizing out-groups, as James Morone has argued, this would seem part of the same structure of feeling.

America is a huge and diverse settler nation marked by a history of slavery and segregation in which free-market capitalism has long been dominant. It is a country in which social schisms are deep and social solidarity is limited. Given these circumstances, one might have expected modern US governments to have done everything possible to remedy these damaging legacies by building solidaristic institutions. President Roosevelt did this in the 1930s and 1940s with Social Security, the G.I. Bill, and the legal recognition of organized labor. And President Johnson continued the project in the 1960s with Medicare, Medicaid, and the War on Poverty. But the subsequent return to free-market fundamentalism marked an end to these solidarity-building efforts.

What America lacks is not a potential for cross-class and cross-race solidarity nor the presence of civic-minded individuals. What it lacks are universalistic institutions that build solidarity across groups otherwise divided by race, region, and social class. Above all, it lacks solidaristic welfare state institutions; a strong, multiracial labor movement; universal health care; high-quality public schools; mixed-income housing; publicly funded childcare; family allowances; and so on—which place people in shared risk pools, provide them with mutual interests, and prompt them to regard each other as fellow citizens who share a common fate.[54] And it lacks these institutions because the US state has failed to build them. As Kathleen Thelen observes, "The role of the state in supporting social solidarity—through its impact on labor unity, on employers' cooperation, and especially on mediating the impact of liberalization, particularly for the most vulnerable groups in society—cannot be overemphasized."[55]

Other large and diverse settler nations such as Canada and Australia have built more comprehensive welfare states and more solidaristic institutions. Partly as a result, neither exhibits America's levels of social disorder and criminal violence. Of course, solidaristic institutions are more easily developed against a background of already-existing solidarity, which is why the most inclusive and generous welfare states emerged in small homogeneous nations such as Norway, Denmark, and Sweden. But the possibility of national solidarity-producing institutions doesn't depend on there being a preexisting national solidarity: it depends on the success of political coalitions in breakthrough moments. When societies build universalist institutions they can extend solidarity beyond its prior extent. As Bo Rothstein puts it, "The level of solidarity in a country is not culturally determined.... [I]ncreased political, social, and economic equality is something that can be manufactured by the design of political institutions."[56]

Welfare States and Solidarity

Welfare state arrangements, insofar as they are universalistic and egalitarian, help reduce divisions, promote solidarity, and supply the resources needed for families and individuals to flourish. At their best, they form interests in common, build mutual trust, provide individuals with security and a sense of citizenship, and promote the public interest. Welfare institutions also shape social relations, structuring the experience, identity, and status of people in need. Universalistic programs can build reciprocity and solidarity, setting up egalitarian, positive-sum relations from which everyone benefits. By contrast, the harsh, means-tested programs so prominent in America's welfare state stigmatize recipients and set up zero-sum divisions between the "welfare dependent" and the "hard-working taxpayer."

Universalistic social institutions—such as strong labor unions, cross-class civic organizations, national service, rituals of national remembrance, and so on—help build broad nationwide solidarities. Where such institutions are in place and higher levels of trust and solidarity are established, there are liable to be positive consequences for crime and criminal justice. Violence and social problems rates are lower in high-welfare, high-trust societies, so there is less demand for punishment and control. Welfare professionals are more likely to occupy leadership positions, so the orientation of criminal justice personnel leans toward more positive ideologies of reform and reentry. And generous welfare states build out an infrastructure of social services, providing various forms of soft power and nonpenal controls with which to prevent crime and manage deviance and disorder.[57] "Social crime prevention is woven into the general Nordic welfare model," Tonry and Lappi-Seppala write. "In this framework, the separation of general social work and specific crime prevention programs is neither necessary nor always easy. Such measures include parental counseling centers, a wide range of school programs, legal education packages, and support for students having difficulty with the curriculum.... Measures aimed at reducing social marginalization and achieving equality also operate as measures against crime."[58]

The American welfare state is, as we saw, a complex structure, large parts of which are hidden in the tax code. It provides decent retirement and health care benefits to seniors who have a lifetime of Social Security contributions and generous tax allowances to better-off individuals who enroll in employer-provided pension schemes and health insurance or borrow money to purchase a home. But the wages, benefits, and employment protections that low-skilled workers receive are among the worst in the developed world. And for people not in work who need income support, housing, healthcare, childcare, or employment, the American welfare state is decidedly ungenerous. Welfare claimants are means-tested, discouraged by convoluted application processes, subjected to work requirements, sanctioned for noncompliance, and stigmatized by political talk about "cultures of dependency" and "welfare queens," with the result that participation rates are low despite high levels of unmet need. And when clients do succeed in making their claims, the benefits they receive are mostly insufficient to lift them out of poverty. Rather than promote cross-class solidarities, these arrangements reinforce social distance and racial division.[59]

America's limited welfare state is in large part a result of the weakness of the labor movement in the United States and the absence of a labor party, characteristics that distinguish the United States from other industrialized nations. But this welfare state is also a result of racial, religious, and regional divisions. Widespread distrust of the national state is, at some level, a distrust of other groups who compose or control or benefit from it, especially other racial groups. That the US federal government, an equal-opportunity employer, has a workforce that is 20 percent Black makes it a target of criticism for aggrieved opponents of affirmative action.[60] For many conservatives, reducing federal taxation and shrinking the federal state are goals that receive top priority.

The American reluctance to develop a welfare state with generalized risk pooling and far-reaching social transfers is partly a reluctance to recognize the worth or deservingness of the groups that would benefit from such arrangements.[61] Rather than seek economic security through such institutions, American governments have opted, time and again, for private, market-based arrangements. The result is that America's welfare state is a class-structured one providing minimal aid to the poorest groups. It divides, demeans, and distances rather than drawing people together in a communal arrangement. As such, it operates in tandem to the penal state, which also functions as a powerful engine of segregation and social division.[62]

If America were to develop a more inclusive labor market, empower labor unions, build a universalistic welfare state, create a fairer tax code, end exclusionary zoning, and replace segregated neighborhoods with mixed-income housing and schools, it could reduce inequality, enhance solidarity, and build greater state capacity for the management of social problems. But over the last fifty years, America's social and economic policies have mostly moved in the opposite direction. Instead of building solidaristic institutions, American administrations have doubled down on market fundamentalism; instead of reducing inequality and insecurity, they have dramatically increased them. By repeatedly choosing the free market, deregulation, and tax cuts over the social state, America's political elites have enriched corporations and the wealthy while reinforcing insecurity, resentment, and distrust among working people.

The hallmarks of "neoliberalism" have been antagonism toward the welfare state, labor unions, the public sector, and progressive taxation, resulting in a raft of policies that, whatever effects they might have on the economy, consistently function to reduce social solidarity. A refusal to pay taxes is, in effect, a rejection of membership in the collectivity, just as a preference for private welfare is a withdrawal from common provision. Such policies constitute individuals as self-interested consumers divided by wealth, not fellow citizens connected by belonging. They undermine solidarity.

Mercy and compassion do not flourish in a context of social division. Nor are they encouraged when many people live in stressful conditions. When working people are economically insecure and afraid for their physical safety, anger and resentment flourish, and criminal offenders or welfare claimants become targets of popular hostility. America's extraordinarily high rates of penal control—like its restrictive welfare state for the poor—are so many indicators of weak social solidarity. Little wonder, then, that the suffering of millions of offenders caught up in penal state could remain a matter of public indifference for so long.

What this analysis shows is that America's extraordinary penal state is structured and sustained by America's extraordinary political economy by the operation of three causal processes. It was the structural shifts in America's political economy in the 1960s and 1970s that triggered an upsurge of social disorganization and criminal violence. It was the structure of America's political economy and the limitations of local and welfare state capacity that ensured that the response to these disruptions would be a massive rollout of penal control. And it was America's racialized political economy that limited solidarity and enabled public indifference toward the millions of people caught up in the controls of the penal state. The extraordinary character of that political economy explains why the resulting levels of disorder and violence, of aggressive policing and punishment, and of public acquiescence and indifference, had no equivalents elsewhere in the developed world.

America's penal state—and the material and symbolic segregation it imposes—is predicated on deep structures of inequality, social division, and racial exclusion. When radicals push for "root causes" to be addressed, these are the structural conditions they wish to see changed.

Epilogue

CONSTRAINTS AND POSSIBILITIES

THE RADICAL analysis is correct. America's extraordinary penal state, like the violence and disorder that form its background, has deep structural sources. If we wish to understand the fundamental causes of America's criminal legal system, its excesses, and its injustices, we must look to the racialized political economy that prevails in America today.[1]

America's penal state is rooted in a peculiar political economy that sets the United States apart from other affluent democracies. It is this ultraliberal form of capitalism that causes the United States to be exceptionally prone to social disorganization and criminal violence and to rely so heavily on aggressive policing and punishment. And it was a specific transformation of that political economy—deindustrialization, the abandonment of central cities, the onset of neoliberalism—that triggered an upsurge of criminal violence and, eventually, a massive buildup of penal controls.

Other affluent nations have lower rates of violence and less extensive penal states because their more constrained markets and more comprehensive welfare states provide greater levels of security, solidarity, and informal social control. Elsewhere in the developed world, the socioeconomic milieus of the lower classes are less disorganized, less gun-laden, and less homicidal. And when crime and disorder do appear, as they do in any society, these other nations have institutional arrangements enabling them to limit their reliance on repressive responses and deploy nonpenal forms of control. America's monstrous penal state is an apparatus of control rooted in the nation's broader social structures, not a contingent policy choice that can be easily undone.

That, in summary, is the comparative, structural analysis set out in the present work. That analysis—and the sociological theory that motivates it—will stand or fall on its arguments and the empirical evidence that bears upon them. Future research on variation between US states, on variation between the United States and other nations, on social control and penal control, and on the causal links between political economy and the penal state will confirm, refute, or refine this explanatory framework. By way of a conclusion, however, I want to draw out what I take to be the implications of this analysis for the politics of penal change. Others may accept the structural analysis developed here while drawing different political inferences.

What does this "root cause" analysis imply for political action? Are abolitionists correct to insist that without root and branch transformation, nothing will change? Must we first dismantle America's capitalist system and its racial order before we can roll back its penal state?

The radical critique that emerged in 2020 has two prescriptive dimensions: one is to address the root causes of crime and violence; the other is to abolish the institutions that America has developed to deal with these. Much of the previous discussion has been concerned with the first of these issues, so let me begin by considering abolition as a basis for political mobilization and policy change.

Abolition

"Abolition" means different things to different people, but it is widely agreed that the distinctive aim of the abolitionist movement is to *abolish* the institutions of police and prison rather than reform them or scale back their use.[2] Abolitionists insist that this is an aim to be pursued here and now, not in some distant future when society will have been remade. And they are frequently dismissive of reforms that stop short of abolition, insisting that such measures have always failed in the past and tend to enhance the penal state rather than reduce its powers. As an article by Mychal Denzel Smith put it, "Incremental change is a moral failure."[3]

Abolitionism is the name of a diffuse, decentralized social movement rather than a well-defined theory, and social movements are complex phenomena with multiple dimensions.[4] If they are to succeed, they need powerful ideals with which to recruit and motivate supporters and a clear message with which to change popular consciousness. In these respects, the idea of total abolition has obvious appeal. It provides the movement with a radical identity, setting abolitionists apart from reformers who are willing to compromise with, and perhaps be coopted by, the system. It echoes the great nineteenth-century campaign to abolish slavery. And it conveys the powerful moral message that America's penal state is broken beyond repair.

But to succeed, social movements must also achieve tangible results. And to build political influence, they must appeal beyond their core group to the wider public and to elected officials. So perhaps it is not surprising that, despite their doubts about reformism, self-described abolitionists are often at the forefront of local reform campaigns that engage with the penal state and seek to remedy its injustices.[5]

So, what should we make of this radical idea and its various expressions? Knowing what we do about the social organization of modern societies, is the abolition of the police or of the prison a serious possibility?

If abolition is taken to mean *institutional* abolition—the abolition of police, of imprisonment, and of the criminal conduct that currently makes them necessary, it seems clear that the answer is no. Not because abolition in the United States seems unlikely any time soon, though this is certainly the case, but because a total abolition of the police and the prison, or of crime and punishment, is inconceivable in societies such as ours.[6]

When pressed to explain how a society without police or prisons might come about, abolitionists point to a future in which capitalism and racism have been overthrown; social relations cease to be antagonistic; and crime as we know it disappears. As Mariame Kaba puts it, "We don't want to just close police departments. We want to make them obsolete."[7] This vision is certainly appealing, and there is value in encouraging imaginative thinking about a world made anew. As Leszek Kolakowski observed, "historical experience... tells us that goals unattainable now will never be reached unless they are articulated when they are still unattainable."[8] But in present-day circumstances, this vision is a deeply unrealistic one, not just in free-market America with its extraordinarily high levels of violent crime but even in well-ordered social democratic societies such as Norway and Sweden.

As a sociological matter, the idea of a crime-free society is an impossibility, as Émile Durkheim famously demonstrated.[9] Crime is an inevitable feature of any stable form of social life, as is punishment, because human groups create social order by establishing norms of conduct backed by sanctions. Group norms vary in their content, with different things being prohibited or required in different times and places. But the obligatory rules of any group are generally set at a level most people can meet most of the time but that some individuals will sometimes choose to breach, either because their subjective desires and interests are not fully aligned with the group or because they momentarily give in to hot anger or easy opportunity. As Philip Selznick puts it, "To explain the persistence and universality of delinquency, we need only postulate that people are active, questing, and self-referring; that they are not puppets or automatons; that they continually make choices between one or another course of conduct, with a view to gaining immediate or long-run satisfactions."[10]

Human beings live in groups; groups establish norms; and these norms, on occasion, are violated by individuals. When such violations occur, they prompt a reaction—by victims, onlookers, or the public—that leads to the imposition of punishment by the group's designated authorities, a process demonstrating that the norms are obligatory and reaffirming the values they express. A social world lacking these features would be a world without group morality or individual freedom—an unrealistic and undesirable aim for any social movement.

Crime will always be with us, and there will always be a need for offenders to be sanctioned. But, of course, imprisonment is only one possible sanction among others, and there have been past societies that have not relied on incarceration. Might *prison* abolition be a realistic goal, even if the abolition of crime and punishment is not? Again, and despite the horrors so often associated with incarceration—Ruth Gilmore describes the American system as "a machine for torture and murder"—sociological analysis suggests that the answer is no.[11]

Since the early nineteenth century, no modern society has existed without some form of imprisonment, though there is enormous variation in the quality and quantity of the prison's use. Imprisonment is inherently problematic, and most actual prisons are sorely in need of remedial transformation. But prisons play an essential role in the penal repertoires of modern societies for reasons that are not liable to disappear.

Any legal system needs an ultimate sanction that can be imposed when offenders withhold cooperation and refuse to submit to legal authority. Following the decline of the death penalty, banishment, and transportation, the prison represents the only effective, culturally acceptable means for doing this. In modern Western culture, reliance on bodily, corporal punishments has come to seem distasteful and uncivilized. The same is true of capital punishment, even if some American states are laggards in this respect.[12] In the absence of capital and corporal sanctions, custodial measures of some kind become essential, not merely to deal with "dangerous" individuals but, more routinely, as a means with which to control noncompliant individuals.

Noncustodial sanctions, such as fines or community penalties, require the cooperation and compliance of the person being sanctioned and assume that the person presents no continuing threat to the well-being of others. Where offenders refuse to comply, or appear to pose a threat, some minimum of coercive control becomes essential.

The prison is the institution upon which modern societies rely to meet this need because, unlike corporal and capital punishments, the prison does not—at least in principle—rely on the deliberate infliction of physical violence. It incapacitates not by killing or maiming but instead by putting people perceived as troublesome behind the scenes of social life.[13] It also imposes a form of retributive suffering—the deprivation of liberty—that accords with the character of modern society and, notionally at least, affects everyone equally. Prison sentences can be calibrated by length of time and by severity of regime, enabling carceral punishments—which range from brief, part-time detention in an open prison to lengthy confinement in maximum security—to be tailored to the offense and to the offender. Imprisonment can even, under certain circumstances, facilitate rehabilitation, education, healthcare, and preparation for work after release, though these positive aspects are grossly underdeveloped in American prisons.[14]

For all these reasons, imprisonment has become an essential institution in modern Western societies. Rates of imprisonment can, of course, be drastically reduced from current American levels. Conditions of confinement can be greatly improved. And perhaps in the future some form of electronic surveillance and control will provide an effective substitute for walled enclosures, and the prison as we know it will begin to disappear.[15] But "imprisonment" will still exist, no doubt with new pathologies to match its electronic form.

What about abolition of the police? Again, this seems a sociological impossibility and a goal that might not be desirable even were it possible. Every developed nation today has a police force, a specialist public agency tasked with crime control, order maintenance, and emergency response authorized to use force in certain circumstances. If criminal laws are to be imperative commands rather than mere suggestions, a coercive backstop of some kind is unavoidable. Enforcing the law, keeping the peace, protecting persons and property, responding to emergencies and disorderly events, using coercion, including deadly force where necessary: these are the distinctive tasks that in modern societies have become the responsibility of police. As Egon Bittner famously observed, "Police are called when something is happening that ought not to happen, about which something ought to be done, now!"[16]

Of course, police activities such as patrolling the streets, apprehending suspects, and delivering them to the justice system ought not to be confused with the whole of public safety, which, as I have argued, depends much more on social control than on penal control. And police work does little to address the root causes of crime and disorder—which is why "defund the police" proponents insist that first-responder responsibilities should be shifted away from armed police to social service agencies. But for all their limitations, the core police functions are essential to the enforcement of law and the maintenance of order in modern societies.

"Ending the police," were that possible, would be a disaster for poor communities.[17] In the absence of tax-funded public police, wealthier people would hire security guards and private police forces, as many already do, leaving the poor more fully exposed to criminal depredation. Analyses that suggest otherwise either assume the (impossible) existence of a crime-free society or else imagine that an alternative law-enforcement agency, operating under a different name, will somehow perform these tasks while avoiding the problems that go with them.

America's problem is not that it has police. It is that it has hyper-local policing with thousands of police departments that are poorly funded, underprofessionalized, racially biased, and trained to operate in ways that are altogether too aggressive. Its problem is that the police discharge extraneous responsibilities—in schools, in public housing, in traffic control, in revenue collection, in social service provision—that nations with more extensive welfare states allocate to other agencies.[18] Its problem is that American police are heavily armed, overly aggressive, underregulated, and for the most part unaccountable. A progressive penal politics would narrow the functions of police departments while improving their funding, quality, professionalism, responsiveness, and accountability. It would not do away with them altogether.

Similarly, the problem with America's penal state is not that utilizes imprisonment. It is that American jails and prisons incarcerate millions of people for unconscionable periods in badly run institutions with harsh regimes and appalling conditions to an extent that is altogether out of line with other developed nations. Radical reductions in America's use of imprisonment—and radical improvements in its prison system—could be made that fall far short of abolition but which would nevertheless be truly transformative.

The scandal of America's criminal legal system is not that it deploys police and prisons: in modern societies these are normal social facts. The scandal is that these institutions are organized and deployed in an extraordinarily excessive, aggressive, and unjust fashion.

Abolitionists have injected a passionate idealism into a field marked by low expectations and weary cynicism. They have altered the terms of political discourse about the penal state, inserting a radical new idea into the debate. But politics requires perspective as well as passion, an ethic of responsibility as well as an uncompromising ethic of conviction, and a sociological understanding of contemporary society makes it clear that abolition in any strict sense—whether of crime, police, or prisons—is not a practical possibility.

Total institutional abolition is a chimera: a sociological impossibility. But there are more limited forms of abolition—let's call them *practical abolitions*—that can be pursued with some likelihood of success. Activists challenging the penal state can and do focus on egregious, harmful, only-in-America practices such as capital punishment, life imprisonment without parole, prolonged solitary confinement, prolonged probation, cash bail, the split-second rule, or criminal justice fees and charges. They can show that these practices have been successfully abolished, or indeed never existed, elsewhere. And they can and do campaign for them to be outlawed in the United States. They might also argue, as many already do, for an end to mass incarceration, an end to unwarranted police violence, and an end of racial discrimination in law enforcement and penal sentencing. None of these are achievable in the short term. Some would become feasible only as a result of major social investments or larger structural change.[19] But unlike total abolition, they are progressive goals with some realistic prospect of success.

Abolition politics takes various forms, many of them well grounded in the realities of penal politics and the difficult work of bringing about change. But where abolitionists embrace an ultraist "all or nothing" approach, they overestimate the possibility of dismantling structural constraints and underestimate the possibility of progressive change within these constraining structures. The analysis developed here casts doubt on both these estimations.

Structural Limits to Reform

That America's penal state is rooted in the nation's political economy means that these larger socioeconomic structures will present serious obstacles to radical penal change. Any movement to bring the United States fully into line with Western norms of policing and punishment would have to overcome the structural constraints of the US political economy and the powerful social interests that uphold them. This raises two questions. What are the possibilities of a transformation in the structures of political economy? And to what extent can the penal state be transformed even in the absence of broader structural change?

On any reasonable assessment, America's political economy is not currently on the verge of a progressive transformation. Antiracists and their liberal allies can point to successes in discrediting racist ideologies and have, over the past sixty years, made significant progress in dismantling racist practices. And because racial discrimination is widely regarded as illegitimate, there are legal and political resources supporting antiracist reforms that will help withstand the current backlash against liberal elites and identity politics. By contrast, American free-market capitalism is widely regarded as legitimate, is very stoutly defended, and is embedded in political institutions that make radical change exceptionally difficult. Any serious challenge to capitalism's hegemony, any major reduction of corporate power, any shift from the neoliberal present to a more social democratic future, would require a series of conditions that includes the following: a massive mobilization of working people and their allies; a radicalized, unified Democratic Party; successive electoral victories bringing full control of Congress and the presidency; and a raft of progressive legislation that would withstand judicial review by a conservative Supreme Court. None of these seems at all likely at present.

America has undergone progressive transformations in the past. The New Deal, the Great Society, and the civil rights revolution were radical upheavals that moved US politics off the well-worn paths of White supremacy, corporate power, and free-market policies.[20] But such changes occur only when the nation's institutions and the power relations backing them are seriously disrupted—by war, by economic collapse, or by popular uprising. And it is notable that neither the global crash of 2008 nor the pandemic of 2020–23 have so far resulted in major transformations. Business-as-usual politics and divided government do not produce big structural change.

Absent structural change of this kind, social problems and lethal violence in the United States will likely remain at extraordinarily high levels, and American policing and punishment will continue to be international outliers, imposing more extensive and intensive penal controls than any comparable nation. This is a sobering thought and a disappointment to the radical hope that emerged in summer 2020. But in the current conjuncture, it seems inescapable.

Structural Change, Crime, and Punishment

That progressive structural change currently appears improbable does not make it impossible in a longer time frame. So, for the sake of argument, let us assume that structural change in America's political economy does take place at some future date and that a progressive movement succeeds in building social democratic institutions that greatly reduce inequalities and insecurities. How would a structural change of this kind impact crime, policing, and punishment?

Here the issues become complicated. We know that political economies and penal systems are correlated and that more social democratic nations have less repressive penal systems. But we don't know much about processes of *transition*—about what would happen if an ultraliberal political economy was restructured to become more social democratic. All things considered, it seems likely that a structural movement toward more social democratic arrangements would not immediately lead to a reduction in crime or a dismantling of the penal state.[21] The establishment of a more comprehensive, universalist welfare state with full employment, strong labor unions, extensive employment protections, and decent social provision would certainly improve the lives of working people and raise up the poor. Over the long term, it could also be expected to curb violent crime and reduce the felt need for penal control. However, it is important to appreciate that these crime control effects would not be automatic, nor would they likely occur in the short term—for reasons implicit in the theory developed in this book.[22]

Political economy and the criminal legal system are loosely linked rather than tightly coupled. They affect one another, but they do not march in lockstep. The linkages that connect political and economic structures with crime rates and penal practices are, as we have seen, indirect and probabilistic, mediated by processes, places, and cultures that have dynamics of their own and are liable to have lingering effects that will not disappear overnight. It is therefore a distinct possibility that the structures of political economy could, over the course of two or three presidential administrations, be significantly altered and that a more inclusive labor market, improved wages and security of employment, a more capacious welfare state, and reduced racial and economic inequality could be put in place, *without* producing concomitant change in levels of violence or in patterns of policing and punishment.

Building social relations of trust and solidarity, altering behavioral norms and cultural beliefs, overcoming generationally transmitted deficits and disadvantages, reducing entrenched patterns of disorganization and violence—these are long-term social undertakings, not easily implemented policy adjustments.[23] When we compare America with other nations and find that social democratic societies exhibit less disorder, less violence, and less aggressive penal controls, we are not observing a short-term, easily reproducible policy effect. We are comparing the characteristics of settled social institutions and social relations that have come into existence over the course of many decades and shaped social behavior over generations.

The social democratic welfare states of societies in Scandinavia and Western Europe were a long time in the making. And they often built on institutional legacies of religious solidarity, cross-class coalitions, strong labor movements, and small, relatively homogeneous populations. If US politics were to undergo a sustained leftward shift, it would be a generation or more before increased levels of solidarity, trust, family formation, and social control took root and began to make a noticeable impact on crime. Even then, the pervasive presence of guns—as well as the size and heterogeneity of the nation—make it unlikely that the United States would ever achieve the low levels of criminal violence and penal control enjoyed in much of Europe. And if, as I have argued, high levels of criminal violence play a key role in legitimizing the penal state, their continuation is liable to act as a brake on efforts to dismantle it.

Economic and social policy reforms do not bring crime-reduction benefits overnight; this aspect of progressive reform is often misunderstood. Creating a more egalitarian, more solidaristic political economy is a long-term project with uncertain prospects. If successful, it would lay the groundwork for secure families, strong communities, solidaristic relations, and informal social controls, all of which reduce the likelihood of social disorder and loosen the grip of criminogenic processes. Universal healthcare would reduce the extent to which people with mental illnesses and addictions become involved with criminal justice.[24] Affordable housing would move homeless people off the streets and reduce jail populations. Strengthened labor unions would improve wages, conditions, and strengthen communities. An adequate minimum wage, together with free childcare, free preschool, and paid parental leave would, over time, enhance the functioning of families, integrate young men, and reduce crime and violence.[25] Prenatal care, nurse home visitation, and early childhood programs could enhance child welfare and reduce adolescent offending.[26] Improved high school retention would reduce adolescent crime and improve the employment prospects of at-risk youth.[27] An end to de facto segregation in housing and schooling would result in stronger communities, less disorder, and less crime.[28]

But—and this point deserves emphasis—in the creation of a social democratic political economy, all of these crime reduction effects would be ancillary and, in a sense, accidental. The prevention of crime would be a virtuous side effect rather than the primary aim of the legislation or the focus of its implementation and evaluation. And because social welfare spending on crime is most effective when aid is received earlier in life—its major crime-control impacts being a lagged effect of improved childhood development—it would be by no means certain in the short term.[29] Bruce Western puts it well when he writes that the full crime-prevention benefits of poverty reduction "may be slow to emerge as children pass through adolescence and into adulthood. As a result, we can't expect the poverty rate to move in lockstep with crime and other social indicators. Instead, we should think of a broad zero-poverty policy regime as laying a foundation on which other change becomes possible."[30]

Viewed purely as a method of crime control, social democratic institution-building would be slow and extraordinarily expensive; indeed, it would not likely be undertaken were this its only effect. But such institutions and policies are not, in the first instance, methods of crime control. They are arrangements designed to enhance the security of working families, to reduce inequality, and to improve the general welfare, and they would be understood and evaluated accordingly. Crime prevention, if and when it occurs, would be a positive externality, not the primary purpose of the social democratic project.

The development of progressive, humane penal institutions would depend not just upon broader socioeconomic change relaxing the restraints of less eligibility but also upon shifts in public attitudes that would make the electorate more amenable to penal reform. As a Norwegian criminologist puts it: "what makes the Nordic prison systems unique is not the mundane regularities and empirical details of their institutions. Rather, it lies, on the one hand, in the web of popular mentalities that envelops the process of punishment, those collective representations that construct and construe both crime and punishment in particular ways; on the other hand, in the structure of the welfare state, particularly the generous and universalistic character of the assistive and social wings of the state."[31] If America's penal state is to become more social democratic in character, it will involve long-term cultural change as well as structural transformations.[32]

The hyper-local character of American criminal justice makes it likely that there will be great unevenness in the pace of change, as has been the case with death penalty abolition.[33] The bipartisan politics and near uniformity with which all fifty states grew their levels of incarceration—when a political chain reaction saw the same measures being enacted all across the country—is unlikely to occur if and when penal expansion gives way to penal retrenchment. Policy developments at the state and municipal level depend on the always contingent alignment of constellations of local forces and interests, which in the United States often differ greatly from place to place. Law and order politics were, for a period, so broadly appealing and politically potent that they were able to shape policy across all regions, states, and localities, though of course to differing degrees. It is highly unlikely that a similar convergence will occur if the penal state begins to be dismantled.[34] Nor does it seem likely that today's Republican Party will ever embrace the issue of decarceration with the enthusiasm that Democrats once brought to "law and order."

If the time frame and uncertainty of social policy's crime prevention effects are underestimated, so too are its costs. Despite the familiar refrain that the current costs of policing and imprisonment are astronomical and that governments would save money by shifting from penal to social policy, such savings are unlikely. Social democratic welfare states are expensive and require high tax rates and a wide tax base.[35] Unlike law enforcement and penal measures, which are narrowly targeted on the population of offenders, the social provision of income support, education, healthcare, housing, and employment would extend to a much larger population of beneficiaries. To implement such policies would require a large-scale increase in social expenditure at the national level, not merely a transfer of funds from one city budget line to another. The politics, price tag, and timeline of a "root cause" approach to crime and violence are more challenging and uncertain than penal control responses. There are no cheap fixes by way of social policy.

The project of building social democracy is distinct from that of dismantling the penal state. No nation ever developed social democratic institutions in order to reduce crime and improve criminal justice. The social actors who might lead the struggle for social democracy—a revived labor movement, a multiracial working-class alliance, a progressive Democratic Party—would likely pursue a reform agenda on which improvements in policing, sentencing, and prison conditions would be a low priority. Sections of the labor movement (such as the police and correctional officer unions) might not embrace penal reform; working-class voters would likely resist the relaxation of policing and penal controls; progressive politicians dependent on a broad popular base would be wary of reforms that might increase crime and alienate voters. At present, penal activism is highly localized because municipalities control most criminal justice policy, but major reform of police, jails, and prisons would require large-scale federal funding, meaning that penal activists would have to organize at the national level.[36] In all these respects, a movement to build social democracy would not necessarily align—in terms of actors, values, and priorities—with a movement to remake the criminal legal system.

To achieve greater alignment and to move criminal legal system issues up the reform agenda, penal state activists and advocacy groups would have to find ways to connect their struggles with those of the larger progressive movement. Those aiming to dismantle the penal state might insist, for example, that social disorder, criminal violence, police abuse, and over-incarceration are social ills generated by free-market capitalism and ought to be addressed by social democratic politics. They might argue, with Michelle Alexander, that mass incarceration undermines the prospect of rebuilding America as a multiracial democracy.[37] They might argue that a twenty-first-century New Deal should go beyond FDR's "Four Freedoms" to include freedom from gun violence, from police violence, and from an overzealous penal state.[38] They might stress that the most effective crime control comes from having strong communities and informal social controls and that the crime problem is, at base, a jobs and families problem. But however they go about it, they would have to make the case for broadening social democratic politics to embrace radical penal reform and find ways to generate popular support for these policies. And they would have to find ways to ensure that their preferred policies align with the material interests of large groups of voters, most of whom will be more affected by crime and violence than they are by the harms of policing and punishment. For that reason, if for no other, crime prevention and crime control must be a central part of any program for curtailing the penal state.

Crime control—above all control of lethal violence—is an urgent matter of social justice for America's poorest communities as well as a political issue that generates broad concern among the electorate. When public safety appears threatened, support for penal reform declines. If there are to be progressive reforms affecting how we police, prosecute, and sentence offenders, these reforms will retain public support only if they can be implemented without causing increases in crime and disorder. At the same time that they work for broader socioeconomic change and reform of the penal state, therefore, progressives will need to develop a platform of crime control measures that can work in the short term, improving policing and public safety without falling back on aggressive penal control. As Thomas Abt remarks, "Progressives must be more than just critics—they must offer an affirmative vision of what law enforcement should do, as well as what it should not do. They must address urban violence directly, and not just through poverty reduction, gun control, and police reform."[39]

Crime control is an emotive, polarizing issue. On one side there is passionate concern about crime, about harm to victims, and about under-policing. On the other is outrage about overpolicing, overpunishment, and the harms to people caught up in the penal state. Liberal elites and working people differ in their exposure to crime and often end up on different sides of the debate. Black communities are often torn between the felt need for more policing and tougher punishment and a righteous concern about abusive policing and the harms of incarceration. A sociologically informed, structural approach to this issue would take care to acknowledge both sides of these issues, seek solutions that might help reconcile them, and do so in a way that is responsive to present-day concerns. Such an approach would likely emphasize a raft of nonpenal crime control measures in the short term—improving the quality and accountability of policing; scaling up nonpenal crime-control measures such as community building, situational crime prevention, and community-based antiviolence initiatives; instituting forms of crisis response that don't involve armed police; and instituting improved social services provision for released offenders—combined with medium- and long-term proposals for radical change in social and economic policy.[40] Dismantling the penal state would require major improvements in public safety as well as structural changes in political economy.

Finally, a major obstacle standing in the way of public safety in America is the ubiquity of guns—an extraordinary feature of America's social environment that markedly increases the frequency and lethality of violence. America's gun problem is a quite specific issue, involving constitutional rights, widespread resistance to any suggestion of disarmament, distrust of government, fears for personal safety, and a cultural politics in which the freedom to own guns has taken on deeply symbolic meaning. Ending America's extraordinary homicide rates would, at a minimum, require that the authorities do much more to get guns off the streets, but the methods previously used to do this—mass stop and frisk and weapon possession sentence enhancements—are deeply problematic, and the Supreme Court has further limited the authority of local governments to impose controls on gun ownership and possession. Most American gun owners report that they have guns for their personal protection, so any voluntary reduction in weapons purchases will necessitate marked and sustained improvements in public safety, such that people no longer feel the need to arm themselves.[41]

The prospects for enacting more stringent firearm controls and gun-safety legislation are bleak at present, though if Democrats were someday to control the House and Senate, that would bring movement in that direction. In the meantime, enforcement of existing controls could be greatly improved, and more could be done to interrupt the illegal gun trade that supplies most of the weapons used in urban violence.[42]

A Bandwidth of Possibility

A major transformation of America's political economy in a progressive direction is an altogether unlikely prospect at present. But this does not mean that Americans are stuck with the forms of policing and penal control that constitute today's penal state. Nor are they fated to endure today's levels of criminal violence and social disorder. Significant, even radical, change in crime and punishment can in fact occur in the absence of broader political and economic restructuring.

To be clear, the outlier status of America's penal state will persist unless and until the nation's political economy is transformed. It is that peculiar political economy that makes American violence, policing, and punishment so extreme compared to other affluent nations. Without a structural transformation in that political economy, the contrasts I have described between the United States and other developed nations will not be altered. However, there *is* a bandwidth of possible variation within which American crime, policing, and punishment *can* be changed: a structurally determined floor and ceiling between which lies the possibility of significant reform. That bandwidth of variation is a key part of the theoretical analysis set out in the present study, and is an empirical fact confirmed by the developments I describe below.

Problems that have "root cause" explanations are not amenable only to "root cause" solutions. Social processes and social structures are not so tightly wound. Criminogenic processes and crime control policies are loosely coupled with political economy, not mechanically and directly determined by it. There is play in the system such that one part can be altered even as other parts remain still. This is what is meant by the "relative autonomy" of the community-level processes that operate in the intermediate area between the macro structures of political economy and street-level activity of crime, policing, and punishment. Crime-control policies can be altered, criminogenic processes interrupted, community work activated without any alternation in larger socioeconomic arrangements.

For those hoping to bring about penal change, the existence of this relative autonomy is vitally important. It means that even if Nordic or Western European levels remain out of reach, there is nevertheless the real possibility of life-altering improvements in policing, punishment, and public safety within the US bandwidth. Ending American penal exceptionalism will not occur until the nation reduces the inequality, insecurity, and disorder that flow from its political economy. But activists, reformers, open-minded officials, and the members of the public who support them can take steps to reduce the power and reach of America's law and order Leviathan without waiting for that larger transformation.

Significant change in levels of violence and penal control is possible in the absence of broader structural change. We know this because we have witnessed many instances of significant change during the last few decades.[43] Between 2008 and 2020, the nation's imprisonment rates declined from a high point of 765 per 100,000 to a new level closer to 600 per 100,000.[44] Between 1991 and 2020, the daily population of New York City's jails dropped from just under 22,000 to around 4,500, while New York State's daily prison population dropped from 70,000 to 47,000.[45] Between 1995 and 2020 the nation's annual homicide rate halved, declining from around 10 murders for every 100,000 people to 5 per 100,000. Over the same period, New York City's annual homicide totals dropped from a high of 2,245 in 1990 to a historic low of 289 in 2018.[46] Between 2000 and 2020, the nation's rate of youth detention fell by 71 percent, while the arrest rate for people under 18 years old fell by more than 80 percent.[47] Shootings of civilians by the NYPD dropped dramatically—from an average of 62 people shot and killed each year in the early 1970s to an average of 9 per year between 2015 and 2021—after new forms of training, guidelines, and accountability were introduced.[48] The NYPD also reduced its deployment of stop and frisk from almost 680,000 per year in 2011 to 11,000 in 2018—again, without experiencing an increase in violent crime.[49] Between 1997 and 2023, two million formerly incarcerated people regained the right to vote, thanks to the campaign against felon disfranchisement.[50] Solitary confinement in jails and prisons is currently being curtailed, with some thirty states introducing legislation to limit its use.[51] And since 2000, the imprisonment rate for Black men has fallen by almost half, meaning that one in five Black men born in 2001 is liable to experience imprisonment within their lifetime: for those born in 1981, the number is one in three.[52]

Each of these changes was significant, even radical, affecting the lives of hundreds of thousands and sometimes millions of people. Together, they amount to an empirical demonstration of the theoretical claim that there is a bandwidth of possibility within which variations in violence levels and penal state policies can occur even in the absence of larger structural change.

America's political economy shapes patterns of criminal violence and penal control but—as we saw in chapter 6—it does not fully determine these outcomes. The neighborhood-level processes that generate rates of violence and the local government processes that enact policy are articulated with these socioeconomic structures and correlated with them. But the linkage is a loose coupling rather than a tight ratchet. And it is this looseness, this relative autonomy, that provides a bandwidth of possibility for major change in the absence of structural transformations.[53]

If intermediate processes are effective causes, then patterns of crime control and punishment can be altered by interventions at that level. Local reforms—in the absence of larger structural change—can succeed in altering levels of criminal violence, the quality of policing, and the extent of state punishment. Structural change in political economy is not an essential precondition for the reduction in levels of violence or the reform of America's penal state, even quite radical reform. A crime-control platform insisting that only expensive, long-term, "root cause" change can improve American crime and punishment is not only politically unavailing; it is also sociologically mistaken.

America's extraordinary regime of policing and punishment is rooted in the structures of the nation's political economy. Fundamental criminal justice reform—reform that would align the United States with other affluent nations and end American penal exceptionalism—is liable to be achieved only if a larger progressive movement succeeds in making America's political economy more egalitarian, its labor markets more secure, its welfare state more comprehensive, and its gun violence less pervasive.

But a structural account of America's penal state and the social disorders that occasioned it does not suggest that nothing can be done short of fundamental reform. America's rates of homicide and incarceration have varied over time and from place to place, and that variation suggests these rates can be brought to lower levels than they are at present without need of prior structural change.[54] Imprisonment rates in specific states have been markedly reduced while the local economy remained unchanged. Police departments have been reformed thanks to local political pressure or federal interventions, not national restructuring. State and local gun controls have reduced shootings and homicides without constitutional amendments and have done so without infringing the rights of Americans who own guns legally and behave responsibly.[55] None of these reforms achieved the low rates enjoyed by other developed nations. Judged by America's current standards, however, they have amounted to significant improvements.

It is a saving grace of American federalism that change can sometimes be achieved at the local level where activists are most impactful, despite gridlock or inertia on the national stage. And the vitality of America's private sector enables community partnerships, not-for-profit organizations, philanthropic foundations, and neighborhood initiatives to experiment with reform and augment the work of the public authorities.

But the gravitational force exerted by structural arrangements—and the powerful interests that support them—is, in the final analysis, ineluctable. America's political economy sets definite limits to what can be achieved and imposes upper bounds on what is possible. Until its structures are transformed, America's penal state will continue to impose a level of punishment and control that has no equivalent in the developed world.

ACKNOWLEDGMENTS

I AM INDEBTED to many friends, colleagues, students, and loved ones for their help in shaping the ideas and arguments that have gone into the making of this book and to New York University for providing me with the freedom and resources to undertake this project.

I extend my warm thanks to the students in my NYU classes on *America's Penal State*, *The People's Welfare*, and *The Sociology of Punishment*; to my research assistants Jordan Olson, Emily Luong, Leila Murphy, Coleman Powell, Shona Hemmady, Rachel Lindy, and Marissa Crook; and to the organizers and audiences of talks I gave at the University of Seattle; Harvard University's Kennedy School; the University of Alberta; Northern Arizona University; NYU Law's Faculty Workshop; Berkeley's Kadish Center; the University of Sydney Law School; University of New South Wales Law and Justice; the Harvard Legal History Workshop; the University of Toronto's Law Faculty Workshop; Edinburgh University Law School; and the University of Zurich Criminal Law Group.

I am especially grateful to my friends Rachel Barkow, Barry Friedman, Jeff Manza, Michael Jacobson, Jerry Karabel, Emma Kaufman, Zach Lewis, Erin Murphy, and Vincent Southerland, who participated in a manuscript workshop at a key stage in the book's development, read the whole manuscript, and provided invaluable advice. Vincent Chiao, Stephen Holmes, Lisa Kerr, Niki Lacey, Steven Lukes, Fergus McNeill, Michael Meranze, Chris Muller, Jonathan Obert, and Rob Sampson offered helpful advice, provided information, and shared ideas. NYU Law librarians Denise To, Janet Kearney, and John Forbis were unfailingly supportive, as were my assistant, Monica Millay; NYU Law School dean Troy McKenzie; and NYU Sociology Department chair Jeff Manza. I also thank my editor Rachael Levay and her colleagues at Princeton University Press for the care, speed, and thoughtfulness with which they shepherded the book through the process, and Martin Schneider for his first-class copyediting.

My daughters, Kasia Garland and Amy Garland, were a constant source of advice, encouragement, and good humor throughout the making of this book. I hope the final version meets with their high standards.

My spouse and life partner, Anne Jowett, was an inspiration in this as in so many things. Anne is the person who makes everything possible and who brightens my life each day. It is to her, with love, that this book is dedicated.

NOTES

Prologue: From Tocqueville to Hobbes

1. De Beaumont and De Tocqueville (1833: 79).
2. On these narratives, together with alternative readings of the historical evidence: Kruse and Zelizer (2022).
3. America's homicide rates reached a high of over 10 per 100,000 in the 1990s. Most developed nations have rates between 1 and 2 per 100,000. Cooper and Smith (2011); Grinshteyn and Hemenway (2019).
4. Rogers (1992).
5. Obert (2018: 259) writes: "Americans have traditionally had an aversion to state violence, yet nevertheless have allowed their government to become a behemoth of coercion."
6. Karabel (2021); King (1999); Hahn (2024).
7. Hobbes (1651).
8. Garland (2001a) shows that these crime fears were overlaid by concerns about social and cultural change, racial status, and economic insecurity and were thematized politically in ways that advanced a New Right agenda.
9. *Law and Order Leviathan* continues a comparative investigation of American difference that began in a previous book, *Peculiar Institution: America's Death Penalty in an Age of Abolition* (Garland 2010). But whereas the extraordinary persistence of capital punishment in (parts of) the United States is a story of Supreme Court jurisprudence, cultural symbols, and political contingencies, the story of America's penal state, more generally, has its roots in the structures of political economy and the material conditions and consequences that flow from it. An earlier book, *The Culture of Control* (Garland 2001a), which traced the causes and consequences of a structural transformation in the field of crime control in both the UK and the United States between the 1970s and the 1990s, bears a more oblique relation to the present study, being primarily historical rather than comparative, and being focused on similar historical trajectories observed in the United States and the UK rather on than differences between America and other developed nations.

1. Challenging Leviathan

1. On the events of 2020: Klinenberg (2024).
2. Estimates of numbers taking part range from 15 to 26 million: Buchanan (2020); Pew Research Center (2020). The Black Lives Matter movement had begun eight years earlier

following the acquittal of George Zimmerman for the killing of Trayvon Martin. On the broader pattern of racism prompting the protests, Michener (2020).

3. As the scholar-activist Ruth Wilson Gilmore remarks, "bipartisan consensus *built* the prison-industrial complex," quoted in Keller (2022a). Reitz (2018: 30) notes: "Before the 2000s, concerns over incarceration rates had virtually no resonance in public or political discourse—or if they did, it was in the form of stout calls for the *greater* use of imprisonment to reduce crime rates."

4. The beating of Rodney King by Los Angeles County police in 1991; the killing of Amadou Diallo by New York City police in 1999; the chokehold death of Eric Garner in Staten Island, New York City, in July 2014; the police shooting of Michael Brown in Ferguson, Missouri, in August 2014; the death from spine injuries of Freddie Gray in Baltimore in April 2015, following a "rough ride" in a police wagon; and the killing of Breonna Taylor by Louisville police in March 2020 were among the most notorious instances. Activists around the country could name hundreds more. A stream of scandals also flowed from the nation's jails and prisons: from individual cases such as Kalief Browder, who committed suicide after being kept in solitary confinement on Rikers Island for three years, to systemic ones, such as California's failure to provide a constitutionally required minimum of health care to prisoners. Gonnerman (2014); Simon (2014).

5. According to the US government's Bureau of Justice Statistics, both property crime and violent crime fell by 71 percent between 1993 and 2022. Pew Research Center (2024).

6. Phelps (2024).

7. On George Floyd-themed memes, Moody-Ramirez et al. (2021).

8. Klinenberg (2024).

9. On the importance of "biographical availability" for social movements, McAdams (1986).

10. Shanahan and Kurti (2022: 30) write that Black Lives Matter was "at once a meme, a social movement, a tangled nexus of formal organizations, and an abstract signifier that guided autonomous organizing across the U.S." For a description of the protesters: Schatz (2020).

11. Smith (2020).

12. On June 12, 2020, the *New York Times* ran an opinion piece by Mariame Kaba, titled, "Yes, We Mean Literally Abolish the Police," which set out a vision of a communitarian society in which police would be "obsolete" and demanded an immediate 50 percent reduction in police numbers and budgets. For a more extended statement: Kaba and Ritchie (2022). For other statements of the case for abolishing police: Vitale (2017); Akbar (2020). On abolition and its cultural impact, Shelby (2022); Keller (2022a). On local activism aiming to dismantle mass incarceration: Simonson (2023).

13. Vitale (2017).

14. For the argument that the carceral state is designed to manage America's surplus population: Shanahan and Kurti (2022). Kaba and Ritchie (2022: 9) write: "While the lure of 'reimagining' and 'reforming' policing is powerful . . . history, experience, and research all point to the reality that policing is not 'broken,' it is operating exactly as was intended: dealing out daily violence to contain control, and criminalize."

15. United States Department of Justice (2015).

16. For example: McLeod (2019); Kaba and Ritchie (2022: 26); Madden et al. (2020).

17. Klinenberg (2024: 68).

18. Shanahan and Kurti (2022: 63ff.).

19. Miller and Parlapiano (2023).

20. On the Black Lives Matter movement: Ransby (2018); Woodly (2021); Movement for Black Lives (2024).

21. In *Graham v. Connor* (1989) the US Supreme Court ruled that because police officers are often "forced to make split-second judgments ... about the amount of force that is necessary in a particular situation," their decisions ought not to be evaluated "with the 20/20 vision of hindsight" (396).

22. The US Supreme Court rejected an appeal against Chauvin's conviction in November 2023. Later that month, Chauvin suffered life-threatening injuries when he was stabbed twenty-two times by a fellow inmate in a federal prison in Arizona. BBC (2023).

23. Keller (2022b: 23).

24. Sklansky (2021) provides details on public concern about abusive policing, citing evidence that it rose and fell along with the crime rate. Fortner (2015); Forman (2017); Clegg and Usmani (2019) show that Black voters were among those who supported get-tough policies, while also calling for social and economic responses.

25. As Page et al. (2017) point out, opposition to the status quo is always present, even in the most hegemonic of circumstances. However, this opposition can remain largely invisible to the wider public for long periods of time.

26. In August 2013, a federal judge ruled the NYPD's use of stop and frisk unconstitutional: Center for Constitutional Rights (2013). Later that year, Bill de Blasio successfully ran for NYC Mayor promising to "end a stop-and-frisk era that unfairly targets people of color." Bergner (2014). On May 24, 2014, *The New York Times* published an editorial titled "End Mass Incarceration Now." The Editorial Board of the paper wrote, "The American experiment in mass incarceration has been a moral, legal, social, and economic disaster. It cannot end soon enough." Berman and Fox (2023: 68) describe the shift in public opinion: "in 1992, 81 percent of Americans said that the justice system was 'not tough enough.' By 2020, this number was cut in half, to 41 percent."

27. Keller (2022b: 23–24). On the movement to end mass incarceration prior to 2020: Eren (2023).

28. Bazelon (2019).

29. Sklansky (2021: 114).

30. On growing opposition to mass incarceration: Ramirez (2013); Keller (2022a); Beckett (2022); Eren (2023).

31. Bobo (2001); Hout and Maggio (2021). On "the antiracism that flared so spectacularly" following George Floyd's killing: Kennedy (2021a).

32. IPSOS (2021). Berman and Fox (2023: 65, 66) provide evidence of "broad support for policing among the American public" citing polling evidence showing that 81 percent of Black Americans and 88 percent of White Americans want the police presence in their neighborhoods to remain the same or to increase. Gallup polls show that Blacks have significantly less confidence in the police than do Whites. The racial gap is a consistent finding since polling on this issue began in the late 1990s. Polls from 2011 to 2014 showed that 59% of White Americans had a great deal of confidence in the police; a further 29% said they had some. Only 12% said they

had very little or none. Among Black Americans, 37% said they had a great deal of confidence, 37% said they had some, and 25% said they had very little or none: Newport (2014). More recent polling continues to show this pattern: Brown and Lloyd (2023). On the ambivalence of Black communities regarding the police: Phelps (2024); Bell (2016).

33. Pickett et al. (2022: 291–330).
34. Cotton (2020).
35. Barker et al. (2021); Collins (2023).
36. The shooter, a seventeen-year-old named Kyle Rittenhouse, was subsequently tried and exonerated.
37. Klinenberg (2024); Devise (2023).
38. Eren (2023). The backlash helped bring about the election of Eric Adams as New York City Mayor in 2021; the recall of District Attorney Chesa Boudin in San Francisco in 2022; and the pushback against New York State bail reform legislation: Bazelon (2023); Londono (2023).
39. On the impact of the BLM protests: Taylor (2021b); Arango and Gabler (2023); Blow (2022). On the return of "tough on crime" policies, Staudt (2024). On 2022 prison numbers: Carson (2023). Mystal (2024) provides data on police killings in 2023. See also Trump-Vance 2024 campaign (2024).
40. Keller (2022b: 31) notes that "the fastest growing subset of the burgeoning anti-mass incarceration movement consists of self-described abolitionists."
41. In a November 2023 survey, 58 percent of respondents said the criminal justice system was not tough enough. Brenan (2023).
42. As a leading homicide expert remarks: "No matter where Americans live, their risk of being murdered is higher than it is in any other first-world democracy." Roth (2009: 3).
43. Klinenberg (2024: 19–20).
44. Berman and Fox (2023: 67) report that, as of 2022, "a majority of Americans support reforming the police." Political scientists consider the American public to be ideologically conservative but programmatically liberal: meaning that a majority of American people express negative views about government programs in general while supporting specific programs such as Social Security and Medicare. Prasad (2016).

2. Toward a Structural Explanation

1. *Law and Order Leviathan* is not a comparative study in the sense of systematically comparing two or more nations in detail. Nor does it aim to idealize the policing and punishment regimes of other nations, all of which have their own problems, as local experts frequently point out. My concern is to establish that the US regime differs markedly from other comparable nations and to explain why. Unless otherwise specified, the comparison group—for penal measures and social indicators—is non-US developed nations: most often, the nations of Western Europe together with Canada, Australia, and New Zealand. This is a "most similar nations" comparison, contrasting the United States to other developed, affluent, liberal-democratic countries, the set with which it is most often compared and which, for policy purposes, is most relevant. Different comparator groups would present the United States in a different light. Regarding rates of lethal violence, or police killings, the United States is much closer to South American nations than to European ones. In terms of incarceration rates, it most resembles

authoritarian regimes such as Stalinist Russia or Maoist China. A comparison with Japan would reveal that the balance of informal social controls and penal state controls found in that nation is the reverse of that of America. For a discussion of the US violence in relation to the nations of South America: Miller (2020). For a global analysis of incarceration rates in which the United States is compared with all nations: Clegg et al. (2024). For an argument that America's poverty levels are comparable to those of developing nations in Africa and Asia: Deaton (2018).

2. I focus on homicide, armed robbery, and gun crime throughout because these are the most politically salient forms of crime: Zimring and Hawkins (1997) and because reliable comparative data are more readily available.

3. On the links between crime, public attitudes, criminal justice policy, and incarceration rates: Enns (2016: 108, 156). On the history of homicide in the United States: Roth (2009). For an account of how the post-1960s violence was thematized politically and woven into the tactical efforts of political actors: Garland (2001a). On the buildup of the penal state: Campbell and Schoenfeld (2013); Gottschalk (2014); Garland (2017).

4. A "political economy" is a specific system of economic action, together with the framework of laws, norms, and institutions within which that system is embedded: see chapter 5. I use the term "America's political economy" as shorthand to describe three interconnected structures: America's polity, economy, and racial order.

5. Holmes (2025).

6. Archer (2007); Karabel (forthcoming).

7. On federalism's consequences for crime control policy: Miller (2008).

8. On America's "incomplete pacification" and its long-term consequences for violence in America in general and the death penalty in particular: Garland (2010: 171–73). On the formation of America's peculiar gun culture: see chapter 5.

9. I am not the first to suggest that America's penal state is linked to its political economy. For other accounts: De Giorgi (2006); Wacquant (2009); Harcourt (2011); Lacey and Soskice (2015); Lacey, Soskice, and Hope (2018).

10. Hacker et al. (2022). Data on economic and social indicators are provided in chapter 5.

11. It is welfare for the poor that is minimized in the United States. Welfare for the rich and better-off, distributed via employment benefits and the tax code, is relatively generous. See chapter 5.

12. Leading examples include Garland (2001a); Simon (2007); Western (2009); Alexander (2010); Gottschalk (2006, 2014); Travis, Western, and Redburn (2014); Schoenfeld (2018); Beckett (2022).

13. An extensive body of empirical research shows penal institutions and welfare institutions to be tightly coupled and mutually reinforcing: the more generous and inclusive a nation's welfare state, the less it relies upon harsh punishment and penal control. This finding holds at the international level when nation states are compared, and at the subnational level, when America's fifty states are compared. See Lappi-Seppala (2018); Garland (2023); Beckett and Western (2001); Downes and Hanson (2006); Sutton (2004); Clegg and Usmani (2019); Lacey (2008); Lacey and Soskice (2018). On the relation between inequality, welfare state provision, and violent crime: Hovermann and Messner (2019); Hummelsheim et al. (2011). A separate set of comparative research studies finds an association between levels of *inequality* on the one hand, and levels of *violence* and *social disorganization* on the other: nations with high levels of

equality have lower levels of violence and fewer social problems than more unequal nations: Messner and Rosenfeld (1997); Savolainen (2000); Messner (2010); Hoverman and Messner (2019). For evidence of links between crime, punishment, and inequality: Lacey et al. (2021); Fajnzylber et al. (2002); Wilkinson and Pickett (2010). Muller (2021) finds a temporal correlation between America's labor market demand and incarceration rates.

14. On the New Deal order and the restructuring after the 1960s: Fraser and Gerstle (1989).

15. For details and sources: see chapters 5 and 6.

16. Muhammad (2019).

17. On the intertwining of race, class, and capitalism in US history: Cox (1948); Michaels and Reed Jr. (2022); Reed (2020).

18. Hispanic and Native Americans are also overrepresented in the criminal legal system, though to a lesser degree than Black Americans: National Conference of State Legislatures (2022). Throughout this study, I focus on the penal state's treatment of Black Americans. A different analysis would be required to explain other racial and ethnic disparities.

19. Sampson (2012: 39) refers to such processes as "mediating social mechanisms."

20. See chapter 6.

21. Sampson and Wilson (1995); Sampson, Wilson, and Katz (2018).

22. I use the term "penal state" to refer to the legal rules, institutional arrangements, personnel, and physical infrastructure through which duly constituted government authorities exercise penal power. See chapter 3.

23. For some thinkers, such as Michel Foucault, any demand for normative compliance can be read as an authoritarian imposition. Against this I would argue that it is a mistake to assume that all controls are the same, or that all are equally objectionable. Without social controls and self-controls group life would be impossible. For a critique of Foucault on this point: Garland (1990: 168–70).

24. On parole: Simon (1993). On policing: Bayley (1994).

25. Selznick (1994: 126).

26. Flamm (2005); Garland (2001a); Enns (2016); Campbell and Schoenfeld (2013); Clegg and Usmani (2019).

27. Wrong (1994); Garland (1995).

28. See chapter 6.

29. On comparative incarceration rates: Lappi-Seppala (2018). On comparative rates of police killings: Zimring (2017). On homicide rates by US state: Center for Disease Control (2022); Cooper and Smith (2011). On homicide rates in European nations: Statista Research Department (2024a).

30. Tonry (2009); Morone (2003 and 2020); Ferguson (2018); Howard (2017).

31. Bobo and Johnson (2004: 151–80); Travis, Western, and Redburn (2014: 13).

32. On racism and punitiveness in Europe and Australia: Davis et al. (2022); Brookman et al. (2022). On racial disparities in England and Wales, Australia, Canada, and France: Ramesh (2010); Jericho (2020); Government of Canada (2022); Fassin (2016).

33. Hout and Maggio (2021: 45, Table on "Racial Resentment by Year and Political Party"); Associated Press (2019); Bobo (2001). Attitudes toward egalitarian racial policies are polarized and becoming more so, with increased support from Democrats and increased opposition from Republicans: Jardina and Ollerenshaw (2022).

34. Garland (2005b).
35. On state capacity, see chapter 7.
36. Weber (2002).

3. America's Penal State

1. On concepts of difference in comparative analysis, including the idea of "American exceptionalism": Garland (2018a).

2. Garland (2015) disguishes between the directive leadership of a penal system (the "penal state") and the system's apparatus of penal control ("penality"). For simplicity, I use "penal state" here to refer to both.

3. For an overview of American penality prior to the 1970s: Garland (2001a, ch. 2).

4. Travis, Western, and Redburn (2014: 35) show that from 1925 to 1970, the US rates of imprisonment, excluding the jail population, averaged just over 100 per 100,000. An earlier estimate by Blumstein (1973) put the average at 110 per 100,000. The combined rate for the United States, including those in jail, between 1940 and 1970, is estimated by International Centre for Prison Studies (2024) to have varied between 201 and 161. The same database provides the following information: England and Wales had an average imprisonment rate of 44 per 100,000 between 1920 and 1970. Between 1932 and 1970, France's average rate was 57; between 1951 and 1970, the Netherlands averaged 40 per 100,000. According to Statistics Canada (n.d.), in 1970, Canada's rate of incarceration was around 35 per 100,000. For data on the earlier twentieth century, see Clegg and Usmani (2019); Muller (2021). On convict labor, see Lichtenstein (1996).

5. International Centre for Prison Studies (2024); Reitz (2018: 3).

6. Sawyer and Wagner (2024).

7. For exemplary accounts of the buildup of the American penal state that stress the articulation of broad national forces with state- and local-level institutional and political arrangements: Campbell and Schoenfeld (2013); Schoenfeld (2018). Sampson and Loeffler (2010) show mass incarceration to be highly localized and uneven in its effects. The phrase "mass incarceration" might best be understood as a critical rhetorical term that takes a heterogeneous phenomenon, spatially dispersed and developed over time, and narrates it as a unitary (and problematic) entity. On this rhetorical process of social construction: Landis (1999).

8. On state incarceration rates: The Sentencing Project (2024).

9. Zimring (2020). Campbell and Schoenfeld (2013: 1379) observe that, between 1980 and 2007, "no state's incarceration rate increase[ed] less than 150% and the vast majority increase[ed] between 200% and 600%."

10. As the US incarceration rate declined from its 2008 peak of 765 per 100,000, some very small nations—El Salvador, Rwanda, Turkmenistan, and Cuba—developed per capita rates that overtook America's. In 2020, Cuba surpassed America's peak rate with a rate of 794 prisoners per 100,000 population: International Centre for Prison Studies (2024). Scholars estimate that Stalinist Russia had an incarceration rate (including political prisoners) somewhere between 1,558 and 2,605 per 100,000: Belova and Gregory (2009).

11. Enns et al. (2019).

12. US Immigration and Customs Enforcement and the United States system of immigration control would require a different explanation and are not included in the present analysis. On

the interaction between the criminal legal system and the immigration control system: De Pena (2022); Das (2020).

13. On guard labor in the United States, which greatly outnumbers public police: Jayadev and Bowles (2006); Bowles and Jayadev (2014).

14. Hyland and Davis (2019). In 2016, police departments employed a total of 468,274 full-time sworn officers and 131,274 civilians. About half of all local departments employ the equivalent of 10 full-time sworn officers.

15. Moskos (2008: ch. 5). More generally: Moore (1992); Balko (2014: 48). For an experiential account: Bratton (2021: ch. 6).

16. CompStat is a computerized system of police management that deploys real-time crime data to map crime events, precinct by precinct, street by street, combined with a system of accountability that holds local precinct commanders responsible for identifying and addressing crime patterns. See US Dept of Justice (2013).

17. Brodeur and Banton (2024).

18. On "stop and frisk" in Britain, where it is known as "stop and search": Delsol and Shiner (2015).

19. Skogan (2023: 1). By 2019, the annual number of stops in NYC had fallen to 13,459: New York Police Department (2021). In 2023, the number was 16,971: McCormack and Lopez (2024).

20. Police foundations are an additional source of funding for many departments. Initially, this private funding was mostly for police officer funerals and the education of slain officers' children. Today, it is also used to provide weaponry, hardware, and public relations for departments. For a critical account: Schwenk (2024).

21. Seventy thousand additional police officers were hired in the six years following the 1994 Violent Crime Control and Law Enforcement Act: Latzer (2016: 222). According to Vitale (2018: 55), in 2013–14, 40 percent of American schools employed a police officer.

22. On police *per capita* in America and other developed nations: Lewis and Usmani (2022). For data on police training in the United States: Reaves (2021); United States Department of Justice (2019). Hirschfield (2023) provides comparative data. On police training in the United States, including use of force training: Walker and Katz (2018: 149ff). For European police training data: Dekanoidze and Khelashvili (2018); Ferreira et al. (2018). Police recruits in the United States receive, on average, 21 weeks training, followed by 12 weeks on-the-job training. In England and Wales, the numbers are 42 and 90; in Sweden, 96 and 48.

23. Hirschfield (2015). According to Godin (2020) there are nineteen nations worldwide where police are typically unarmed.

24. Most people killed in the United States by police are white. African Americans account for about 25 percent of victims—double their proportion in the general population: Hirschfield (2023); Karabel (2017); Zimring (2017).

25. Sklansky (2021: 113). Zimring (2017: 76–77) calculates that "the US rate of police killings is 4.6 times that of Canada, twenty-two times that of Australia, forty times higher than Germany's, and more than 140 times the rate of police shooting deaths of England and Wales."

26. Karabel (2017).

27. Porter and Meheut (2023).

28. Associated Press (2024).

29. Subramanian et al. (2022).

30. *The Guardian* (2015). For background details: Katzenstein and M. Waller (2015).

31. Tonry (2012a). Tonry (2016b: 3) writes: "Prosecutors dominate sentencing in the United States but have little or no role in sentencing in most developed countries."

32. Pfaff (2017: 127ff.).

33. Lynch (2023). For a defense of these practices: National Association of Assistant United States Attorneys (2015).

34. Travis, Western, and Redburn (2014).

35. Enns (2016: 107). The US Department of Justice (2011) estimates that over 90 percent of state court cases result in a guilty plea.

36. Kohler-Hausmann (2018).

37. Campbell and Schoenfeld (2013); National Association of Assistant United States Attorneys (2015).

38. Goldstein (2025); Gaskins (2024).

39. On American sentencing law developments since 1975: Tonry (2016a). On sentencing policies and practices in other western nations: Tonry (2016b). According to Justice Policy Institute (2011), in the United States 69.9% of all court sentences, felony and misdemeanor, involve incarceration. In Canada the figure is 33.8%; England and Wales 9.2%; Germany 7.5%; and Finland 7.2%. Weigend (2016) reports that between 2000 and 2015, 5% of convicted offenders in Germany were sentenced to immediate imprisonment, a further 12% received a suspended prison sentence, and the rest were fined. For research showing that the US is an international outlier in its use of long sentences: Kazemian (2022).

40. Garland (2017); see also chapter 7.

41. Death Penalty Information Center (2023).

42. Arnsdorf (2020). For the theory: Garland (2010).

43. Nellis (2021); Mauer and Nellis (2018). Nellis (2021) reports that in America one in seven prisoners, and one in five Black prisoners, is serving a life sentence.

44. Sweden, Denmark, and Finland permit sentences of life imprisonment, though these are rarely imposed and typically involve a term of less than fifteen years: Van Zyl Smit and Appleton (2019); Schartmueller (2015).

45. O'Flaherty and Sethi (2019: 200). Breivik may be subject to preventive detention if he is judged to be dangerous when his twenty-one-year prison sentence concludes.

46. The War on Drugs has been scaled back since the late 1990s, with penalty levels reduced and enforcement relaxed. As a result, Black/White disparities in state prisons have decreased considerably: Ghandnoosh et al. (2024); Gramlich (2019).

47. Kleiman (2013). In nations such as Portugal drug use is addressed as a public health issue rather than a criminal justice problem: Justice Policy Institute (2011).

48. Tonry (2012a: 77).

49. Tonry (2016b: 484).

50. Weigend (2016).

51. Tonry (2023), citing Reaves (2013). The European figures typically combine what in America would be called felony and misdemeanor convictions.

52. Subrananian and Shames (2013).

53. Tonry (2023).

54. This is the standard definition of "mass imprisonment" or "mass incarceration": Garland (2001b).

55. Sawyer and Wagner (2024). On the methodology used by the Prison Policy Initiative for counting the total number incarcerated in American prisons and jails: Prison Policy Initiative (n.d.). For a different estimate using a different methodology: Kaeble et al. (2015: 3, table 2).

56. Doob and Webster (2018).

57. Sampson and Loeffler (2010).

58. Angela Davis, a leading critic of the prison-industrial complex, explains the origin and meaning of the term as follows: "as the US prison system expanded, so did corporate involvement in construction, provision of goods and services, and use of prison labor. Because of the extent to which prison building and operation began to attract vast amounts of capital—from the construction industry to food and health provision—in a way that recalled the emergence of the military-industrial complex, we began to refer to a 'prison-industrial complex.'" Davis (2003: 12). On correctional profits made by commercial firms: Wagner and Rabuy (2017); Subramanian et al. (2022).

59. Since 2008, prison numbers have declined in the range of 0.5 to 3% annually, excluding 2020, when a larger number of pandemic-related releases occurred: Nellis (2024).

60. On *Brown v Plata*: see Simon (2014).

61. Widra (2024).

62. Prison Policy Initiative (2024).

63. Morgenstern et al. (2024); Walmsley (2014).

64. Liptak (2008) reports that "commercial bail bond companies dominate the pretrial release systems of only two nations, the United States and the Philippines." He adds, "In England, Canada, and other countries, agreeing to pay a defendant's bond in exchange for money is a crime akin to witness tampering or bribing a juror."

65. Subramanian et al. (2015).

66. Prison Policy Initiative (2024); Federal Bureau of Prisons (n.d.).

67. National Institute of Corrections (2021). On women's prisons in the United States: Keller (2022b). On incarcerated women and girls, Budd (2024), who notes that between 1980 and 2022 there was a 585 percent increase in women's imprisonment; this rate of growth is nearly twice as high as that of men, though from a much lower base. Keller (2022b: 22) notes that 7 percent of state prison inmates are housed in private prisons and about 17 percent in the federal system. See also Wildeman et al. (2018).

68. USA Facts (2024).

69. Lynch (2010); Campbell and Schoenfeld (2013).

70. On violence in America's prisons: Sklansky (2021: ch. 6). On European prison conditions: Keller (2022a); Benko (2015). On solitary confinement in US and European prisons: Reiter (2016); Shalev (2015). According to Gottschalk (2021) 20 percent of prisoners in the United States spend time in "administrative segregation" in any one year. For a comparison of prison staff and working conditions in the United States and Germany: Keller (2022a: 58). On rehabilitative prison programming throughout the world: Vanstone and Priestley (2022). Tonry (2016b: 463) claims that "the quality of life in American prisons is incomparably worse than in most continental European countries" and contrasts crowded federal and state prisons in the United States with Northern European countries, which, he says, "typically provide single-occupancy cells and often maintain waiting lists for admission in order to avoid overcrowding."

71. On less eligibility in America's prisons: Bonnet (2019). On the principle of normalization: Van de Rijt et al. (2023); De Vos (2023). On open prisons in Norway, where about one third of prisoners are housed: Shammas (2015, 2017a); Ugelvik and Dullum (2012). Bhuller et al. (2019) provide details of Norwegian imprisonment and reentry. For a more critical account of Nordic penality: Barker (2013).

72. Keller (2022a: 64–65).

73. Gottschalk (2014: 39) notes that "[i]ndependent oversight of US prisons and jails is minimal or nonexistent compared to other Western countries." See also Dolovich (2022). European prison inmates are, at least in theory, protected by Article 3 of the European Convention on Human Rights, which prohibits torture and "inhuman or degrading treatment or punishment," and by the European Committee for the Prevention of Torture and Inhuman or Degrading Treatment of Punishment.

74. Where decent reentry programs do exist in the United States, they are usually private programs, financed by donors, and run by volunteers: Keller (2022b: 97–98).

75. Katz and Yi (2020).

76. Fridhov (n.d.); Mammen (n.d.). On prisoner reentry and resettlement programs in other nations: Dünkel (2019).

77. Nellis (2024); Phelps (2020).

78. Corda (2016); Smit and Corda (2018); Reitz (2018: 9, 12). By 2022 the combined number had declined to 3.7 million.

79. K Reitz (2018, chs. 9, 10); Schiraldi (2023).

80. On probation practice in the UK: McNeill (2018); on probation in Europe: Confederation of European Probation (2024).

81. Simon (1993). On the use of "flash incarceration" to enforce probation: Shanahan and Kurti (2022: 111).

82. Schiraldi (2023).

83. Stroud and King (2020); Daems (2020).

84. Ewald (2017).

85. Corda et al. (2023); Demleitner (2018). According to the 2023 Report of Safehome.org, in 2021 some 800,000 people were listed on sex offender registries in the United States. See also Gabriele (2023).

86. Travis (2002); Jacobs (2015). Since collateral consequences such as felon disfranchisement came to light in the early 2000s, reformers have succeeded in modifying them to some extent. On the number of Americans with criminal records: Widra (2023).

87. Widra (2023); Kirk et al. (2020).

88. Harris (2016); Page and Soss (2017).

89. Gottschalk (2014: 36). On "pay to stay" fees, which are used by all fifty states to defray the costs of imprisonment: Brennan Center for Justice (2019).

90. Page and Soss (2017: 146).

4. The Control Imperative

1. Garland (1990: 129–30).

2. Schumpeter (1942). See also chapter 5.

3. Balko (2020); Soss and Weaver (2017).

4. Between 2004 and 2012, when the NYPD mounted a large-scale stop and frisk campaign, of the 4.4 million stops that occurred, 80 percent were of Blacks and Latinos. These groups together make up less than 50 percent of the city's population: NYCLU (2019). A lawsuit against the state of New Jersey found that police stops on the New Jersey Turnpike in the late 1990s were overwhelmingly of drivers of color: ABC News (2000). For data on highway racial profiling: Epp et al. (2014). Fryer (2019) reports that Blacks and Hispanics "are more than 50% more likely to experience some form of force in interactions with police."

5. Hirschfield (2023); Karabel (2017).

6. Statista Research Department (2024b); Fernandes and Crutchfield (2018).

7. Nellis (2024, 2021).

8. Travis, Western, and Redburn (2014: 5). According to Raphael and Stoll (2009: 10) in California at the end of the 1990s, "over 90 percent of black male high-school dropouts . . . [had] served prison time in the state." BJS data show that between 1980 and 1993, the percentage of sentenced prisoners who were Black rose from 46.5% to 50.8%. This increase likely resulted from the War on Drugs with its racially disparate enforcement: Stanglin (2020). The scaling back of the War on Drugs has caused the number of Black prisoners to decrease. In 2000, Black offenders were 8 times more likely to be admitted to prison than White offenders. By 2020, that disparity had fallen to 5.5 times more likely: Ghandnoosh (2024); Gramlich (2019).

9. Beck and Blumstein (2018); Federal Bureau of Investigation (2020); Thompson and Tapp (2023).

10. Balko (2020); Tonry (2012b). On race and class in America's criminal courts: Clair (2020).

11. Reported in DeVuono-Powell (2015) and *New York Times* Editorial Board (2014). See also Western and Wildeman (2009); Johnson (2020).

12. Pfaff (2017: 137) reports that "80 percent of defendants in serious criminal cases need a state-appointed lawyer." According to Wang et al. (2022) the typical state prisoner has a 10th-grade education. Forty-two percent of prisoners surveyed by the BJS in 2016 reported that their family received public assistance before they were eighteen years old and 49 percent met the criteria for substance use disorder. On the class status of people in prison: Muller and Roehrkrasse (2021); Western and Muller (2013). Lara-Millan (2021: 6) notes that "In 2010, roughly 65% of incarcerated adults in prisons or jails met the medical criteria for an alcohol or drug use disorder, seven times likelier than individuals in the community."

13. On the underenforcement of the criminal law in respect of corporations and corporate settings: Coffee (2020); Garrett (2021 and 2014); Taub (2020); Hagan (2010).

14. Muller and Roehrkrasse (2022).

15. Muller and Roehrkrasse (2022).

16. Muller (2021).

17. A Justice Policy Institute Report (2011) provides the following comparisons: In 2008, African Americans made up 37% of people in American prisons but 12% of the general population. In Australia in 2006, Indigenous people made up 24% of people in prison but 2% of the general population. In Canada in 2006, Aboriginal people were 24% of those admitted to custody in the provinces and 18% of those admitted to federal custody, but 4% of the general population. In Germany in 2008, "foreign born" people made up 26.3% of the prison population but

12.9% of the general population. Muller and Roehrkrasse (2021: 3) observe that "racial inequality in [American] prison admission declined in the early twenty-first century, while class inequality in prison admissions reached alarming new extremes."

18. For a discussion of the normative status of mass incarceration: Usmani and Lewis (forthcoming).

19. Barr (1992). In the same year, a Heritage Foundation author wrote that: "In the 1960s and early 1970s, incarceration rates dropped and violent crime rates skyrocketed. Conversely, when incarceration rates jumped in the 1980s, the rate of increase of crime was substantially reduced" (Cary 1992). See, generally, United States Department of Justice (1992). For an estimate of the supposed crime prevention effects of mass stop and frisk, see self-described conservative criminologists, Wright and Delisi (2016: 70) who write, "The 'stop and frisk' policies of the New York Police Department are estimated to have saved some 15,000 predominantly black lives."

20. Davis (2003: 12) writes that "the practice of mass incarceration during that period [the 1980s] had little or no effect on official crime rates." Beckett (2022: 7) states that "mass incarceration does not make us safer." See also Roeder et al. (2015).

21. For these estimates: Western (2006); Travis, Western, and Redburn (2014); Spelman (2006: 97–129); Rosenfeld and Fomango (2007). On policing and the New York City crime drop: Zimring (2013). On the methodological problems involved: Levitt and Miles (2007); Bun et al. (2020).

22. On the criminogenic effects of imprisonment: Vieraitis et al. (2007). On the correlation of increased imprisonment rates and decreased crime rates over time: Enns (2016). Sampson (2011) observes that the removal of so many males increased family disruption and rates of violence.

23. On these nonpenal crime control mechanisms: Garland (2001a); Sharkey, Torrats-Espinosa, and Takyar (2017); Sharkey (2018); Clarke (1997).

24. Johnson (2024); National Center for Health Statistics (2022). The states are Louisiana, Mississippi, Arkansas, Kentucky, Georgia, Texas, and Arizona.

25. Dholakia (2023).

26. Glazer and Sharkey (2021); Austin and Jacobson (2013); Stemen (2017).

27. Sharkey (2018); Sharkey, Torrats-Espinosa, and Takyar (2017).

28. Skogan (2023: 9). Butler (2017) describes how Black men experience stop and frisk.

29. Massoglia and Pridemore (2015).

30. Lerman and Weaver (2014).

31. O'Flaherty and Sethi (2019: 69). On America's low clearance rates: Thompson (2022).

32. Hinton (2021).

33. Garland (2017, 2020).

34. Ferguson (2018); Whitman (2003); Alexander (2010).

35. For other analyses stressing the centrality of control: Feeley and Simon (1992); Kaufman et al. (2018); Campbell and Schoenfeld (2013: 1379).

36. The death penalty, when executed, is a total and permanent form of control; incarceration is virtually total but generally time-limited; correctional supervision is partial and intermittent; exclusions and disqualifications are focused and partial. Fines do not impose controls but instead levy resources. And deferred or suspended sentences are psychological rather than

physical controls, depending on the offender being deterred by the prospect of a later more severe sentence.

37. For an analysis of the basic modes of penal action—penal afflictions, penal levies, penal controls, and penal assistance: Garland (2017). On the official purposes and social functions of punishment more generally: Garland (1990).

38. Jacobs (2015); Simon (1993); Anderson (1995).

39. Whitman (2003); Lynch (2009).

40. Weigend (2016) notes that in Germany from 2000 to 2015, around 80 percent of criminal cases were dealt with by a stand-alone fine. A further 12 percent received suspended sentences of imprisonment. On the widespread use of stand-alone fines in criminal justice systems outside the United States: Justice Policy Institute (2011: 20ff); Reitz (2018: 35): Kahan (1996); Subramanian and Shames (2013).

41. Reitz (2018: 35n40) writes that "American legal systems have not found it possible to substitute economic penalties for jail or prison terms—and it is likely that they do not stand in for probationary sentences either. Instead, in American legal culture, fines, restitution, fees, and surcharges are 'add-ons,' rarely viewed as adequate sentences in themselves."

42. One might suppose that America's comparative underuse of fines as a stand-alone, court-imposed penalty results from the fact that so many offenders lack the financial means to pay. But sentencers show little hesitation in imposing add-on fines. Similarly, administrative fees and charges are frequently imposed on impecunious individuals and their families: Harris (2016).

43. Subramanian and Shames (2013); Reitz (2018).

44. Balko (2023); Hirschfield (2023).

45. Barkow (2019).

46. On this culture of control: Garland (2001a). On cultural narratives conflating race and crime: Muhammad (2019).

47. Bennett et al. (1996); DiIulio (1994, 1995). For more recent examples: Wootson and Berman (2017).

48. Garland (2001a) argues that postwar changes in the social organization of the UK and the United States led to the relaxation of informal social controls, which in turn led to rises in crime and disorder. The increased penal controls that both nations imposed in the 1980s and 1990s were, in part, a response to these problems, though they were also shaped by political, economic, and cultural developments.

49. Reitz (2018) generally.

50. See chapters 5 and 6. Grinshteyn and Hemenway (2019) provide comparative data showing the US homicide rate in 2015 to be an international outlier. Gallup polls show that the poorest Americans fear for their safety at levels similar to people in developing nations such as Chad or Nicaragua: Kluch (2018).

51. Polanyi (1944).

52. Merton (1996) provides the best account of this idea.

53. Early research suggesting that public opinion was led by political actors and had little relation to crime rates, such as Beckett (1997), has been shown to be poorly supported by empirical evidence. A more recent review of public opinion data, Pickett (2019), concludes that "public opinion moves in response to crime rates and . . . both criminal justice policy and practice respond to opinion movements." Focusing on rates of change, Enns (2016) reaches a similar conclusion after assembling and reviewing an extensive database.

54. Garland (2001a, 2001b: epilogue); Campbell and Schoenfeld (2013).
55. See Sampson (2012); Sharkey (2018).
56. Clegg and Usmani (2019).
57. Ramsay (2023).
58. Sklansky (2020: 55).
59. Sharkey (2018: 22).
60. Zimring and Hawkins (1997: 6).
61. Miller (2016). From the mid-1960s, much of the developed world experienced increasing rates of violent crime and homicide. But these were generally increases from a low base line. Even at their peak, West European rates never came close to the rates experienced in the United States when US homicide rates were at their lowest: Cooper and Smith (2011); Grinshteyn and Hemenway (2015).
62. See chapter 7.
63. See chapter 3.
64. Shammas (2017).

5. America's Political Economy

1. The term "political economy" is sometimes used in a second sense to describe the application of economic models, such as "public choice" theory, to the explanation of political behavior. That is not how I use the term here.
2. Skogan (1990) describes how neighborhoods are shaped by political economy.
3. Lacey, Soskice, and Hope (2018).
4. Hacker et al. (2022: 56) note, "Studies focused on postindustrial democracies find a negative relationship between the number of veto points and a country's redistributive efforts, social spending, and income equality." Frequent, first-past-the-post elections, primary elections, and private financing of candidates for office weaken party discipline and the capacity of governing parties to enact wide-ranging economic and social policy measures. On peculiarly American obstacles to policy-implementation: Kagan (2019).
5. Stuntz (2001).
6. Hacker et al. (2022: 15); King and Lieberman (2009).
7. Hacker et al. (2022: 17); Sutton (2000: 364). Older scholarship frequently refers to the American state as "weak," a characterization that has been vigorously disputed: Novak (2008). As I note later in this chapter, the US federal government is distinctive in the extent to which it pursues its objectives by coordinating with local and private actors.
8. Vogel (1978: 48); Beckert (2015).
9. Lehne (2013: 10). Holmes (forthcoming: 81, 103) describes how, in the early years of the republic, "a relatively weak confederacy" used "civilians rather than soldiers, to seize and hold half a continent." Holmes adds, "The foot soldiers of westward expansion were armed civilian farmers."
10. Vogel (1978: 56–57, 65–66).
11. Rogers (2018). "Market fundamentalism" is an ideology that assumes that markets are the answer to all problems of production, distribution, and social welfare; claims that government social programs always fail; and insists that social provision is a matter for individuals and their families, not for the state.

12. Archer (2007).
13. Korpi (2018); Esping-Anderson (1985); Refslund and Arnholtz (2021).
14. Karabel (2021); Hochschild (2022).
15. Archer (2007); Kolin (2016).
16. Archer (2007).
17. Hacker et al. (2022: 3); Lieberman (1998: 234); Bensel (1984). See also Quadagno (1996); Katznelson (2005).
18. On wealth and race: Conley (1999). On racial patterns in hiring: Pager (2007). Policies of "affirmative action" aiming to counter these effects have generally been controversial and unpopular: Newport (2020).
19. Bonilla-Silva (2003).
20. Sugrue (2005: xviii) writes that "the story of American metropolitan areas... is a history of the ways that whites, through the combined advantages of race and residence, were able to hoard political and economic resources—jobs, public services, education, and other goods—to their own advantage at the expense of the urban poor." On segregation: Beckett (2021). On opportunity hoarding: Desmond (2023). On structural racism: Bonilla-Silva (2003).
21. Desmond (2023); Tilly (1998).
22. Ellen (2001); Conley (1999).
23. American corporations bitterly complain about government regulation but compared with European economies the United States is "much less regulated... both in the labor and in the goods market." Alesina and Glaeser (2004: 43).
24. Baldwin (2009).
25. Frank (2024).
26. Wilensky (2018). Thelen (2014: 47) describes the US economy as a "limiting case" overdetermined by "weak power resources, lack of a dedicated 'left' political party, and the absence of corporatist interest intermediation."
27. Hall and Soskice (2001); Esping-Andersen (1990). The "varieties of capitalism" (VOC) framework has dominated research for much of the last twenty years, but it is not uncritically accepted. Critics such as Streeck (2010), Thelen (2012), and Menz (2018) note that there has been more change than the static, functionalist, VOC framework would predict; that there has been a trend toward convergence at the neoliberal end of the spectrum; and that the "coordinated market economy" category fails to distinguish between those nations that stress coordination, such as Germany and Japan, and those committed to egalitarian outcomes, such as Denmark and Sweden.
28. On corporatist institutions, which bring organized interest groups (unions, business, government, etc.) together in regular dialogue to promote coordination, planning, and agreements: Kenworthy (2020: 83ff.); Hall and Soskice (2001).
29. Hacker et al. (2022: 12). Wilensky (2018: 157) lists a series of features of America's political economy "that are so extreme that we can say they are unique to the United States: the lack of national health insurance; the greatest concentration of wealth; the most poverty and inequality; family break up without family policies to cushion the shock; and related mayhem [violent crime, homicide]; and very high military spending."
30. The comparative data cited in this chapter, and elsewhere in this book, have been assembled from a variety of sources and from various years in the period under discussion.

Standardized data across all the economic and social indicators would be preferable but because the ratios between the United States and comparator nations have stayed relatively stable over this period, this variation does not greatly detract from the analysis. Wherever changes in the comparisons have occurred, I have pointed this out.

31. Baldwin (2009: 21–22) reports that, in a comparison with fifteen European nations, the United States has the least labor market regulation, and gives employers the most firing flexibility. Also Stansbury and Summers (2020).

32. Karabel (2021); Hochschild (2022); Archer (2007).

33. Karabel (2011); Smeeding (2005: 34). According to Rosenfeld (2014) union membership halved between 1980, when it was 20%, to 2023, when it was 10%. Public sector unionization is much stronger than in the private sector, at around 32% of the public employee workforce in 2023: United States Department of Labor (2024). Police and prison officer unions are often especially powerful: see chapter 7.

34. Manufacturing's share of jobs in the US fell from 28% in 1965, to 16% in 1994, and to 9% in 2020, an earlier and more dramatic deindustrialization than in many other old economies: Rowthorn and Ramaswamy (1997).

35. Safier and Harrison (2024); Leicht (2024).

36. Haider (2021).

37. Clegg and Usmani (2019: 51).

38. Ghilarducci (2023). Welfare and employment protections for poor and working people are generally more limited in the United States than in other developed countries: Alesino and Glaser (2006); Laurison (2011); Miller and Parlapiano (2023).

39. Andrias and Hertel-Fernandez (2021: 4) note, "In no other rich democracy do private-sector businesses have as much latitude to dismiss workers without justification as in the US." See also Thelen (2019: 8); Henderson (2023).

40. Henderson (2023). Lynch (2014) reports that the United States is one of only four nations worldwide that does not offer paid leave with job protection for women following childbirth. Among twenty-one rich countries, America is the only one that does not guarantee its workers paid vacation and holidays. Almost 1 in 4 American workers receives neither paid vacation nor paid holidays: Maye (2019). See also Henderson (2023).

41. Schumpeter (1942); Streeck (2012).

42. Garland (2016).

43. Garfinkel et al. (2010).

44. Katznelson (2013).

45. Our World in Data (n.d.). The other nations were Australia, Italy, Canada, Sweden, France, Germany, Greece, Japan, Netherlands, and the UK. In 2019, US public social spending was 18.7% of GDP, well below the OECD average. France spends 31%; the Nordic countries, Belgium, Italy, Germany, and Spain all spend 25% or more.

46. Karabel and Laurison (2011); Smeeding et al. (2001). Garfinkel et al. (2010: 89) write, "The United States spends the least on cash transfers and has the highest poverty rates and greatest inequality.... Among rich nations, the United States currently ranks last or nearly last in promoting education, health, and equality of opportunity."

47. Kenworthy (2014, 2020).

48. Garland (2016); Alesina and Glaeser (2004): Marmor et al. (1990).

49. As Lynch (2014: 113) observes, the US welfare state is unusual in "its extensive reliance on private markets to produce public social goods; its geographic variability; its insistence on deservingness as an eligibility criterion; and its orientation toward benefits for the elderly rather than children and working-age adults." On race and the US welfare state: Lieberman (1998); Quadagno (1996).

50. Alesina and Glaeser (2004: 2) write: "Not only does government spending in Europe favor the poor much more than in the United States, but government tax policy as well is much more redistributive. Income tax rates are more progressive in Europe than in the United States."

51. Desmond (2023).

52. Melhuish and Petrogiannis (2006); Garfinkel et al. (2005); Currie (2020); Desmond (2016, 2023); White (2015). On public housing in the United States compared to Europe, see Wilson (2002).

53. On inequality: Baldwin (2009: 190); Forster and Vleminck (2004); Karabel and Laurison (2011); Massey (2009: 10). On poverty and social problems: Desmond and Western (2018); Hacker (2006).

54. Collyer et al. (2022); Strauss (2020).

55. Smeeding et al. (2001). Rank et al. (2021) estimate that "nearly 60 percent of Americans will experience poverty between ages twenty and seventy-five." Quoted in DeParle (2021).

56. Confronting Poverty (2024). Kenworthy (2014: 55) reports that the extent of material deprivation (share of households experiencing food insecurity, inability to heat home, overcrowding, arrears in bill payment, arrears in rent, difficulty in making ends meet) is worse in the United States than most other developed nations.

57. Statista Research Department (2023). See also Sharkey (2008).

58. Baldwin (2009); Wilson (2011). The American rate has been declining since 1995 but is still the highest of its peers: Ely and Driscoll (2022); Gunja et al. (2023).

59. Starr (2023); Wallace-Wells (2023).

60. Baldwin (2009); Baumgartner et al. (2022); Gunja et al. (2023).

61. Kristof (2017); Wilkinson and Pickett (2010).

62. Wilkinson and Pickett (2010).

63. Sampson and Wilson (1995).

64. Kearney (2023); Berger (2004); Wilensky (2012).

65. Putnam (2015: 69).

66. Putnam (2015: 62, 63, 70).

67. Kearney (2023). For evidence that these developments have destabilized families and childrearing, Kenworthy (2014: 46–47). Family specialist Isabel Sawhill writes, "Generalizations are dangerous; many single parents are doing a terrific job under difficult circumstances. But on average, children from single-parent families do worse in school and in life." Quoted in Putnam (2015: 79).

68. Gustavson (1995).

69. Kristof (2023).

70. Kristof (2023). See also Chetty et al. (2020).

71. Sedgh et al. (2015). Guttmacher Institute (2015) reports that US rates have declined considerably in recent years but remain the highest of those nations that have complete data.

72. Hacker et al. (2022: 133) report, "In 2016, the median net worth of Black and Hispanic households nationwide was $17,000 and $20,700 respectively, compared to $171,000

for whites." They note even bigger disparities between households with children: "In 2016 Black households with children held 1 percent of the wealth of non-Hispanic white households with children."

73. Case and Deaton (2020).

74. Enns (2016).

75. Grinshteyn and Hemenway (2019).

76. Cooper and Smith (2011); Grinshteyn and Hemenway (2019).

77. White (2016); Grinshteyn and Hemenway (2019). The frequency of mass shootings is also exceptionally high in the United States: Violence Project (2023).

78. *The Economist* (2021); Centers for Disease Control (2023).

79. In 2019, the rate for homicides by white Americans was 2.2 per 100,000: *The Economist* (2021); Sharkey (2018: 90–91); Currie (2020).

80. Currie (2020: 23).

81. Benson (2023) reports that just over 10 percent of Americans over 65 live in poverty. The rate for children is over 16 percent.

82. Cowie (2017) argues that New Deal social policies were enabled by immigration controls, which restricted mass immigration between 1918 and 1965. On the reconfiguration of party politics that occurred after the Civil Rights and Voting Rights Acts re-enfranchised Black people: Fraser and Gerstle (1989). On neoliberalism: Gerstle (2022).

83. Together with the Civil Rights and Voting Rights Acts of 1964 and 1965, the War on Poverty was a major attempt to remedy the racial injustices that had persisted through the New Deal era: Zelizer (2015).

84. Katz et al. (2005); Muller (2021). For an analysis of how other nations mitigated the impact of deindustrialization on working people: Therborn (1986).

85. Clegg and Usmani (2019: 24).

86. Fraser and Gerstle (1989); Gerstle (2022: Part 1).

87. Massey (2009: 18); Gerstle (2022).

88. On the impact of "New Federalism" on public housing and poor city dwellers: Venkatesh (2000: 114ff.).

89. Massey (2009: 12).

90. Wilson (1987, 1996); Sharkey (2018).

91. Glazer and Sharkey (2021: 8); Sharkey (2018); Wilson (2011).

92. See, for example, National Advisory Commission on Civil Disorders (1967).

93. Guetzkow (2020). For examples of right-wing analysis and commentary: Wilson (1975); DiIulio (1994, 1995, 1996a, 1996b); Bennett et al. (1996). On the history of this process: Flamm (2005); Garland (2001a).

94. Hinton (2016).

95. Gebeloff et al. (2024).

96. Currie (2020).

97. On lynching deaths: Garland (2005b). On plantation violence: Stubbs (2019). On race riots and massacres: Petruzzello (2024).

98. Leovy (2015).

99. Small Arms Survey (2018); Schaeffer (2023).

100. Winkler (2011).

101. Katznelson (2002); Obert (2018). On EU data: Krusselmann et al. (2021). Fisher (2022) describes how Britain, Australia, New Zealand, and Norway tightened restrictions following violent events.

102. European Commission (2020).

103. Obert (2018: 258).

104. Winkler (2011).

105. Yaname (2019: 173). For this history generally: Obert (2018); Haag (2016); Mennell (2007); Bellesiles (2000); Anderson (2021); Cornell (2006); Carlson (2020); Kaufman (2001); Katznelson (2002); Obert et al. (2019), especially the chapters by Zimring and Yaname.

106. Kaufman (2001: 88–102).

107. Carlson (2020: 31–32).

108. Obert (2018: 14).

109. Cornell (2006); Dunbar-Ortiz (2018).

110. Cornell (2006).

111. Cornell (2006: 214).

112. Kaufman (2001: 94); Skeen (1999); Obert (2018: 248).

113. Dunbar-Ortiz (2018).

114. Bellesiles (1996: 455). The claims made by Bellesiles (2000) about the scarcity of guns in early America were hotly disputed: Lindgren and Heather (2002). By contrast, his observation that guns became pervasive in late nineteenth-century America is uncontroversial: Cramer (2018: 165).

115. Bellesiles (2000: 429, 431); Lansford (2015: 28).

116. Bellesiles (2000: 443) On the nineteenth-century gun industry, see Haag (2016).

117. Haag (2016: 355, 357) describes how gun manufacturers such as Colt and Winchester competed in what he calls the "myth market." He writes, "The gun was retrospectively fetishized. Where it had played a role in American history, it was now the star of the show."

118. Brearley (1932) quoted in Haag (2016: 381). The leading historical study of homicide in the United States notes: "By the end of the Civil War, homicide rates among unrelated adults were substantially higher in the North than in Canada or western Europe, and higher still by one or two orders of magnitude in the South and Southwest." Roth (2009: 299).

119. Kaufman (2001).

120. Kaufman (2001: 96).

121. Kaufman (2001: 90).

6. Political Economy and Disorder

1. This chapter draws on the work of Robert Sampson and his associates, building on the framework set out in Sampson and Wilson (1995: 49): "Boiled down to its essentials, our theoretical framework, linking social disorganization theory with research on urban poverty and political economy suggests that macrostructural forces (e.g., segregation, migration, housing discrimination, structural transformation of the economy) interact with local community-level factors (e.g., residential turnover, concentrated poverty, family disruption) to impede social organization."

2. After the 1960s, federal investment in central city neighborhoods was generally on a small scale and for a limited time: Sharkey (2018); Sharkey and Marsteller (2022).

NOTES TO CHAPTER 6   159

3. Sampson and Wilson (1995); Sharkey (2018); Vankatesh (2002); Glazer and Sharkey (2021: 8).

4. Sampson and Wilson (1995: 43).

5. See generally Wilson (1987, 1996).

6. At the start of the 1960s, America's homicide rate was 4 per 100,000; during the 1980s and 1990s, it fluctuated between 8 and 10 per 100,000, its peak year being 1980 when it reached 10.2 per 100,000: Cooper and Smith (2011).

7. Sharkey (2018: 22).

8. Rosenfeld and Messner (2013: 83–84).

9. Sampson and Wilson (1995: 45) define "social disorganization" as "the inability of a community structure to realize the common values of its residents and maintain effective social controls." Sampson and Groves (1989) note that social disorganization is a measurable phenomenon, "distinct from the structural conditions that prompt it and the deviant outcomes to which it gives rise."

10. On neighborhood disorder: Skogan (1990).

11. Skogan (1990); Klinenberg (2002).

12. Sampson (2019: 5) shows that "neighborhood structures are a persistent feature of urban systems that exert causal effects on a wide variety of aspects of everyday life." Sampson and Raudenbush (2001: 2) describe the "self-regulating capacity of a social unit" as including "informal social control mechanisms" which "intervene in preventing truancy, public drinking, vandalism, or other manifestations of disorder."

13. Sampson (2012: 127) describes this capacity as "collective efficacy" defined as "the linkage of cohesion and mutual trust among residents with shared expectations for intervening in support of neighborhood social control." Sampson's research shows collective efficacy is reduced by concentrated disadvantage, immigration, and residential instability. It is increased by networks of community-based organizations. On the impact of mass incarceration on social capital and social organization: Rose and Clear (1998).

14. Klinenberg (2002) describes and explains the differential capacity of neighborhoods to withstand natural disasters.

15. Sampson and Raudenbush (2001); Skogan (1990: 65); Rosenfeld and Messner (2013: 42).

16. Massey and Denton (1993: 8).

17. Massey and Denton (1993: 9).

18. Katz (2005); Sugrue (2005).

19. Sampson and Wilson (1995: 42).

20. Massey and Denton (1993: 8).

21. Garland (2001a).

22. Messner and Rosenfeld (1997); Messner et al. (2012); Savage et al. (2008); Savolainen (2000); Wilensky (2002); Wilkinson and Pickett (2009). For overviews of the evidence: Pratt and Cullen (2005); Peterson and Krivo (2005).

23. Sampson (2006, 2012); Sampson et al. (1997).

24. Fernandes and Crutchfield (2018: 401); Sampson (2012: 100).

25. Hagan (2010).

26. Zimring and Hawkins (1999: 141) cite studies from the 1980s estimating that more than 50 percent of all homicides in New York City and Washington, D.C., were drug-related.

27. Abt (2019: 159).

28. For the claim that the growth of US incarceration was unrelated to problems of crime and violence: Wacquant (2009); Alexander (2010).

29. Sampson and Wilson (1995).

30. See Sampson et al. (1997).

31. Rosenfeld and Messner (2013: 37); Sampson and Wilson (1995).

32. Sampson and Wilson (1995); Sampson et al. (2018); Sampson (1986); Sampson et al. (1997).

33. Wilson (1996).

34. Sampson and Wilson (1995: 47).

35. Sampson, Wilson, and Katz (2018). On cycles of gun violence: Kennedy (2012); Bourgois (2003); Anderson (2000).

36. On the techniques required to use interpersonal violence effectively: Collins (2009).

37. Sharkey (2018). Sampson et al. (2005). Western (2018: 66) summarizes the research literature.

38. Sampson and Wilson (1995: 40) show that the prevalence of family disruption is substantially related to murder and robbery rates and closely linked to rates of juvenile offending.

39. On illegal economic activity and "hustles" in a declining neighborhood: Venkatesh (2002). Rios (2011) notes that when deviant norms emerge, individuals must adapt to the perceptions, expectations, and challenges of others. Being law-abiding may lead to being viewed with suspicion by neighbors who perceive the law-abiding individual as weak, or a snitch, or of thinking themselves better than others.

40. O'Flaherty and Sethi (2019: 74).

41. Sampson and Wilson (1995: 52):

42. Bourgois (2003); Goffman (2014); Anderson (2000); Katz (1988).

43. O'Flaherty and Sethi (2024). Braga and Cook (2023: 174) report that arrest and conviction rates for nonfatal shootings are below 10 percent in many American cities, and not much higher for fatal shootings.

44. Crutchfield (2014: 4–5). Sampson and Wilson (1995: 45) reject the "materialist fallacy" that falsely assumes that the causal relevance of economic factors works through motivation to commit acquisitive crimes. See also Rosenfeld and Messner (2013).

45. Pfaff (2017).

46. Klinenberg (2002).

47. This was the fate of Daniel Patrick Moynihan's 1965 report, *The Negro Family: The Case for National Action*. Moynihan was widely perceived as blaming the social problems of poor neighborhoods on Black women for having children out of wedlock, Black men for failing to support their children's mothers, and Black parents for failing to discipline their children. For recent and more nuanced discussions of the Report, see Coates (2015); Massey and Sampson (2009).

48. Messner and Rosenfeld (2013: 93).

49. Kearney (2023); Berger (2004).

50. On childhood development and crime: Farrington (2020); Font and Kennedy (2022); Smith et al. (2005).

51. For data about Black and White involvement in crimes of violence: Federal Bureau of Investigation (2020). Krivo and Peterson (1996) show that high violence rates are racially invariant when controlling for socioeconomic conditions.

52. Sampson et al. (2018: 14, 21) show that "concentrated disadvantage predicts crime similarly across racial groups" and "the gap between Black and White rates of violence is socially explicable and not due to intrinsic racial features." They also show that Black crime rates vary by neighborhood, just as White rates do.

53. Marx (1852).

7. Political Institutions and Crime Control

1. Kohler-Hausmann (2019).

2. Abend (2014) analyzes the "moral background" that shapes decision making in business. Here I discuss the unstated social background that shapes criminal justice decisions.

3. Lacey and Soskice (2015: 458).

4. Tonry (2012a).

5. Savelsberg (1994).

6. According to Ellis (2012) the United States is the only country where prosecutors are elected. Originally, American prosecutors were appointed by governors, judges, or legislators, but between 1832 and 1860 state constitutional conventions made most prosecutors and state judges electable. Federal prosecutors are not elected but they are appointed in a political process and given direction by a politically appointed chief prosecutor, the US Attorney.

7. Page (2011); National Association of Assistant US Attorneys (2015); Page et al. (2020); Zimring et al. (2001).

8. Pfaff (2017: 154).

9. Garland (2018a); Reitz (2020); Savelsberg (1994).

10. Berry (2015); Dieter (1996).

11. Weaver (2017: 11). Zimring and Hawkins (1991) described this arrangement as a "correctional free lunch."

12. Kleiman (2009); Lewis and Usmani (2022). As police scholar Lawrence Sherman remarks, "In England and Wales, the spending on police is twice as high as on corrections. In Australia it's more than three times higher. In Japan, it's seven times higher. Only in the United States it's lower." Quoted in Tierney (2013).

13. Hirschfield (2023). On police training: US Department of Justice (2019). On the "danger narrative" in police training and police culture: Eisenberg (2023); Sierra-Arevalo (2024).

14. Balko (2013); Kommenda and Kirk (2020).

15. Dienst and Paredes (2019); Zimring (2017: 249). It seems likely that police violence—lethal and nonlethal—declined over the course of the twentieth century. There were 994 police-involved shootings in New York City in 1972. In 2018, following a series of reforms, there were 35. For a detailed evaluation of the department's firearm procedures: Rostker et al. (2008). Over time, policing in the United States has likely become less brutal, less corrupt, and more professionalized while also becoming more militarized, more proactive, and more aggressive in its engagement with poor communities. For critical histories: Felker-Kantor (2018); Go (2023); and Balto (2018). Phelps (2023) points to the dual characteristics of American policing—the promise of state protection and the threat of state violence—which helps explain the ambivalence felt toward police by many residents in poor Black communities. Police funding has become a highly contentious issue in the United States, with some critics arguing that the police

are overfunded and that some part of their funding ought to be diverted to social services and others arguing that the United States has relatively few police per capita, given the high levels of serious crime: Lewis and Usmani (2022). The point I wish to stress here is that the *quality* of policing in the United States is adversely affected by the resource limitations of the local state.

16. Hirschfield (2015).

17. Schwartz (2023).

18. Schwartz (2023); Kirkpatrick (2021).

19. Sharkey (2018).

20. Clegg and Usmani (2019: 46); Laskin (2011).

21. On homeowner influence in local politics: Hall and Yoder (2022).

22. Lacey et al. (2018). Miller (2008, 2015) observes that cities and municipalities lack the resources needed to enact redistributive policies and that poor Americans, hard-hit by disorder and violence, are typically underrepresented at the federal level where resources are more available. On local policy choices in respect of crime control: Beck (2022).

23. Subramanian and Shames (2013). For examples of austerity measures in US prisons: Keller (2022a); Gottschalk (2014).

24. As Rusche (1980: 12) observed, the conditions of life in penal institutions "are inevitably limited by the situation of the lowest socially significant proletarian class." See also Bonnet (2019).

25. Gottschalk (2014: 49).

26. Lynch (2010); Campbell and Schoenfeld (2013).

27. Making offenders pay the costs of their punishment is a long-standing practice in some American states: McLennan (2008). Albin-Lackey (2014) reports that, as of 2013, twelve states contracted probation out to commercial firms which charged fees to probationers.

28. Forman (2017); Fortner (2015).

29. Gilens (1999); Bailey and Danziger (2013); Jencks (2015); Zelizer (2015).

30. Lacey and Soskice (2015); Edsall (2018); King (1997); Gilens (1999); Miller (2016); Baldwin (2009).

31. Political barriers are low because proposals to increase police powers or punishments rarely meet with organized opposition: Stuntz (2001).

32. Mann (1993: 59); Lindsey (2021).

33. Soifer and vom Hau (2008). State capacity, which encompasses resources, administrative and logistical arrangements, personnel, expertise, institutional routines, relationships, and so on, is an infrastructure that accumulates slowly over time as the product of repeated actions and acquisitions. In normal times, state capacity is relatively fixed, though in moments of radical change, such as FDR's New Deal in the 1930s or the start of the second Trump administration in 2025, transformations in state capacity can occur quite rapidly.

34. Zimring (2013).

35. Weaver (2000); Mink (1998).

36. For detailed accounts of the social responses that other western nations mount in respect of crime and disorder: Boutellier (2001); Gilling (2001); Lappi-Seppala (2011); Albrecht (2004); Junger-Tas (2004); Kyvsgaard (2004); Janson (2004); Kristoff (2017); Gottschalk (2006).

37. In places such as New York City government action is supplemented by a rich network of charitable, private, and public-private interventions. But nongovernmental initiatives of this

kind are not uniformly present in the nation as a whole, and tend to be under-financed, uncoordinated, and not to scale.

38. The National Research Council (Travis, Western, and Redburn 2014) reports that 64% of America's jail inmates have mental illness and 68% have drug or alcohol dependence. In state prisons, the prevalence is 56% and 53%. Eighty percent of inmates are without private or public health insurance upon reentry, and several states make former inmates ineligible for Medicaid.

39. Quoted in Dennis et al. (2016). The quotation continues, "Not enough mental health funding, let the cops handle it. . . . Here in Dallas we got a loose dog problem; let's have the cops chase loose dogs. Schools fail, let's give it to the cops. . . . That's too much to ask. Policing was never meant to solve all those problems."

40. Forman (2016); Hinton (2016).

41. Hirschfield (2023); Sherman (2018). On "warrior style" policing: Balko (2013). On the militarization of US police: Go (2023).

42. The macho character of police culture generally prohibits open expressions of such fears. For an exceptional occasion when these fears were openly admitted: Brown (2023).

43. Skogan (2023: 4); Sierra Arevalo (2021 and 2024). Swedler et al. (2014: 35) note that most officers (67%) were killed by short-barrel firearms; 10% with their own service weapon. They also report, "The most frequent encounter with a suspect prior to a homicide was responding to a disturbance call."

44. O'Flaherty and Sethi (2019: 124).

45. USAFacts (2023); O'Flaherty and Sethi (2019: 122); Zimring (2019: 158).

46. Zimring (2019). Sierra-Arevalo (2020a) reports that between 79% and 86% of all firearm assaults on police in any given year are non-fatal. As Sierra-Arevalo (2024: 4) notes, "Bureau of Labor Statistics data show that policing has a violent injury rate of 121.7 per 100,000, more than 16 times the national average for all occupations."

47. Braga and Cook (2023: 149).

48. Zimring (2017: 86) writes, "In a major city police force of 10,000 officers, a fatal risk of 7.1 per 100,000 [the rate at which US police officers are killed] translates into one killing in an average two-year period . . . the threat of lethal attack is a palpable part of being a police officer in the United States." For data on police officers shot with their own firearms: Swedler (2014). On police fears: O'Flaherty and Sethi (2019).

49. Sierra Arevalo (2021: 74).

50. Sierra-Arevalo (2020b: 5); Moskos (2009: ch. 6).

51. O'Flaherty and Sethi (2019: 123); Zimring (2017); Karabel (2017).

52. O'Flaherty and Sethi (2019: 131).

53. Sierra-Arevalo (2024); Simon (2024).

54. Brooks (2021: 312).

55. Quoted in Baker (2015).

56. For evidence that police use greater force in neighborhoods they perceive as dangerous: O'Flaherty and Sethi (2019: 27); Terrill and Reisig (2003).

57. O'Flaherty and Sethi (2019) observe that American police officers are influenced by racist stereotypes and behave in ways that make them self-fulfilling.

58. Kohler-Hausmann (2018: 72, 76, 265). On the chaotic lives of many offenders: Western (2019).

59. Morgenstern (2024).

60. Western (2018: 4) hints at this in the following passage, though the contrast he draws is between the lives of poor Americans and middle-class Americans: "So much of the ethical talk about incarceration . . . is naïve about the empirical reality in which it is administered." Its moral logic "imports assumptions from middle-class life, in which a basic level of order and security prevails."

61. In Scotland, for example, probation officers are known as "criminal justice social workers," must have a university degree in social work, and are employed by local authority social work departments: Prospects (2024). On probation practice in Norway, with its client-centered focus on reintegration: Todd-Kvam (2022). For information about probation in specific European nations: Confederation of European Probation (2024). On probation in the United States: Phelps (2020). On US parole: Simon (1993). Donna Sytek, the New Hampshire parole board chairperson, commented that the lack of a social safety net or a safe place to live is the most common reason for refusing parole to applicants who otherwise have good risk profiles. Quoted in Schwartzapfel (2015).

62. Keller (2022a: 58–61) highlights the contrasts between American and European prisons in this respect. On America's jails: Littman (2021).

63. See chapter 3.

8. Social Sources of Indifference

1. Sklansky (2021: 110–12) presents evidence that public concern about police violence, prompted by the events of the 1960s, waned as crime rates rose in the 1970s and 1980s. He adds (2021: 108), "There is a long history of complaints about police brutality and efforts to rein in violence by the police, but there is also a long history of looking the other way, and of vocal defenses of tough, aggressive police tactics." On public support for punitive policies, which peaked in the late-1990s: Enns (2016: 35).

2. I make no claim here about the comparative punitiveness of the American public relative to the publics of other nations. My claim is that, for decades, majorities of the American public have, by and large, supported a penal state that is extraordinarily punitive relative to those of other nations.

3. Here I follow the social theory of emotions outlined by Nussbaum (2001: 302).

4. Garland (1990: 242); Elias (2000).

5. Sampson and Loeffler (2010).

6. Simon (2021).

7. Matza and Uggen (2006).

8. US Department of Justice (2015).

9. Enns (2016).

10. Travis, Western, and Redburn (2014); Sharkey (2018).

11. Western (2006).

12. Ofer (2021).

13. Cohen (2001); Press (2021).

14. On racist attitudes that identify young Black men with violent crime: Rucker and Richeson (2021).

15. Quoted in Keller (2022a: 80).

16. Drakulich et al. (2023); Sklansky (2021).

17. Travis, Western, and Redburn (2014: 123) write that "public opinion on crime and punishment is highly racialized. Whites tend to associate crime and violence with being black and are more likely than blacks to support harsh penal policies. Whites who harbor racial resentments are especially likely to endorse tougher penal policies and to reject claims that the criminal justice system discriminates against blacks." See also Bobo and Johnson (2004: 172).

18. Rucker and Richeson (2021).

19. Woodhill (2014) summarizes the right-wing critique.

20. Bobo and Johnson (2004).

21. National Conference of State Legislatures (2022).

22. Carson (2023); Zeng (2022); United States Department of Justice (2023).

23. Alexander (2010).

24. Connaughton (2022); Burn-Murdoch (2023).

25. Wacquant (2022): Katz (1995).

26. Bennett et al. (1996); DiIulio (1995); Reinerman and Levine (1997); Ramsay (2023).

27. Currie (2020).

28. O'Flaherty and Sethi (2019: 233); Wilson (2011).

29. Durkheim (1973).

30. Klinenberg (2024, 179).

31. Durkheim, quoted in Lukes (1973). See also Miller (2017); Stjernø (2005).

32. Rothstein (2011b).

33. Hirst (1994).

34. Rothstein (2011b); Horton and Gregory (2009).

35. Hall (2017).

36. Kymlicka (2015); Banting and Kymlicka (2017). For empirical evidence linking Canada's higher levels of trust and solidarity (relative to the United States) to its more universal welfare state: Johnston et al. (2017). On the role of trade unions and social democratic parties in building solidarity at the national level: Hall (2017).

37. On social distance: Enos (2017). Rothstein and Stolle (2003: 197) write that "in their essence, [non-universal] welfare states are designed to plot groups of the population against one another."

38. Social Capital Project (2017); Bellah (1985); Putnam (2000); Tocqueville (1835).

39. On the importance of ethnic fractionalization in shaping America's political economy in general and its welfare state in particular: Alesina and Glaeser (2004).

40. Burn-Murdoch (2023); Vallier (2020); Menendian (2021). On the association between levels of social trust and rates of incarceration in OECD countries and in each of the American states: Lappi-Seppala (2018: 233).

41. Desmond (2023).

42. Burn-Murdoch (2023); Connaughtan (2020).

43. Personal communication from Bo Rothstein, quoted in Chan (2022). For data on racial and economic inequality, and on child poverty, see chapter 5.

44. In a comparative study, Johnson et al. (2007) show that, of the five countries compared, the United States exhibits the most ethnic residential segregation, with Blacks being America's most segregated group. For an older US/Canada comparison, see Fong (1996).

45. Enos and Celaya (2018). Massey and Denton (1993: 14) note that the segregation of Black Americans means that public resources allocated to their neighborhoods benefit only Blacks, making it difficult for Black residents to build mutually self-interested coalitions with other ethnic groups.

46. Burn-Murdoch (2023).

47. Vallier (2020).

48. Enos (2017); *The Economist* (2018); Reardon and Owens (2014).

49. Putnam (2015: 41); Desmond (2023).

50. Sharkey (2008). Katz et al. (2005: 79) note that "At the end of the twentieth century, the typical African American still lived in a neighborhood where two-thirds of the other residents were blacks."

51. Desmond (2023); Massey and Denton (1993). Levels of residential segregation in the United States fell from 1970 to 1980 and then stayed level. For recent research on segregation in the United States: *The Economist* (2018); Beckett (2021); Tatum (2017).

52. For research showing that inequality reduces the prospects of solidarity in societies: Paskov and Dewilde (2012).

53. Morone (2003, 2020).

54. On welfare state institutions and solidarity: Banting and Kymlicka (2017).

55. Thelen (2014: 205).

56. Rothstein (2011b: 2); Horton and Gregory (2009).

57. Lappi-Seppala (2018: 227).

58. Tonry and Lappi-Seppala (2011: 23–24).

59. Desmond (2023). On the divisive impacts of welfare states like the American one: Rothstein and Stolle (2003: 197). On the public sphere and its implications for solidarity: Marquand (2004). On American meritocracy and how it exacerbates inequality: Markovits (2020).

60. Williams (2019). On the racist trope that the federal government is somehow "African American": Haney Lopez (2011); Edsall and Edsall (1991: 202–7).

61. On American welfare policy as premised upon worth and deservingness: Dauber (2013).

62. Lappi-Seppala (2008); Rothstein (2011b).

Epilogue: Constraints and Possibilities

1. For examples of this radical, "root cause" analysis, see the section titled "Getting to the Root: Racial Capitalism and Neoliberalism" in Kaba and Ritchie (2022: 26–32) or Mariame Kaba's statement that "You're not going to be able to end policing without ending capitalism." Quoted in Madden, Leeds, and Carmichael (2020). See also Vitale (2017: 34).

2. Shelby (2022) provides an overview of prison abolition arguments and positions. Taylor (2021a) notes the calls of some activists "for an end to policing as we know it" and of others "that the institution of policing should be abolished completely."

3. Smith (2020). For a discussion and attempted rebuttal of this claim: Fox and Berman (2023). On prison abolition generally: Shelby (2022).

4. For the original statement of the theory of prison abolition: Mathiesen (1974). On social movements: Goodwin and Jasper (2014).

5. As Berger et al. (2017: 2) remark, "Prison abolitionists aren't naïve dreamers. They're organizing for concrete reforms, animated by a radical critique of state violence." The concept

of "non-reformist reforms" is an attempt to smooth over the tension between abolitionist theory and this reform-oriented practice: Stahly-Butts and Akbar (2022); Akbar (2023).

6. Kennedy (2021b: 444, 447) writes that "it is morally imperative for a polity to maintain agencies of collective self-defense, including police and prisons. Justice requires that arbitrariness, prejudice, and cruelty be removed from such agencies. But that is a project of reform, not abolition . . . Abolitionism has erred . . . in choosing to target for erasure (actually or even only rhetorically) public institutions that are essential." See also Gopnik (2024).

7. Kaba (2020). For an early statement: Smith (2015).

8. Kolakowski (1969).

9. Durkheim (1982).

10. Selznick (1994: 126). Selznick (1994: 127) continues: "we must think of delinquency as a normal feature of social life, constrained in most settings by the claims of conscience and the strength of the social fabric. When either one weakens, so does self-control. We can expect delinquency to be correlated with the prevalence of temptation and with conditions that produce low self-control."

11. Gilmore (2024)

12. Garland (2010).

13. Putting troublesome people behind the scenes—hiding them away—may serve the ends of government but the practice has a despotic aspect, as Blackstone (1765) long ago observed: "[C]onfinement of the person, by secretly hurrying him to jail, where his sufferings are unknown or forgotten, is a . . . dangerous engine of arbitrary government."

14. Kleiman (2009: 123) notes that prisons and jails are settings in which healthcare and social services could be provided to people greatly in need of them.

15. On electronic monitoring: Daems (2020).

16. Jones et al. (2017: 632); Kennedy (2021b); Bittner (1990: 249).

17. For an argument for "the end of policing": Vitale (2017).

18. Dodd (2023) reports that the London Metropolitan Police no longer accept calls to attend mental health emergencies, except where life is in danger.

19. Gottschalk (2014 : 261) writes that "successful decarceration will cost money. The people reentering society after prison need significant educational, vocational, housing, medical, and economic support to ensure that the communities they are returning to are not further destabilized by waves of former prisoners." Lobuglio and Piehl (2015: 56) similarly note that "unwinding mass incarceration will neither be cheap nor easy, and to be done responsibly, will require a new infrastructure of coordinated community-based facilities and services."

20. Cowie (2017).

21. Progressives are prone to overestimate the crime-control efficacy of social welfare measures: Fogel (2021: 9).

22. On the temporal aspects of the links between economic policy change and crime rate change: Farrall and Gray (2024).

23. Once welfare states are established, all else being equal, they tend to influence criminal justice by reducing poverty-related social problems but also by revising sentencing principles and the ideologies of criminal justice personnel in a welfarist direction: Garland (2018b).

24. Vogler (2020) finds that in states that expanded Medicaid eligibility reported crime decreased relative to non-expansion states.

25. Fishback et al. (2010) estimate that New Deal spending on work relief significantly reduced property crime.
26. Kleiman (2009: 126).
27. Lochner and Moretti (2004).
28. Sharkey (2008).
29. Savage et al. (2008).
30. Western (2023: 58).
31. Shammas (2015: 5).
32. The critique of mass incarceration has created a cultural current that strives to humanize people caught up in the penal state, seeking to undo the demonization of offenders that was part of the law and order era. Changes in the language used to describe justice-involved people is one aspect of this cultural shift. See Fortune Society (n.d.); The Marshall Project (n.d.).
33. Garland (2010).
34. On the contrast between the politics of state building and state retrenchment: Pierson (2010).
35. Kleiman (2009: 119) points out: "By comparison with education or health care, criminal-justice operations are fairly cheap in dollar terms. If we abolished prisons and jails entirely, or cut the police budget in half, and spend all of the money on public elementary and secondary education, the savings could finance about a 10 percent budget boost for schools.... Even the public share of health care spending—about half the total—is five times the entire criminal justice budget." Criminal justice—even in America's massive penal state—is targeted and tightly focused relative to other programs such as education, health, and welfare programs that serve a much broader clientele. On the relative costs of policing and corrections as compared to social democratic social policy: Clegg and Usmani (2019); Lewis and Usmani (2022).
36. Miller (2008).
37. Alexander (2010).
38. Engel (2015).
39. Abt (2019: 174).
40. On community building as crime control: Skogan (1990: 16–17); Glazer and Sharkey (2021); Welsh and Pfeffer (2013). On situational crime prevention: Clarke (1997). On nonpenal crime control: Kleiman (2009: ch. 7); Welsh and Pfeffer (2013); Sherman et al. (1997). On the importance of "urban guardians": Sharkey (2018: 53), who notes, "As the number of non-profits rises, every kind of violent crime falls."
41. Rabin (2023).
42. Jacobs and Zuhr (2019); Braga and Cook (2023: ch. 10); Abt (2019). On the efficacy of local gun controls in reducing homicides: Sharkey and Kang (2023), who write thus: "Stricter gun laws passed by 40 states from 1991 to 2016 reduced gun deaths by nearly 4,300 in 2016, or about 10 percent of the nationwide total." Abt (2019: 135) notes that "urban violence is perpetrated with guns that are loaned, stolen, or bought on the black market. Relatedly, only about one in every six guns used in the commission of a crime is legally obtained."
43. As Gottschalk (2015) writes: "Comprehensive changes in penal policy, not an assault on structural problems and the root causes of crime, have been the main drivers of successful decarcerations elsewhere, including Finland in the 1960s and 1970s, Germany in the 1980s, and California under Governor Ronald Reagan."

44. Widra (2024).

45. New York City Mayor's Office of Criminal Justice (2024). According to Loopoo et al. (2023: 32): "The story of New York's turnaround, from a bleak landscape to what we have today—arguably the most decarcerated major urban area in the United States—was the result of several factors: (a) incremental changes to the criminal legal system; (b) durable, sizeable investments in social policy to preempt system involvement; (c) efforts by highly organized advocacy organizations; and (d) open-minded officials willing to implement changes."

46. For details of the New York City developments: Fox and Berman (2023: ch. 5); Glazer and Sharkey (2021: 12).

47. Rovner (2023).

48. Binion (2023). The same period saw large declines in other cities such as Los Angeles, Detroit, and Chicago.

49. NYCLU (2019).

50. Porter and McLeod (2023).

51. Reiter (2023); Boghani (2017).

52. Ghandnoosh (2023).

53. For a discussion of interventions of this kind: Glazer and Sharkey (2021: 18). The authors describe how New York City undertook a shift "away from policies of negation (arrest and incarcerate) and toward policies of creation (strengthen family, nurture neighborhood connections and networks, transform public spaces, and open up jobs.)" On proposals for "affirmative action for neighborhoods," and durable investments in disadvantaged urban spaces: Sampson et al. (2018: 27).

54. Zimring (2006, 2013).

55. Sharkey and Kang (2023).

BIBLIOGRAPHY

ABC News. 2000. "NJ Knew of Racial Profiling for Years." October 12. https://abcnews.go.com/US/story?id=95406&page=1.

Abend, G. 2014. *The Moral Background: An Inquiry into the History of Business Ethics*. Princeton: Princeton University Press.

Abt, T. 2019. *Bleeding Out: The Devastating Consequences of Urban Violence—and a Bold New Plan for Peace in the Streets*. New York: Basic Books.

Akbar, A. 2020. "An Abolitionist Horizon for (Police) Reform." *California Law Review* 108: 1781–1846.

Akbar, A. 2023. "Non-Reformist Reforms and Struggles Over Life, Death, and Democracy." *Yale Law Journal* 132, no. 8.

Albin-Lackey, C. 2014. "Profiting from Probation: America's 'Offender-Funded' Probation Industry." *Human Rights Watch*, February 5. https://www.hrw.org/report/2014/02/05/profiting-probation/americas-offender-funded-probation-industry.

Albrecht, H. 2004. "Youth Justice in Germany." *Crime and Justice* 31: 443–93.

Alesina, A., and E. L. Glaeser. 2004. *Fighting Poverty in the US and Europe: A World of Difference*. New York: Oxford University Press.

Alesina, A., and E. L. Glaeser. 2006. "Why Are Welfare States in the US and Europe So Different?" *Horizons Stratégiques* 2, no. 2: 51–61.

Alexander, M. 2010. *The New Jim Crow: Mass Incarceration in the Age of Colorblindness*. New York: The New Press.

Anderson, C. 2021. *The Second: Race and Guns in a Fatally Unequal America*. New York: Bloomsbury.

Anderson, D. 1995. *Crime and the Politics of Hysteria: How the Willie Horton Story Changed American Criminal Justice*. New York: Crown.

Anderson, E. 2000. *Code of the Street: Decency, Violence, and the Moral Life of the Inner City*. New York: Norton.

Andrias, K., and A. Hertel-Fernandez. 2021. "Ending At-Will Employment: A Guide for Just Cause Reform." Roosevelt Institute. https://rooseveltinstitute.org/wp-content/uploads/2021/01/RI_AtWill_Report_202101.pdf.

Arango, T., and E. Gabler. 2023. "Amid Criticism, Elite Crime Teams Dwindled. Then Cities Brought Them Back." *New York Times*, February 6. https://www.nytimes.com/2023/02/06/us/police-teams-memphis-scorpion-unit.html.

Archer, R. 2007. *Why Is There No Labor Party in the United States?* Princeton: Princeton University Press.

Arnsdorf, I. 2020. "Inside Trump and Barr's Last-Minute Killing Spree." ProPublica, December 23. https://www.propublica.org/article/inside-trump-and-barrs-last-minute-killing-spree.
Associated Press. 2019. "Changing Attitudes about Racial Inequality." NORC Center for Public Affairs Research, University of Chicago, March. https://apnorc.org/wp-content/uploads/2020/02/APNORC_GSS_race_relations_report_2019-1.pdf.
Associated Press. 2024. *"All Cases." Lethal Restraint.* https://apnews.com/projects/investigation-police-use-of-force/all-cases/.
Austin, J., and M. Jacobson. 2013. "How New York City Reduced Mass Incarceration." Brennan Center for Justice. https://www.brennancenter.org/our-work/research-reports/how-new-york-city-reduced-mass-incarceration-model-change.
Bailey, M. J., and S. Danziger, eds. 2013. *Legacies of the War on Poverty.* New York: Russell Sage Foundation.
Baker, A. 2015. "U.S. Police Leaders, Visiting Scotland, Get Lessons on Avoiding Deadly Violence." *New York Times*, December 11. https://www.nytimes.com/2015/12/12/nyregion/us-police-leaders-visiting-scotland-get-lessons-on-avoiding-deadly-force.html.
Baldwin, P. 2009. *The Narcissism of Minor Differences: How America and Europe Are Alike.* New York: Oxford University Press.
Balko, R. 2013. *Rise of the Warrior Cop: The Militarization of America's Police Forces.* New York: PublicAffairs.
Balko, R. 2020. "There Is Overwhelming Evidence That the Criminal Justice System Is Racist. Here Is the Proof." *Washington Post*, June 10. https://www.washingtonpost.com/graphics/2020/opinions/systemic-racism-police-evidence-criminal-justice-system/.
Balto, S. 2018. *Occupied Territory: Policing Black Chicago from Red Summer to Black Power.* Chapel Hill: University of North Carolina Press.
Banting, K., and W. Kymlicka, eds. 2017. *The Strains of Commitment: The Political Sources of Solidarity in Diverse Societies.* New York: Oxford University Press.
Barker, K., M. Baker, and A. Watkins. 2021. "In City after City, Police Mishandled Black Lives Matter Protests." *New York Times*, March 20. https://www.nytimes.com/2021/03/20/us/protests-policing-george-floyd.html.
Barker, V. 2013. "Nordic Exceptionalism Revisited: Explaining the Paradox of a Janus-Faced Penal Regime." *Theoretical Criminology* 17, no. 1: 5–25.
Barkow, R. E. 2019. *Prisoners of Politics: Breaking the Cycle of Mass Incarceration.* Cambridge: Harvard University Press.
Barr, W. 1992. "Foreword." *The Case for More Incarceration*, report, United States Department of Justice, Office of Policy Development. https://www.ojp.gov/ncjrs/virtual-library/abstracts/case-more-incarceration.
Baumgartner, J. C., E. D. Gumas, and M. Z. Gunja. 2022. "Too Many Lives Lost: Comparing Overdose Mortality Rates and Policy Solutions Across High-Income Countries." Commonwealth Fund, May 19. https://www.commonwealthfund.org/blog/2022/too-many-lives-lost-comparing-overdose-mortality-rates-policy-solutions.
Bayley, D. 1994. *Police for the Future.* New York: Oxford University Press.
Bazelon, E. 2019. *Charged: The New Movement to Transform American Prosecution and End Mass Incarceration.* New York: Random House.

Bazelon, E. 2023. "The Response to Crime: Republican Lawmakers Are Putting Limits on Progressive Prosecutors." *New York Times*, April 7. https://www.nytimes.com/2023/04/07/briefing/legislators-response-to-crime.html.

BBC. 2023. "Ex-Policeman Derek Chauvin Stable After Prison Stabbing." November 26. https://www.bbc.com/news/world-us-canada-67529163.

Beck, A. J., and A. Blumstein. 2018. "Racial Disproportionality in U.S. State Prisons: Accounting for the Effects of Racial and Ethnic Differences in Criminal Involvement, Arrests, Sentencing, and Time Served." *Journal of Quantitative Criminology* 34: 853–83.

Beck, B. 2022. "Do Austerity Cuts Spare Police Budgets? Recessions and the Budgetary Shift from Social Services to Law Enforcement in U.S. Cities." Punishment and Society Digital Speakers Series, YouTube, November 9. https://www.youtube.com/watch?v=pneL1OxilCg.

Beckert, S. 2015. *Empire of Cotton: A Global History*. New York: Vintage Books.

Beckett, K. 1997. *Making Crime Pay: Law and Order in Contemporary Politics*. New York: Oxford University Press.

Beckett, K. 2022. *Ending Mass Incarceration: Why it Persists and How to Achieve Meaningful Reform*. New York: Oxford University Press.

Beckett, K., and B. Western. 2001. "Governing Social Marginality: Welfare, Incarceration, and the Transformation of State Policy." *Punishment and Society* 3, no. 1: 43–59.

Beckett, L. 2021. "Where You Live Determines Everything: Why Segregation Is Growing in the US." *The Guardian*, June 28. https://www.theguardian.com/us-news/2021/jun/28/us-racial-segregation-study-university-of-california-berkeley.

Bell, M. 2016. "Situational Trust: How Disadvantaged Mothers Reconceive Legal Cynicism." *Law and Society Review* 50, no. 2: 314–47.

Bellah, R. N., R. Madsen, W. M. Sullivan, A. Swidler, and S. M. Tipton. 1985. *Habits of the Heart: Individualism and Commitment in American Life*. Berkeley and Los Angeles: University of California Press.

Bellesiles, M. A. 1996. "The Origins of Gun Culture in the United States, 1760–1865." *Journal of American History* 83, no. 2: 425–55.

Bellesiles, M. A. 2000. *Arming America: The Origins of a National Gun Culture*. New York: Knopf.

Belova, E., and P. Gregory. 2014. "Political Economy of Crime and Punishment under Stalin." *Public Choice* 140, no. 3/4: 463–78.

Benko, J. 2015. "The Radical Humaneness of Norway's Halden Prison." *New York Times Magazine*, March 26. https://www.nytimes.com/2015/03/29/magazine/the-radical-humaneness-of-norways-halden-prison.html.

Bennett, W. J., J. J. DiIulio, and J. P. Walters. 1996. *Body Count: Moral Poverty . . . And How to Win America's War Against Crime and Drugs*. New York: Simon & Schuster.

Bensel, R. F. 1984. *Sectionalism and American Political Development, 1880–1980*. Madison: University of Wisconsin Press.

Benson, C. 2023. "Child Poverty Rate Still Higher Than for Older Populations But Declining." United States Census Bureau, Washington, D.C., December 4. https://www.census.gov/library/stories/2023/12/poverty-rate-varies-by-age-groups.html.

Berger, D., M. Kaba, and D. Stein. 2017. "What Abolitionists Do." *Jacobin*, August 24. https://jacobin.com/2017/08/prison-abolition-reform-mass-incarceration.

Berger, L. 2004. "Income, Family Structure, and Child Maltreatment Risk." *Children and Youth Services Review* 26, no. 8: 725–48.

Berman, G., and A. Fox. 2023. *Gradual: The Case for Incremental Change in a Radical Age*. New York: Oxford University Press.

Berry, K. 2015. "How Judicial Elections Impact Criminal Cases." Brennan Center for Justice. https://www.brennancenter.org/sites/default/files/publications/How_Judicial_Elections_Impact_Criminal_Cases.pdf.

Bhuller, M., G. B. Dahl, and K. Løken. 2019. "Policies to Reintegrate Former Inmates into the Labor Force." Aspen Institute, February 4.

Binion, B. 2023. "Police Killed 1,183 People in 2022. Despite a Viral Claim, That's Not a "Record High.'" *Reason*, January 12. https://reason.com/2023/01/12/police-killed-1183-people-in-2022-despite-a-viral-claim-thats-not-a-record-high/.

Bittner, E. 1990. *Aspects of Police Work*. Boston: Northeastern University Press.

Bivens, J., and J. Kandra. 2023. "CEO Pay Slightly Declined in 2022." Economic Policy Institute, September 21. https://www.epi.org/publication/ceo-pay-in-2022/.

Blackstone, W. 1765. "On the Absolute Rights of Individuals." Facsimile edition. *Commentaries on the Laws of England*. Repr. Chicago: University of Chicago Press, 1979.

Blow, C. M. 2022. "'Defund the Police' Is Dead. Now What?" *New York Times*, August 31.

Bobo, L. 2021. "Racial Attitudes and Relations at the Close of the Twentieth Century." In *America Becoming: Racial Trends and Their Consequences: Volume 1*, ed. N. J. Smesler, W. J. Wilson, and F. Mitchell. Washington, DC: National Academy Press.

Bobo, L. D., and D. Johnson. 2004. "A Taste for Punishment: Black and White Americans' Views on the Death Penalty and the War on Drugs." *Du Bois Review* 1, no. 1: 151–80.

Boesche, R. 1980. "The Prison: Tocqueville's Model for Despotism." *Western Political Quarterly* 33, no. 4: 550–63.

Boghani, P. 2017. "Reducing Solitary Confinement, One Cell at a Time." PBS, April 18. https://www.pbs.org/wgbh/frontline/article/reducing-solitary-confinement-one-cell-at-a-time/.

Bonilla-Silva, E. 2003. *Racism Without Racists: Color-Blind Racism and the Persistence of Racial Inequality in the United States*. Lanham, MD: Rowman & Littlefield.

Bonnet, F. 2019. *The Upper Limit: How Low-Wage Work Defines Punishment and Welfare*. Oakland: University of California Press. https://www.aspeninstitute.org/longform/expanding-economic-opportunity-for-more-americans/policies-to-reintegrate-former-inmates-into-the-labor-force/.

Bourgois, P. 2003. *In Search of Respect*. 2nd ed. New York: Cambridge University Press.

Boutellier, H. 2001. "A Letter from the Netherlands—on Safety, Criminal Law and Humanism." *Crime Prevention and Community Safety* 3: 71–79.

Bowles, S., and A. Jayadev. 2014. "One Nation Under Guard." *New York Times*, February 15. https://archive.nytimes.com/opinionator.blogs.nytimes.com/2014/02/15/one-nation-under-guard/.

Braga, A. A., and P. J. Cook. 2023. *Policing Gun Violence: Strategic Reforms for Controlling Our Most Pressing Crime Problem*. New York: Oxford University Press.

Bratton, W. 2021. *The Profession: A Memoir of Community, Race, and the Arc of Policing in America*. New York: Penguin Press.

Brearley, H. C. 1932. *Homicide in the United States*. Chapel Hill: University of North Carolina Press.

BIBLIOGRAPHY

Brenan, M. 2023. "Americans More Critical of U.S. Criminal Justice System." Gallup, November 16.

Brennan Center for Justice. 2019. "Is Charging Inmates to Stay in Prison Smart Policy?" September 9. https://www.brennancenter.org/our-work/research-reports/charging-inmates-stay-prison-smart-policy.

Brodeur, J-P., and M. Banton. 2024. "Decentralized Police Organizations." Britannica. https://www.britannica.com/topic/police/Decentralized-police-organizations.

Brookman, R., K. Wiener, W. DeSoto, and H. Tajalli. 2022. "Racial Animus and Its Association with Punitive Sentencing and Crime Types: Do Australian Community Attitudes Reflect the United States'?" *Journal of Criminology* 55, no. 1: 23–46.

Brooks, R. 2021. *Tangled Up in Blue: Policing the American City*. New York: Penguin Books.

Brown, L. 2023. "Police Admit They Were Too Scared of School Shooter's AR-15 'Battle Rifle.'" *New York Post*, March 21. https://nypost.com/2023/03/21/uvalde-cops-were-too-scared-of-shooters-battle-rifle-ar-15/.

Brown, M., and C. Lloyd. 2023. "Black Americans Less Confident, Satisfied with Local Police." Gallup, September 18. https://news.gallup.com/poll/511064/black-americans-less-confident-satisfied-local-police.aspx.

Buchanan, L., Q. Bui, and J. Patel. 2020. "Black Lives Matter May Be the Largest Movement in U.S. History." *New York Times*, July 3.

Budd, K. 2024. "Incarcerated Women and Girls." The Sentencing Project, July 24. https://www.sentencingproject.org/fact-sheet/incarcerated-women-and-girls/.

Bun, M.J.G., et al. 2020. "Crime, Deterrence, and Punishment Revisited." *Empirical Economics* 59: 2303–2333.

Burn-Murdoch, J. 2023. "Collapsing Social Trust is Driving American Gun Violence." *Financial Times*, May 12.

Butler, P. 2017. *Chokehold: Policing Black Men*. New York: The New Press.

Campbell, M. C., and H. Schoenfeld. 2013. "The Transformation of America's Penal Order: A Historicized Political Sociology of Punishment." *American Journal of Sociology* 118, no. 5: 1375–1423.

Carlson, J. 2020. *Policing the Second Amendment: Guns, Law Enforcement, and the Politics of Race*. Princeton: Princeton University Press.

Carson, A. 2023. "Prison Report Series: Preliminary Data Release." *Bureau of Justice Statistics, US Department of Justice*, September. https://bjs.ojp.gov/library/publications/prisons-report-series-preliminary-data-release.

Cary, M. 1993. *How States Can Fight Violent Crime: Two Dozen Steps to a Safer America*. The Heritage Foundation, June 7. https://www.heritage.org/crime-and-justice/report/how-states-can-fight-violent-crime-two-dozen-steps-saferamerica.

Case, A., and A. Deaton. 2020. *Deaths of Despair and the Future of Capitalism*. Princeton: Princeton University Press.

Center for Constitutional Rights. 2013. "Landmark Decision: Judge Rules NYPD Stop and Frisk Practices Unconstitutional, Racially Discriminatory." August 12. https://ccrjustice.org/home/press-center/press-releases/landmark-decision-judge-rules-nypd-stop-and-frisk-practices.

Center for Disease Control. 2022. "Homicide Mortality by State." https://www.cdc.gov/nchs/pressroom/sosmap/homicide_mortality/homicide.htm.

Center for Disease Control. 2023. "Leading Causes of Death—Males—Non-Hispanic Black—United States, 2018." https://www.cdc.gov/minorityhealth/lcod/men/2018/nonhispanic-black/#age-group.

Chan, W. 2022. "American Exceptionalism: Trust, Social Capital, and Solidarity." Undergraduate research apprenticeship thesis, supervised by Jerome Karabel, University of California, Berkeley. On file with author.

Chetty, R., D. Grusky, M. Hell, N. Hendren, R. Manduca, and J. Narang. 2017. "The Fading American Dream: Trends in Absolute Income Mobility Since 1940." *Science* 356, no. 6336: 398–406.

Chetty, R., N. Hendren, M. R., Jones, and S. R. Porter. 2020. "Race and Economic Opportunity in the United States: An Intergenerational Perspective." *Quarterly Journal of Economics* 135, no. 2: 711–83.

Clair, M. 2020. *Privilege and Punishment: How Race and Class Matter in Criminal Court*. Princeton, NJ: Princeton University Press.

Clarke, R. V. 1997. *Situational Crime Prevention: Successful Studies*. 2nd ed. New York: Harrow and Heston.

Clegg, J., and A. Usmani. 2019. "The Economic Origins of Mass Incarceration." *Catalyst* 3, no. 3: 9–53.

Clegg, J., and A. Usmani. Forthcoming. *From Plantation to Prison*.

Clegg, J., S. Spitz, A. Usmani, and A. Wolcke. 2024. "Punishment in Modern Societies: The Prevalence of Incarceration Around the World." *Annual Review of Criminology* 7: 211–31.

Coaston, J. 2023. "The Libertarian vs. Conservative Impulses in G.O.P. Policy on Crime." *New York Times*, September 25. https://www.nytimes.com/2023/09/25/opinion/conservative-criminal-justice-lehman.html.

Coates, T. 2015. "The Black Family in the Age of Mass Incarceration." *Atlantic*, October 15. https://www.theatlantic.com/magazine/archive/2015/10/the-black-family-in-the-age-of-mass-incarceration/403246/.

Coffee, J. C. 2020. *Corporate Crime and Punishment: The Crisis of Underenforcement*. Oakland: Berrett-Koehler.

Cohen, S. 2001. *States of Denial: Knowing about Atrocities and Suffering*. Malden: Polity.

Collins, D. 2023. "146 NYC Police Committed Misconduct in 2020 Protests: Report." APNews. February 6. https://apnews.com/article/politics-protests-and-demonstrations-george-floyd-new-york-city-505491e2bf8657df2448fcc99520ba6e.

Collins, R. 2009. "The Microsociology of Violence." *British Journal of Sociology* 60, no. 3: 566–76.

Collyer, S., M. Curran, I. Garfinkel, D. Harris, D., Richardson, and C. Wimer. 2022. "A Step in the Right Direction: The Expanded Child Tax Credit Would Move the United States' High Child Poverty Rate Closer to Peer Nations." *Center on Poverty and Social Policy Joint Report* 6, no. 7: 1–8. https://www.povertycenter.columbia.edu/publication/2022/child-tax-credit-and-relative-poverty.

Confederation of European Probation. 2024. "Probation in Europe." https://www.cep-probation.org/knowledgebases/probation-in-europe/.

Confronting Poverty. 2024. "Poverty Facts and Myths: America's Poor Are Worse Off Than Elsewhere." https://confrontingpoverty.org/poverty-facts-and-myths/americas-poor-are-worse-off-than-elsewhere/.

Conley, D. 1999. *Being Black, Living in the Red: Race, Wealth, and Social Policy in America.* Berkeley and Los Angeles: University of California Press.

Connaughton, A. 2020. "Social Trust in Advanced Economies Is Lower among Young People and Those with Less Education." Pew Research Center, December 3. https://www.pewresearch.org/short-reads/2020/12/03/social-trust-in-advanced-economies-is-lower-among-young-people-and-those-with-less-education/.

Cooper, A. D., and E. L. Smith. 2011. "Homicide Trends in the United States, 1980–2008." Bureau of Justice Statistics, November. https://bjs.ojp.gov/library/publications/homicide-trends-united-states-1980-2008.

Corda, A. 2016. "American Exceptionalism in Parole Supervision." Robina Institute Data Brief, May 23. https://robinainstitute.umn.edu/articles/american-exceptionalism-parole-supervision.

Corda, A., M. Rovira, and A. Henley. 2023. "Collateral Consequences of Criminal Records from the Other Side of the Pond: How Exceptional is American Penal Exceptionalism?" *Criminology and Criminal Justice* 23, no. 4: 519–27.

Cornell, S. 2006. *A Well-Regulated Militia: The Founding Fathers and the Origins of Gun Control in America.* New York: Oxford University Press.

Cotton, T. 2020. "Send in the Troops." *New York Times,* June 3. https://www.nytimes.com/2020/06/03/opinion/tom-cotton-protests-military.html.

Cowie, J. 2017. *The Great Exception: The New Deal and the Limits of American Politics.* Princeton: Princeton University Press.

Cox, O. C. 1948. *Cast, Class, and Race: A Study in Social Dynamics.* Garden City: Doubleday and Company.

Cramer, C. 2018. *Lock, Stock, and Barrel: The Origins of American Gun Culture.* Santa Barbara, CA: Praeger.

Crime Report Staff. 2020. "How 'Warrior Policing' Undermines U.S. Law Enforcement." *Crime Report,* September 8. https://thecrimereport.org/2020/09/08/how-warrior-policing-undermines-u-s-law-enforcement/.

Crutchfield, R. D. 2014. *Get a Job: Labor Markets, Economic Opportunity, and Crime.* New York: NYU Press.

Currie, E. 2020. *A Peculiar Indifference: The Neglected Toll of Violence on Black America.* New York: Metropolitan Books.

Daems, T. 2020. *Electronic Monitoring: Tagging Offenders in a Culture of Surveillance.* New York: Palgrave Macmillan.

Das, A. 2020. *No Justice in the Shadows: How America Criminalizes Immigrants.* New York, Bold Type Books.

Dauber, M. L. 2013. *The Sympathetic State: Disaster Relief and the Origins of the American Welfare State.* Chicago: University of Chicago Press.

Davis, A. Y. 2003. *Are Prisons Obsolete?* New York: Seven Stories Press.

Davis, A., M. Gibson-Light, E. Bjorklund, and T. Nunley. 2022. "Institutional Arrangements and Power Threat: Diversity, Democracy, and Punitive Attitudes." *Justice Quarterly* 39, no. 7: 1545–1564.

De Beaumont, G., and De Tocqueville, A. 1833. *On the Penitentiary System in the United States.* Repr. 1964 Carbondale: Southern Illinois University Press.

De Tocqueville, A. 1835. *Democracy in America*. Repr. 2002 Chicago: University of Chicago Press.

Death Penalty Information Center. 2023. "The Death Penalty in 2023: Year End Report." December 1. https://deathpenaltyinfo.org/facts-and-research/dpic-reports/dpic-year-end-reports/the-death-penalty-in-2023-year-end-report.

Deaton, A. 2018. "America Can No Longer Hide Its Deep Poverty Problem." *New York Times*, January 24. https://www.nytimes.com/2018/01/24/opinion/poverty-united-states.html.

Dekanoidze, K., and M. Khelashvili. 2018. *Police Education and Training Systems in the OSCE Region*. Kyiv: OSCE. https://www.osce.org/files/f/documents/f/7/423401.pdf.

Delsol, R., and M. Shiner, eds. 2015. *Stop and Search: The Anatomy of a Police Power*. New York: Palgrave Macmillan.

Demleitner, N. V. 2018. "Collateral Sanctions and American Exceptionalism: A Comparative Perspective." In *American Exceptionalism in Crime and Punishment*, ed. K. R. Reitz. New York: Oxford University Press.

Dennis, B., M. Berman, and E. Izadi. 2016. "Dallas Police Chief Says 'We're Asking Cops to Do Too Much in This Country.'" *Washington Post*, July 11. https://www.washingtonpost.com/news/post-nation/wp/2016/07/11/grief-and-anger-continue-after-dallas-attacks-and-police-shootings-as-debate-rages-over-policing/.

DeParle, J. 2021. "A Historic Decrease in Poverty." *New York Review of Books*, November 18.

De Peña, K. 2022. "The Legal Snarls Between Criminal and Immigration Law: Tackling Crimmigration in the 21st Century." Niskanen Center, February 10. https://www.niskanencenter.org/the-legal-snarls-between-criminal-immigration-law-tackling-crimmigration-in-the-21st-century/.

Desmond, M. 2016. *Evicted: Poverty and Profit in the American City*. New York: Crown.

Desmond, M. 2023. *Poverty, By America*. New York: Crown.

Desmond, M., and B. Western. 2018. "Poverty in America: New Directions and Debates." *Annual Review of Sociology* 44: 305–18.

Devers, L. 2011. "Plea and Charge Bargaining: Research Summary." Bureau of Justice Statistics, United States Department of Justice, January 24. https://bja.ojp.gov/sites/g/files/xyckuh186/files/media/document/pleabargainingresearchsummary.pdf.

De Visé, D. 2023. "Americans Bought Almost 60 Million Guns during the Pandemic." *The Hill*, April 21. https://thehill.com/policy/national-security/3960527-americans-bought-almost-60-million-guns-during-the-pandemic/.

De Vos, H. 2023. *Beyond Scandinavian Exceptionalism: Normalization, Imprisonment, and Society*. Cham, Switzerland: Palgrave Macmillan.

DeVuono-Powell, S., C. Schweidler, A. Walters, and A. Zohrabi. 2015. "Who Pays? The True Cost of Incarceration on Families." Ella Baker Center for Human Rights, Oakland, California, September. https://static.prisonpolicy.org/scans/who-pays%20Ella%20Baker%20report.pdf.

Dholakia, N. 2023. "Prisons and Jails Are Violent: They Don't Have to Be." Vera Institute of Justice, October 18. https://www.vera.org/news/prisons-and-jails-are-violent-they-dont-have-to-be.

Dienst, J., and D. Paredes. 2019. "NYPD Shootings Dramatically Decrease over Decades Data Shows." NBC New York, March 1. https://www.nbcnewyork.com/news/local/nypd-police-involved-shootings-decrease-dramatically-nyc/19351/.

Di Giorgi, A. 2006. *Rethinking the Political Economy of Punishment: Perspectives on Post-Fordism and Penal Politics*. Ashgate: Routledge.

Dieter, R. 1996. *Killing for Votes: The Dangers of Politicizing the Death Penalty Process*. Washington, DC: DPIC.

DiIulio, J. J. 1994. "Let 'em Rot." *Wall Street Journal*.

DiIulio, J. J. 1995. "The Coming of the Super-Predators." *Weekly Standard*, November 22, 1995.

DiIulio, J. J. 1996a. "The Cycle of Poverty Produces "Super-Predators.'" *Star Ledger*, June 23.

DiIulio, J. J. 1996b. "My Black Crime Problem, and Ours." *City Journal* 6, no. 2: 14–28.

Dirks, S. 2023. "These California Police Officers Have Created a Scandal. They Sent Racist Texts." NPR, April 27. https://www.npr.org/2023/04/27/1171369375/california-police-scandal-racist-texts.

Dodd, V. 2023. "Met Wins Battled with NHS Over Not Attending Mental Health Calls." *Guardian*, August 17. https://www.theguardian.com/uk-news/2023/aug/17/met-police-mental-health-calls-nhs-mark-rowley.

Dolovich, S. 2022. "The Failed Regulation and Oversight of American Prisons." *Annual Review of Criminology* 5: 153–77.

Doob, A., and C. Webster. 2018. "Penal Optimism: Understanding Mass Incarceration from a Canadian Perspective." In *American Exceptionalism in Crime and Punishment*, ed. K. Reitz. New York: Oxford University Press.

Downes, D., and K. Hansen. 2006. "Welfare and Punishment in Comparative Perspective." In *Perspectives on Punishment*, ed. S. Armstrong and L. McAra. Oxford: Oxford University Press.

Drakulich, K., E. Rodriguez-Whitney, and J. Robles. 2023. "Why White Americans More Frequently Fail to View the Police Critically." *Du Bois Review* 20, no. 1: 57–88.

Dunbar-Ortiz, R. 2018. *Loaded: A Disarming History of the Second Amendment*. San Francisco: City Lights Books.

Dünkel, F. 2019. *Prisoner Resettlement in Europe*. London: Routledge, Taylor, & Francis..

Durkheim, E. 1973. "Two Laws of Penal Evolution." *Economy and Society* 2, no. 3: 285–308.

Durkheim, E. 1982. *The Rules of Sociological Method*. Basingstoke, UK: Palgrave Macmillan.

Edsall, T. B., and M. Edsall. 1991. *Chain Reaction: The Impact of Race, Rights, and Taxes on American Politics*. New York: Norton.

Eisenberg, A. K. 2023. "Policing the Danger Narrative." *Journal of Criminal Law and Criminology* 113, no. 3: 473–540.

Elias, N. 2000. *The Civilizing Process: Sociogenetic and Psychogenetic Investigations*. Rev. ed. London: Blackwell.

Ellen, I. G. 2001. *Sharing America's Neighborhoods: The Prospects for Stable Racial Integration*. Cambridge: Harvard University Press.

Ellis, M. J. 2012. "The Origins of the Elected Prosecutor." *Yale Law Journal* 121, no. 6: 1528–1569.

Ely, D., and A. Driscoll. 2022. *Infant Mortality in the United States 2020*. National Vital Statistics Report, US Department of Health and Human Services, vol. 71, no. 5, September 29.

Engel, J. 2015. *The Four Freedoms: FDR and the Evolution of an American Idea*. New York: Oxford University Press.

Enns, P. K. 2016. *Incarceration Nation: How the United States Became the Most Punitive Democracy in the World*. New York: Cambridge University Press.

Enns, P. K., Y. Yi, M. Comfort, A. Goldman, H. Lee, C. Muller, S. Wakefield, E. Wang, and C. Wildeman. 2019. "What Percentage of Americans have ever had a Family Member Incarcerated?" *Socius: Sociological Research for a Dynamic World* 5: 1–45.

Enos, R. D. 2017. *The Space between Us: Social Geography and Politics*. New York: Cambridge University Press.

Enos, R. D., and C. Celaya. 2018. "The Effect of Segregation on Intergroup Relations." *Journal of Experimental Political Science* 5, no. 1: 26–38. https://scholar.harvard.edu/files/renos/files/enoscelaya.pdf.

Epp, C. R., S. Maynard-Moody, and D. Haider-Markel. 2014. *Pulled Over: How Police Stops Define Race and Citizenship*. Chicago and London: University of Chicago Press.

Eren, C. P. 2023. *Reform Nation: The First Step Act and the Movement to End Mass Incarceration*. Stanford: Stanford University Press.

Esping-Andersen, G. 1985. *Politics against Markets: The Social Democratic Road to Power*. Princeton, NJ: Princeton University Press.

Esping-Andersen, G. 1990. *The Three Worlds of Welfare Capitalism*. Cambridge: Polity Press.

European Commission. 2020. *Firearms in the European Union*. Directorate-General for Communication. Flash Eurobarometer 383. https://home-affairs.ec.europa.eu/system/files/2020-09/fl383_firearms_report_en.pdf.

Ewald, A. "Collateral Sanctions." 2017. *Oxford Research Encyclopedia of Criminology*, December 16. https://doi.org/10.1093/acrefore/9780190264079.013.224.

Ewing, J. 2020. "United States Is the Richest Country in the World, and It Has the Biggest Wealth Gap." *New York Times*, September 23. https://www.nytimes.com/2020/09/23/business/united-states-is-the-richest-country-in-the-world-and-it-has-the-biggest-wealth-gap.html.

Fajnzylber, P., D. Lederman, and N. Loayza. 2002. "Inequality and Violent Crime." *Journal of Law and Economics* 45, no. 1: 1–39.

Farrall, S., and E. Gray. 2024. *The Politics of Crime, Punishment, and Justice: Exploring the Lived Reality and Enduring Legacies of the 1980's Radical Right*. New York: Routledge.

Farrington, D. 2020. "Human Development and Criminal Careers." In *Crime, Inequality, and the State*, ed. M. Vogel. London: Routledge.

Fassin, D. 2016. *Prison Worlds: An Ethnography of the Carceral Condition*. New York: Wiley.

Federal Bureau of Investigation. 2020. "Arrests by Race and Ethnicity, 2019." *Crime in the United States, 2019*, Uniform Crime Reports, table 43. https://ucr.fbi.gov/crime-in-the-u.s/2019/crime-in-the-u.s.-2019/tables/table-43.

Federal Bureau of Prisons. n.d. "About Our Facilities." https://www.bop.gov/about/facilities/federal_prisons.jsp.

Feeley, M., and J. Simon. 1992. "The New Penology: Notes on the Emerging Strategy of Corrections." *Criminology* 30, no. 4: 449–47.

Felker-Kantor, M. 2018. *Policing Los Angeles: Race, Resistance, and the Rise of the LAPD*. Chapel Hill: University of North Carolina Press.

Ferguson, R. A. 2018. *Inferno: An Anatomy of American Punishment*. Cambridge: Harvard University Press.

Fernandes, A. D., and R. Crutchfield. 2018. "Race, Crime, and Criminal Justice: Fifty Years Since The Challenge of Crime in a Free Society." *Criminology and Public Policy* 17, no 2: 397–417.

Ferreira, E., S. Gomes, and N. Perez. 2018. "Police Recruitment and Training in Democratic Societies: A Socio-Legal Comparative Perspective." In *Comparative Policing from a Legal Perspective*, ed. Monica Van Den Boer. Cheltenham, UK: Edward Elgar.

Fishback, P. V., R. S. Johnson, and S. Kantor. 2010. "Striking at the Roots of Crime: The Impact of Welfare Spending on Crime during the Great Depression." *Journal of Law and Economics* 53, no. 4: 715–40.

Fisher, M. 2022. "Other Countries Had Mass Shootings. Then They Changed Their Gun Laws." *New York Times*, May 25. https://www.nytimes.com/2022/05/25/world/europe/gun-laws-australia-britain.htm.

Flamm, M. W. 2005. *Law and Order: Street Crime, Civil Unrest, and the Crisis of Liberalism in the 1960s*. New York: Columbia University Press.

Fogel, B. 2021. "Lower the Crime Rate." *Jacobin*, November 11. https://jacobin.com/2021/11/lower-the-crime-rate.

Foner, E. 2023. "The Little Man's Big Friends." *London Review of Books* 45, no. 11.

Fong, E. 1996. "A Comparative Perspective on Racial Residential Segregation: American and Canadian Experiences." *Sociological Quarterly* 37, no. 2: 199–226.

Font, S., and R. Kennedy. 2022. "The Centrality of Child Maltreatment to Criminology." *Annual Review of Criminology* 5: 371–96.

Forman, J. 2016. "Fortress America: How 20th-Century Liberals Helped Create Our Age of Mass Incarceration." *Nation*, September 27. https://www.thenation.com/article/archive/fortress-america/.

Forman, J. 2017. *Locking Up Our Own: Crime and Punishment in Black America*. New York: Farrar, Straus and Giroux.

Förster, M. F., and K. Vleminckx. 2004. "International Comparisons of Income Inequality and Poverty: Findings from the Luxembourg Income Study." *Socio-Economic Review* 2: 191–212.

Fortner, M. J. 2015. *Black Silent Majority: The Rockefeller Drug Laws and the Politics of Punishment*. Cambridge: Harvard University Press.

Fortune Society. n.d. "Words Matter: Using Humanizing Language." https://fortunesociety.org/wordsmatter/.

Foucault, M. 1977. *Discipline and Punish: The Birth of the Prison*. Translated by Alan Sheridan. London: Allen Lane.

Frank, J. 2024. "The US Is the Top Country for Millionaires and Billionaires." CNBC, March 22. https://www.cnbc.com/2024/03/22/the-us-is-the-top-country-for-millionaires-and-billionaires.html.

Fraser, S., and G. Gerstle, eds. 1989. *The Rise and Fall of the New Deal Order, 1930–1980*. Princeton: Princeton University Press.

Fridhov, I. n.d. "Norwegian Reintegration Guarantee Aims to Provide Ex-Prisoners the Right Tools for Resocialization." Confederation of European Probation. https://www.cep-probation.org/norwegian-reintegration-guarantee-aims-to-provide-ex-prisoners-the-right-tools-for-resocialization/.

Fryer, R. G. 2019. "An Empirical Analysis of Racial Differences in Police Use of Force." *Journal of Political Economy* 127, no. 3: 973–1473.

Gabriele, R. 2024. "Sex Offender Registry Statistics: 2024 Data for All 50 States." Safehome, September 17. https://www.safehome.org/data/registered-sex-offender-stats/.

Garfinkel, I., L. Rainwater, and T. Smeeding. 2010. *Wealth and Welfare States: Is America a Laggard or Leader?* New York: Oxford University Press.

Garland, D. 1990. *Punishment and Modern Society: A Study in Social Theory.* Chicago: University of Chicago Press.

Garland, D. 1995. "*The Problem of Order: What Unites and Divides Society?* by Dennis Wrong." Book review. *British Journal of Criminology* 35, no. 4: 639–41.

Garland, D. 2001a. *The Culture of Control: Crime and Social Order in Contemporary Society.* Chicago: University of Chicago Press.

Garland, D., ed. 2001b. *Mass Imprisonment: Social Causes and Consequences.* Thousand Oaks, CA: Sage.

Garland, D. 2005a. "Capital Punishment and American Culture." *Punishment and Society* 7, no. 4: 347–76.

Garland, D. 2005b. "Penal Excess and Surplus Meaning: Public Torture Lynchings in 20th Century America." *Law and Society Review* 39, no. 4: 793–834.

Garland, D. 2010. *Peculiar Institution: America's Death Penalty in an Age of Abolition.* Cambridge: Harvard University Press.

Garland, D. 2013. "Penality and the Penal State: The 2012 Sutherland Address." *Criminology* 51, no. 3: 475–517.

Garland, D. 2016. *The Welfare State: A Very Short Introduction.* New York: Oxford University Press.

Garland, D. 2017. "Penal Power in America: Forms, Functions, and Foundations." *Journal of British Academy* 5: 1–35.

Garland, D. 2018a. "The Concept of American Exceptionalism." In *American Exceptionalism in Crime and Punishment*, ed. K. Reitz. New York: Oxford University Press.

Garland, D. 2018b. *Punishment and Welfare: A History of Penal Strategies.* Reprint edition. New Orleans: Quid Pro Books.

Garland, D. 2020. "Penal Controls and Social Controls: Toward a Theory of American Penal Exceptionalism." *Punishment and Society* 22, no. 3: 321–52.

Garland, D. 2023. "The Punishment-Welfare Relationship: History, Sociology, and Politics." In *The Oxford Handbook of Criminology, 7th Edition*, ed. A. Liebling, S. Maruna, and L. McAra. New York: Oxford University Press.

Garrett, B. L. 2014. *Too Big to Jail: How Prosecutors Compromise with Corporations.* Cambridge: Harvard University Press.

Garrett, B. L. 2021. "How Biden Should Prosecute Corporate Crime: In Top-to-Bottom Criminal Justice Reform, Let's Not Forget the Top." *The American Prospect*, January 29. https://prospect.org/culture/books/how-biden-should-prosecute-corporate-crime/.

Gaskins, K. 2024. "Rough Election for Progressive Prosecutors as Voters Oust Soft-on-crime DA's." ABC News (Channel 4), Charleston, South Carolina, November 7. https://abcnews4.com/news/beyond-the-podium/rough-election-for-progressive-policies-as-voters-oust-soft-on-crime-da-district-attorney-los-angeles-county-california-san-francisco-colorado-donald-trump-politics.

Gebeloff, R., R. Lai, E. Murray, J. William, and R. Lieberman. 2024. "How the Pandemic Reshaped Gun Violence." *New York Times*, May 24.

Gerstle, G. 2022. *The Rise and Fall of the Neoliberal Order: America and the World in the Free Market Era.* New York: Oxford University Press.

Ghandnoosh, N., L. Trinka, and C. Barry. 2024. "One in Five: How Mass Incarceration Deepens Inequality and Harms Public Safety." The Sentencing Project, January 16. https://www.sentencingproject.org/publications/one-in-five-how-mass-incarceration-deepens-inequality-and-harms-public-safety/.

Ghilarducci, T. 2023. "New Study: U.S. Tops Rich Nations as Worst Place to Work." *Forbes*, June 14. https://www.forbes.com/sites/teresaghilarducci/2023/06/14/new-study-us-tops-rich-nations-in-worst-place-to-work/?sh=168968653be6.

Gilens, M. 1999. *Why Americans Hate Welfare: Race: Media, and the Politics of Antipoverty Policy.* Chicago: University of Chicago Press.

Gilling, D. 2001. "Community Safety and Social Policy." *European Journal on Criminal Policy and Research* 9: 381–400.

Gilmore, R. W. 2024. Remarks at "Dismantling Racial Capitalism" seminar. NYU School of Law, September 5.

Glazer, E., and P. Sharkey. 2021. *Social Fabric: A New Model for Public Safety and Vital Neighborhoods.* The Square One Project. https://squareonejustice.org/wp-content/uploads/2021/03/Social-Fabric-A-New-Model-for-Public-Safety-and-Vital-Neighborhoods_Liz-Glazer-and-Pat-Sharkey_WEB_FINAL.pdf.

Go, J. 2023. *Policing Empires: Militarization, Race, and the Imperial Boomerang in the US and Britain.* New York: Oxford University Press.

Godin, M. 2020. "What the U.S. Can Learn from Countries Where Cops Don't Carry Guns." *Time*, June 19. https://time.com/5854986/police-reform-defund-unarmed-guns/.

Goffman, A. 2014. *On the Run: Fugitive Life in an American City.* Chicago: Chicago University Press.

Goldstein, R. 2025. "Toplash: Progressive Prosecutors Under Attack from Above." *American Criminal Law Review* 61.

Gonnerman, J. 2014. "Before the Law." *The New Yorker*, September 29. https://www.newyorker.com/magazine/2014/10/06/before-the-law.

Goodwin, J., and J. Jasper. 2014. *Social Movements: Concepts and Cases.* New York: Wiley Blackwell.

Gopnik, A. 2024. "Should We Abolish Prisons?" *The New Yorker*, July 22.

Gottschalk, M. 2006. *The Prison and the Gallows: The Politics of Mass Incarceration in America.* New York: Cambridge University Press.

Gottschalk, M. 2014. *Caught: The Prison State and the Lockdown of American Politics.* Princeton: Princeton University Press.

Gottschalk, M. 2015. "Raze the Carceral State." *Dissent*, Fall. https://www.dissentmagazine.org/article/criminal-justice-reform-minimum-sentencing-mass-incarceration/.

Government of Canada. 2022. "Overrepresentation of Black People in Canadian Criminal Justice System." Research and Statistics Division, December. https://www.justice.gc.ca/eng/rp-pr/jr/obpccjs-spnsjpc/pdf/RSD_JF2022_Black_Overrepresentation_in_CJS_EN.pdf.

Graham v. Connor. 490 US 386 1989.

Gramlich, J. 2019. "The Gap between the Number of Blacks and Whites in Prison Is Shrinking." Pew Research Center, April 30, https://www.pewresearch.org/short-reads/2019/04/30/shrinking-gap-between-number-of-blacks-and-whites-in-prison/.

Grinshteyn, E., and D. Hemenway. 2019. "Violent Death Rates in the US Compared to Those of the Other High-Income Countries, 2015." *Preventative Medicine* 123: 20–26.

Guetzkow, J. 2020. "Common Cause? Policymaking Discourse and the Prison/Welfare Trade-Off." *Politics and Society* 48, no. 3: 321–56.

Gunja, M. Z., E. D. Gumas, and R. D. Williams. 2022. "The U.S. Maternal Mortality Crisis Continues to Worsen: An International Comparison." *Commonwealth Fund*, December 1. https://www.commonwealthfund.org/blog/2022/us-maternal-mortality-crisis-continues-worsen-international-comparison.

Gustavson, S. 1995. "Single Parents in Sweden: Why is Poverty Less Severe?" In *Poverty, Inequality, and the Future of Social Policy*, ed. K. McFate et al. New York: Russell Sage Foundation.

Guttmacher Institute. 2015. "Teen Pregnancy Rates Declined in Many Countries Between the Mid-1990s and 2011." January 23. https://www.guttmacher.org/news-release/2015/teen-pregnancy-rates-declined-many-countries-between-mid-1990s-and-2011.

Haag, P. 2016. *The Gunning of America: Business and the Making of American Gun Culture*. New York: Basic Books.

Hacker, J. S. 2006. *The Great Risk Shift: The Assault on American Jobs, Families, Health Care, and Retirement and How You Can Fight Back*. New York: Oxford University Press.

Hacker, J. S., A. Hertel-Fernandez, P. Pierson, and K. Thelen. 2022. *The American Political Economy: Politics, Markets, and Power*. New York: Cambridge University Press.

Hagan, J. 2010. *Who Are the Criminals? The Politics of Crime Policy from the Age of Roosevelt to the Age of Reagan*. Princeton: Princeton University Press.

Hahn, S. 2024. *Illiberal America: A History*. New York: Norton.

Haider, A. 2021. "The Basic Facts About Children in Poverty." *American Progress*, January 12. https://www.americanprogress.org/article/basic-facts-children-poverty/.

Hall, A., and J. Yoder. 2022. "Does Home Ownership Influence Political Behavior?" *Journal of Politics* 84, no. 1. https://www.andrewbenjaminhall.com/homeowner.pdf.

Hall, P. 2017. "The Political Sources of Social Solidarity." In *The Strains of Commitment*, ed. K. Banting and W. Kymlicka. Oxford: Oxford University Press.

Hall, P., and D. Soskice, eds. 2001. *Varieties of Capitalism: The Institutional Foundations of Comparative Advantage*. New York: Oxford University Press.

Haney-Lopez, I. 2011. "Freedom, Mass Incarceration, and Racism in the Age of Obama." *Alabama Law Review* 62, no. 5.

Harcourt, B. 2011. *The Illusion of Free Markets*. Cambridge: Harvard University Press.

Harris, A. 2016. *A Pound of Flesh: Monetary Sanctions as Punishment for the Poor*. New York: Russell Sage Foundation.

Henderson, K. 2023. "Where Hard Work Doesn't Pay Off: An Index of US Labor Policies Compared to Peer Nations." Oxfam, May 3. https://www.oxfamamerica.org/explore/research-publications/where-hard-work-doesnt-pay-off/.

Hinton, E. 2016. *From the War on Poverty to the War on Crime*. Cambridge: Harvard University Press.

Hinton, E. 2021. *America on Fire: The Untold History of Police Violence and Black Rebellion since the 1960s*. New York: Liveright.

Hirschfield, P. J. 2015. "Lethal Policing: Making Sense of American Exceptionalism." *Sociological Forum* 30, no. 4: 1109–1117.

Hirschfield, P. J. 2023. "Exceptionally Lethal: American Police Killings in a Comparative Perspective." *Annual Review of Criminology* 6: 471–98.

Hirst, P. 1994. *Associative Democracy: New Forms of Economic and Social Governance.* Amherst: University of Massachusetts Press.

Hitt, J. 2015. "Police Shootings Won't Stop Unless We Also Stop Shaking Down Black People: The Dangers of Turning Police Officers into Revenue Generators." *Mother Jones*, September/October. https://www.motherjones.com/politics/2015/07/police-shootings-traffic-stops-excessive-fines/.

Hobbes, T. 1651. *Leviathan.* Repr. New York: Penguin Classics, 2017.

Hochschild, A. 2022. *American Midnight: The Great War, A Violent Peace, and Democracy's Forgotten Crisis.* New York: Mariner Books.

Holmes, S. 2025. *Flesh of our Flesh: Imperial Ambition and Republican Ideology in the American Constitution.* New York: Knopf.

Horton, T., and J. Gregory. 2009. *The Solidarity Society: Why We Can Afford to End Poverty, and How to Do It with Public Support.* London: Fabian Society.

Hout, M., and C. Maggio. 2021. "Immigration, Race, and Political Polarization." *Daedalus* 150 (Spring).

Hövermann, A., and S. F. Messner. 2019. "Institutional Anomie Theory across Nation States." In *Oxford Research Encyclopedia of Criminology and Criminal Justice*, ed. H. Pontell. New York and Oxford: Oxford University Press.

Howard, M. 2017. *Unusually Cruel: Prisons, Punishment, and the Real American Exceptionalism.* New York: Oxford University Press.

Hummelsheim, D., H. Hirtenlehner, J. Jackson, and D. Oberwittler. 2011. "Insecurities and Fear of Crime: A Cross-National Study on the Impact of Welfare State Policies on Crime-Related Anxieties." *European Sociological Review* 27, no. 3: 327–45.

Hutchinson, B., 2020. "Breonna Taylor Case Sparks Renewed Scrutiny of Grand Juries in Police Misconduct Cases." ABC News, October 9. https://abcnews.go.com/US/breonna-taylor-case-sparks-renewed-scrutiny-grand-juries/story?id=73438566.

Hyland, S. S., and E. Davis. 2019. "Local Police Departments, 2016: Personnel." Bureau of Justice Statistics, United States Department of Justice, October.

International Centre for Prison Studies. 2024. *World Prison Brief.* https://www.prisonstudies.org/.

IPSOS. 2021. "Americans' Trust in Law Enforcement, Desire to Protect Law and Order on the Rise." March 5. https://www.ipsos.com/en-us/americans-trust-law-enforcement-desire-protect-law-and-order-rise.

Jacobs, J. B. 2015. *The Eternal Criminal Record.* Cambridge: Harvard University Press.

Jacobs, J. B., and Z. Zuhr. 2019. *The Toughest Gun Control Law in the Nation: The Unfulfilled Promise of New York's SAFE Act.* New York: New York University Press.

Janson, C.-G. 2004. "Youth Justice in Sweden." *Crime and Justice* 31: 391–441.

Jardina, A., and T. Ollerenshaw. 2022. "The Polarization of White Racial Attitudes and Support for Racial Equality in the U.S." *Public Opinion Quarterly* 86: 576–87.

Jayadev, A., and S. Bowles. 2006. "Guard Labor." *Journal of Developmental Economics* 79, no. 2: 328–48.

Jencks, C. 2015. "The War on Poverty." *New York Review of Books*, April 2.

Jericho, G. 2020. "No, Australia Is Not the US. Our Shocking Racial Injustice Is All Our Own." *The Guardian*, June 6. https://www.theguardian.com/business/grogonomics/2020/jun/07/no-australia-is-not-the-us-our-shocking-racial-injustice-is-all-our-own.

Johns Hopkins Bloomberg School of Public Health. 2013. "93% of Homicides of U.S. Law Enforcement Officers Result from Firearms." May 30. https://publichealth.jhu.edu/2013/pollack-swedler-police-homicides.

Johnson, D., ed. 2020. "Connections among Poverty, Incarceration, and Inequality." Institute for Research on Poverty, May. https://www.irp.wisc.edu/resource/connections-among-poverty-incarceration-and-inequality/.

Johnson, S. 2024. "Ten States with the Highest Incarceration Rates." *US News & World Report*, June 10. https://www.usnews.com/news/best-states/slideshows/10-states-with-the-highest-incarceration-rates.

Johnston, R., M. Poulsen, and J. Forrest. 2007. "The Geography of Ethnic Residential Segregation: A Comparative Study of Five Countries." *Annals of the Association of American Geographers* 97, no. 4: 713–38.

Johnston, R., M. Wright, S. Soroka, and J. Citrin. 2017. "Diversity and Solidarity: New Evidence from Canada and the US." In *The Strains of Commitment*, ed. K. Banting and W. Kymlicka. Oxford: Oxford University Press.

Jones, T., T. Newburn, and R. Reiner. 2023. "Policing and the Police." In *The Oxford Handbook of Criminology*, ed. A. Liebling, S. Maruna, and L. McAra. New York: Oxford University Press.

Junger-Tas, J. 2004. "Youth Justice in the Netherlands." *Crime and Justice* 31: 293–347.

Justice Policy Institute. 2011. "Finding Direction: Expanding Criminal Justice Options by Considering Policies of Other Nations." April. https://justicepolicy.org/wp-content/uploads/2022/02/finding_direction-full_report.pdf.

Kaba, M. 2020. "Yes, We Mean Literally Abolish the Police." *New York Times*, June 12. https://www.nytimes.com/2020/06/12/opinion/sunday/floyd-abolish-defund-police.html.

Kaba, M., and A. J. Ritchie. 2022. *No More Police: A Case for Abolition*. New York: The New Press.

Kaeble, D., L. Glaze, A. Tsoutis, and T. Minton. 2015. "Correctional Populations in the United States, 2014." Bureau of Justice Statistics, United States Department of Justice, December. https://bjs.ojp.gov/content/pub/pdf/cpus14.pdf.

Kagan, R. 2019. *Adversarial Legalism: The American Way of Law*. 2nd ed. Cambridge: Harvard University Press.

Kahan, D. 1996. "What Do Alternative Sanctions Mean?'" *University of Chicago Law Review* 632: 591–653.

Karabel, J. 2017. "Police Killings Surpass the Worst Years of Lynching, Capital Punishment, and a Movement Responds." *Huffington Post*, December 6. https://www.huffpost.com/entry/police-killings-lynchings-capital-punishment_b_8462778.

Karabel, J. 2021. "Let's Honor the True Spirit of Labor Day." *New York Times*, September 5. https://www.nytimes.com/2021/09/05/opinion/labor-day-us-history.html.

Karabel, J. Forthcoming. *Outlier Nation: The Epochal History of How the United States Became a Country Like No Other*.

Karabel, J., and D. Laurison. 2011. "Outlier Nation? American Exceptionalism and the Quality of Life in the United States." Working paper, Institute for Research on Labor and Employment, University of California at Berkeley.

Katz, J. 1988. *Seductions of Crime: Moral and Sensual Attractions in Doing Evil*. New York: Basic Books.

Katz, M., and K. Yi. 2020. "NJ Gave 2,200 Prisoners Freedom, But Not What They Needed to Restart Their Lives." *Gothamist*, November 14. https://gothamist.com/news/nj-gave-2200-prisoners-freedom-not-what-they-needed-restart-their-lives.

Katz, M. B. 1995. *Improving Poor People: The Welfare State and the Underclass*. Princeton: Princeton University Press.

Katz, M. B., M. J. Stern, and J. J. Fader. 2005. "The New African American Inequality." *Journal of American History* 92, no. 1: 75–108.

Katzenstein, M., and M. Waller. 2015. "Taxing the Poor." *Perspectives on Politics* 13, no. 3: 638–56.

Katznelson, I. 2002. "Flexible Capacity: The Military and Early American Statebuilding." In *American Political Development*, ed. I. Katznelson and M. Shefter. Princeton: Princeton University Press.

Katznelson, I. 2005. *When Affirmative Action Was White*. New York: Norton.

Katznelson, I. 2013. *Fear Itself: The New Deal and the Origins of Our Time*. New York: Liveright.

Kaufman, J. 2001. "Americans and Their Guns: Civilian Military Organizations and the Destabilization of American National Security." *Studies in American Political Development* 15: 88–102.

Kaufman, N., J. Kaiser, and C. Rumpf. 2018. "Beyond Punishment: The Penal State's Interventionist, Covert, and Negligent Modalities of Control." *Law and Social Inquiry* 43, no. 2: 468–95.

Kazemian, J. 2022. "Long Sentences: An International Perspective." Council on Criminal Justice, December. https://counciloncj.foleon.com/tfls/long-sentences-by-the-numbers/an-international-perspective.

Kearney, M. S. 2023. *The Two-Parent Privilege: How the Decline in Marriage Has Increased Inequality and Lowered Social Mobility, and What We Can Do About It*. Chicago: University of Chicago Press.

Keller, B. 2022a. "Reform or Abolish?" *New York Review of Books* 69, no. 17: 12–16.

Keller, B. 2022b. *What's Prison For? Punishment and Rehabilitation in the Age of Mass Incarceration*. New York: Columbia Global Reports.

Kennedy, D. 2012. *Don't Shoot: One Man, A Street Fellowship, and the End of Violence in Inner City America*. New York: Bloomsbury USA.

Kennedy, R. 2021a. *Say It Loud! On Race, Law, and Culture*. New York: Pantheon Books.

Kennedy, R. 2021b. "Why We Need Good Police." *Dissent Magazine* Summer. https://www.dissentmagazine.org/article/why-we-need-good-police/.

Kenworthy, L. 2014. *Social Democratic America*. New York: Oxford University Press.

Kenworthy, L. 2020. *Social Democratic Capitalism*. New York: Oxford University Press.

King, D. 1999. *In the Name of Liberalism: Illiberal Social Policy in the USA and Britain*. New York: Oxford University Press.

King, D., and R. C. Lieberman. 2009. "Review: Ironies of State Building: A Comparative Perspective on the American State." *World Politics* 61, no. 3: 547–88.

Kirk, G., A. Fernandes, and B. Friedman. 2020. "Who Pays for the Welfare State? Austerity Politics and the Origin of Pay-to-Stay Fees as Revenue Generation." *Sociological Perspectives* 63, no. 6: 921–38.

Kirkpatrick, D. D. 2021. "Split-Second Decisions: How a Supreme Court Case Shaped Modern Policing." *New York Times*, April 25. https://www.nytimes.com/2021/04/25/us/police-use-of-force.html.

Kleiman, M.A.R. 2009. *When Brute Force Fails: How to Have Less Crime and Less Punishment*. Princeton: Princeton University Press.

Kleiman, M.A.R. 2013. "Smart on Crime." *Democracy*, no. 28 (Spring). https://democracyjournal.org/magazine/28/smart-on-crime/.

Klinenberg, E. 2002. *Heatwave: A Social Autopsy of Disaster in Chicago*. Chicago: University of Chicago Press.

Klinenberg, E. 2012. *Going Solo: The Extraordinary Rise and Surprising Appeal of Living Alone*. New York: Penguin Books.

Klinenberg, E. 2024. *2020: One City, Seven People, and Year When Everything Changed*. New York: Knopf.

Kluch, S. 2018. "Low-Income Non-Whites in US Feel as Safe as Nicaraguans." Gallup, July 12. https://news.gallup.com/opinion/gallup/236969/low-income-nonwhites-feel-safe-nicaraguans.aspx.

Kohler-Hausmann, I. 2018. *Misdemeanorland: Criminal Courts and Social Control in an Age of Broken Windows Policing*. Princeton and Oxford: Princeton University Press.

Kolakowski, L. 1969. "The Concept of the Left." In *The New Left Reader*, ed. C. Oglesby. New York: Grove Press. https://platypus1917.org/wp-content/uploads/readings/kolakowski leszek_conceptleft1968.pdf.

Kolin, A. 2016. *Political Economy of Labor Repression in the United States*. Lanham, MD: Lexington Books.

Kommenda, N., and A. Kirk. 2020. "Why Are Some US Police Forces Equipped Like Military Units?" *Guardian*, June 20. https://www.theguardian.com/world/2020/jun/05/why-are-some-us-police-forces-equipped-like-military-units.

Koop, A. 2021. "Mapped: The 25 Richest Countries in the World." *Visual Capitalist*, April 22. https://www.visualcapitalist.com/mapped-the-25-richest-countries-in-the-world/.

Korpi, W. 2018. *The Democratic Class Struggle*. London: Routledge.

Kristof, N. 2017. "How to Win the War on Drugs." *New York Times*, September 22. https://www.nytimes.com/2017/09/22/opinion/sunday/portugal-drug-decriminalization.html.

Kristof, N. 2023. "The One Privilege Liberals Ignore." *New York Times*, September 13. https://www.nytimes.com/2023/09/13/opinion/single-parent-poverty.html.

Krivo, L. J., and R. D. Peterson. 1996. "Extremely Disadvantaged Neighborhoods and Urban Crime." *Social Forces* 75, no. 2: 619–48.

Kruse, K. M., and J. E. Zelizer, eds. 2022. *Myth America: Historians Take on the Biggest Legends and Lies About Our Past*. New York: Basic Books.

Krüsselmann, K., P. Aarten, and M. Liem. 2021. "Firearms and Violence in Europe—A Systematic Review." *PLOS ONE* 16, no. 4. https://doi.org/10.1371/journal.pone.0248955.

Kymlicka, W. 2015. "Solidarity in Diverse Societies: Beyond Neoliberal Multiculturalism and Welfare Chauvinism." *Comparative Migration Studies* 3:17.

Kyvsgaard, B. 2004. "Youth Justice in Denmark." *Crime and Justice* 31: 349–90.

Lacey, N. 2008. *The Prisoner's Dilemma: The Political Economy of Punishment in Comparative Perspective*. Cambridge: Cambridge University Press.

Lacey, N., and D. Soskice. 2015. "Crime, Punishment, and Segregation in the United States: The Paradox of Local Democracy." *Punishment and Society* 17, no. 4: 454–81.

Lacey, N., D. Soskice, L. Cheliotis, and X. Sappho, eds. 2021. *Tracing the Relationship between Inequality, Crime, and Punishment: Space, Time, and Politics.* Oxford: Oxford University Press.

Lacey, N., D. Soskice, and D. Hope. 2018. "Understanding the Determinants of Penal Policy: Crime, Culture, and Comparative Political Economy." *Annual Review of Criminology* 1: 195–217.

Landis, M. 1999. "Fate, Responsibility, and 'Natural' Disaster Relief: Narrating the American Welfare State." *Law and Society Review* 33, no. 2: 257–318.

Lansford, T. 2015. "The Early History of Guns: From Colonial Times to the Civil War." In *Guns and Contemporary Society: The Past, Present, and Future of Firearms and Firearm Policy,* ed. G. H. Utter. Santa Barbara, CA; Praeger.

Lappi-Seppala, T. 2008. "Trust, Welfare, and Political Culture: Explaining Differences in National Penal Policies." *Crime and Justice* 8, no. 4: 313–87.

Lappi-Seppala, T. 2011. "Explaining Imprisonment in Europe." *European Journal of Criminology* 8, no. 4: 303–28.

Lappi-Seppala, T. 2018. "American Exceptionalism in Comparative Perspective: Explaining Trends and Variation in the Use of Incarceration." In *American Exceptionalism in Crime and Punishment,* ed. K. R. Reitz. New York: Oxford University Press.

Lara-Millán, A. 2021. *Redistributing the Poor: Jails, Hospitals, and the Crisis of Law and Fiscal Austerity.* New York: Oxford University Press.

Laskin, J. 2011. "Camden on the Brink: The Poverty-Ridden New Jersey City Faces Police Cuts Amid Increasing Crime." *City Journal*, February 9. https://www.city-journal.org/article/camden-on-the-brink.

Latzer, B. 2016. *The Rise and Fall of Violent Crime in America.* New York: Encounter Books.

Lehne, R. 2013. *Government and Business: American Political Economy in Comparative Perspective.* Los Angeles: Sage.

Leicht, A. 2024. "Here's How Much Credit Card Debt the Average American Has—And How to Pay It Off." CBS News, April 26. https://www.cbsnews.com/news/heres-how-much-credit-card-debt-the-average-american-has-and-how-to-pay-it-off/.

Leovy, J. 2015. *Ghettoside: A True Story of Murder in America.* New York: One World.

Lerman, A. E., and V. M. Weaver. 2014. *Arresting Citizenship: The Democratic Consequences of American Crime Control.* Chicago: University of Chicago Press.

Levitsky, S., and D. Ziblatt. 2018. *How Democracies Die.* New York: Crown.

Levitt, S. D., and T. J. Miles. 2007. "Empirical Study of Criminal Punishment." *Handbook of Law and Economics* 1: 455–95.

Lewis, C., and A. Usmani. 2022. "The Injustice of Under-Policing in America." *American Journal of Law and Equality* 2: 85–106.

Lichtenstein, A. 1996. *Twice the Work of Free Labor: The Political Economy of Convict Labor in the New South.* New York: Verso.

Lieberman, R. 1998. *Shifting the Color Line.* Cambridge: Harvard University Press.

Lindgren, J., and J. Heather. 2002. "Counting Guns in Early America." *William and Mary Law Review* 3:5.

Lindsey, B. 2021. "State Capacity: What Is It, How We Lost It, and How to Get It Back." Niskanen Center, November 18. https://www.niskanencenter.org/state-capacity-what-is-it-how-we-lost-it-and-how-to-get-it-back/.

Lipset, S. M. 1990. *Continental Divide: The Values and Institutions of the United States and Canada.* New York: Routledge.

Liptak, A. 2008. "Illegal Globally, Bail for Profit Remains in U.S." *New York Times*, January 29. https://www.nytimes.com/2008/01/29/us/29bail.html.

Littman, A. 2021. "Jails, Sheriffs, and Carceral Policymaking." *Vanderbilt Law Review* 74, no. 4: 861–950.

Lobuglio, S. F., and A. M. Piehl. 2015. "Unwinding Mass Incarceration." *Issues in Science and Technology* 32, no. 1.

Lochner, L., and E. Moretti. 2004. "The Effect of Education on Crime: Evidence from Prison Inmates, Arrests, and Self-Reports." *American Economic Review* 94, no. 1: 155–89.

Londoño, E. 2023. "How 'Defund the Police' Failed." *New York Times*, June 16. https://www.nytimes.com/2023/06/16/us/defund-police-minneapolis.html.

Lopez, G. 2023. "A Drop in American Gun Violence." *New York Times*, November 1. https://www.nytimes.com/2023/11/01/briefing/gun-violence.html.

Lopoo, E., V. Schiraldi, and T. Ittner. 2024. "How Little Supervision Can We Have?" *Annual Review of Criminology* 6: 23–42.

Lukes, S. 1973. *Emile Durkheim: His Life and Work: A Historical and Critical Study.* Stanford: Stanford University Press.

Lynch, J. 2014. "A Cross-National Perspective on the American Welfare State." in *Oxford Handbook of U.S. Social Policy*, ed. D. Beland, K. J. Morgan, and C. Howard. New York: Oxford University Press.

Lynch, M. 2010. *Sunbelt Justice: Arizona and the Transformation of American Punishment.* Stanford: Stanford University Press.

Lynch, M. 2023. "Prosecutors as Punishers: A Case Study of Trump-Era Practices." *Punishment and Society* 25, no. 5: 1312–1333.

Mac Donald, H. 2016. *The War on Cops: How the New Attack on Law and Order Makes Everyone Less Safe.* New York: Encounter Books.

Madden, S., S. Leeds, and R. Carmichael. 2020. "'I Want Us to Dream a Little Bigger': Noname and Mariame Kaba on Art and Abolition." NPR, December 19. https://www.npr.org/2020/12/19/948005131/i-want-us-to-dream-a-little-bigger-noname-and-mariame-kaba-on-art-and-abolition.

Mammen, N. n.d. "Prisoner Reintegration: Lessons from Norway." Impartial Justice for All. https://impartial.one/prisoner-reintegration-lessons-from-norway/.

Mann, M. 1993. *The Sources of Social Power.* Vol. 2. Cambridge: Cambridge University Press.

Manza, J., and C. Uggen. 2006. *Locked Out: Felon Disenfranchisement and American Democracy.* New York: Oxford University Press.

Markovits, D. 2020. *The Meritocracy Trap: How America's Foundational Myth Feeds Inequality, Dismantles the Middle Class, and Devours the Elite.* New York: Penguin Books.

Marmor, T., J. Mahaw, and P. Harvey. 1990. *America's Misunderstood Welfare State.* New York: Basic Books.

Marquand, D. 2004. *Decline of the Public: The Hollowing-Out of Citizenship.* Malden, MA: Polity Press.

The Marshall Project. n.d. *The Language Project.* https://www.themarshallproject.org/2021/04/12/the-language-project.

Marx, K. 1852. *The 18th Brumaire of Louis Napoleon.* Repr. New York: International Publishing, 1994.

Massey, D. S. 2009. "Globalization and Inequality: Explaining American Exceptionalism." *European Sociological Review* 25, no. 1: 9–23.

Massey, D. S., and N. A. Denton. 1993. *American Apartheid: Segregation and the Making of the Underclass.* Cambridge: Harvard University Press.

Massey, D. S., J. Rothwell, and T. Domina. 2009. "The Changing Bases of Segregation in the United States." *The ANNALS of the American Academy of Political and Social Science* 626, no. 1: 74–90.

Massey, D. S., and R. Sampson. 2009. *Moynihan Redux: Legacies and Lessons.* Special issue, *Annals of the American Academy of Political and Social Science* 62, no. 11 (January).

Massoglia, M., and W. A. Pridemore. 2015. "Incarceration and Health." *Annual Review of Sociology* 41: 291–310.

Mathiesen, T. 1974. *The Politics of Abolition.* New York: Wiley.

Mauer, M., and A. Nellis. 2018. *The Meaning of Life: The Case for Abolishing Life Sentences.* New York: The New Press.

Maye, A. 2019. "No-Vacation Nation." *Center for Economic and Policy Research.* https://cepr.net/images/stories/reports/no-vacation-nation-2019-05.pdf.

McAdam, D. 1986. "Recruitment to High-Risk Activism: The Case of the Freedom Summer" *American Jounral of Sociology* 92: 64–90.

McBride, A. G., S. R. Schlesinger, S. D. Dillingham, and R. B. Buckman. 1992. "Combatting Violent Crime: 24 Recommendations to Strengthen Criminal Justice." Office of the Attorney General, United States Department of Justice. https://www.ojp.gov/ncjrs/virtual-library/abstracts/combating-violent-crime-24-recommendations-strengthen-criminal.

McCarthy, J. 2022. "Americans Remain Steadfast on Policing Reform Needs in 2022." Gallup, May 27. https://news.gallup.com/poll/393119/americans-remain-steadfast-policing-reform-needs-2022.aspx.

McCormack, S., and M. Lopez. 2024. "NYPD Stops Are Rocketing under Mayor Adams." NCLU Commentary, March 22. https://www.nyclu.org/commentary/nypd-stops-are-skyrocketing-under-mayor-adams.

McLennan, R. M. 2008. *The Crisis of Imprisonment: Protest, Politics, and the Making of the American Penal State, 1776–1941.* New York: Cambridge University Press.

McLeod, A. 2019. "Envisioning Abolition Democracy." *Harvard Law Review* 132, no. 6: 1613–1649.

Melhuish, E., and K. Petrogiannis. 2006. *Early Childhood Care and Education: International Perspectives.* New York: Routledge.

Menendian, S. 2021. "US Neighborhoods Are More Segregated Than a Generation Ago, Perpetuating Racial Inequality." *Think: Opinion, Analysis, Essays,* NBC News, August 16. https://www.nbcnews.com/think/opinion/u-s-neighborhoods-are-more-segregated-generation-ago-perpetuating-racial-ncna1276372.

Mennell, S. 2007. *The American Civilizing Process.* Malden, MA: Polity Press.

Menz, G. 2018. *Comparative Political Economy.* New York: Oxford University Press.

Merton, R. 1996. "Paradigm for Functional Analysis in Sociology." In *On Social Structure and Science,* ed. Piotr Sztompka. Chicago: University of Chicago Press.

Messner, S. F., L. E. Raffalovich, and G. M. Sutton. 2010. "Poverty, Infant Mortality, and Homicide Rates in Cross-National Perspective: Assessments of Criterion and Construct Validity." *Criminology* 48, no. 2: 509–37.

Messner, S. F., and R. Rosenfeld. 1997. "Political Restraint of the Market and Levels of Criminal Homicide: A Cross-National Application of Institutional-Anomie Theory." *Social Forces* 75, no. 4: 1393–1416.

Messner, S. F., and R. Rosenfeld. 2013. *Crime and the American Dream*. 5th ed. Belmont: Wadsworth.

Michaels, W. B., and A. Reed, 2022. *No Politics but Class Politics*. London: ERIS.

Michener, J. 2020. "George Floyd's Killing Was Just the Spark. Here's What Really Made the Protests Explode." *Washington Post,* June 11. https://www.washingtonpost.com/politics/2020/06/11/george-floyds-killing-was-just-spark-heres-what-really-made-protests-explode/.

Miller, C. C., and A. Parlapiano. 2023. "The U.S. Built a European-Style Welfare State. It's Largely Over." *New York Times*, May 11. https://www.nytimes.com/interactive/2023/04/06/upshot/pandemic-safety-net-medicaid.html.

Miller, D. 2017. "Solidarity and its Sources" in *The Strains of Commitment*, ed. K. Banting and W. Kymlicka. Oxford: Oxford University Press.

Miller, L. L. 2008. *The Perils of Federalism: Race, Poverty, and the Politics of Crime Control*. New York: Oxford University Press.

Miller, L. L. 2015. "What's Violence Got to Do with It? Inequality, Punishment, and State Failure in US Politics." *Punishment and Society* 17, no. 2: 184–210.

Miller, L. L. 2016. *The Myth of Mob Rule: Violent Crime and Democratic Politics*. New York: Oxford University Press.

Miller, L. L. 2020. "American Exceptionalism or Exceptionalism of the Americas: The Politics of Lethal Violence, Punishment, and Inequality." In *Tracing the Relationship between Inequality, Crime, and Punishment*, ed. N. Lacey, D. Soskice, L. Cheliotis, and S. Xenakis. Oxford, UK: Oxford University Press.

Mink, G. 1998. *Welfare's End*. Ithaca, NY: Cornell University Press.

Moody-Ramirez, M., G. B. Tait, and D. Bland. 2021. "An Analysis of George-Floyd-Themed Memes: A Critical Race Theory Approach to Analyzing Memes Surrounding the 2020 George Floyd Protests." *Journal of Social Media in Society* 10, no. 12: 373–401.

Moore, M. H. 1992. "Problem-Solving and Community Policing." *Crime and Justice* 15: 99–158.

Morgenstern, C., W. Hammerschick, and M. Rogan, eds. 2024. *European Perspectives on Pre-Trial Detention: A Means of Last Resort?* New York: Routledge.

Morone, J. A. 2003. *Hellfire Nation: The Politics of Sin in American History*. New Haven: Yale University Press.

Morone, J. A. 2020. *Republic of Wrath: How American Politics Turned Tribal, From George Washington to Donald Trump*. New York: Basic Books.

Moskos, P. 2008. *Cop in the Hood: My Year Policing Baltimore's Eastern District*. Princeton: Princeton University Press.

Movement for Black Lives. 2024. *The Movement for Black Lives*. https://m4bl.org/.

Moynihan, D. 1965. *The Negro Family: The Case for National Action*. Washington, DC: US Department of Labor.

Muhammad, K. G. 2019. *The Condemnation of Blackness: Race, Crime, and the Making of Modern Urban America*. Cambridge: Harvard University Press.

Muller, C. 2021. "Exclusion and Exploitation: The Incarceration of Black Americans from Slavery to the Present." *Science* 374, no. 6565: 282–86.

Muller, C., and A. F. Roehrkasse. 2022. "Racial and Class Inequality in U.S. Incarceration in the Early Twenty-First Century." *Social Forces* 101, no. 2: 803–28.

Mystal, E. 2024. "The Cops Killed More People in 2023 Than They Had in Years." *The Nation*, January 11. https://www.thenation.com/article/archive/cops-killed-more-people-in-2023-than-in-years/.

National Advisory Commission on Civil Disorders. 1967. *Kerner Commission Report on the Causes, Events and Aftermath of the Civil Disorders of 1967*. Washington, DC: US Department of Justice.

National Association of Assistant United States Attorneys. 2015. "The Dangerous Myths of Drug Sentencing 'Reform.'" *Federal Sentencing Reporter* 28, no. 1: 18–23.

National Center for Health Statistics. 2022. "Homicide Mortality by State." March 2. https://www.cdc.gov/nchs/pressroom/sosmap/homicide_mortality/homicide.htm.

National Conference of State Legislatures. 2022. *Racial and Ethnic Disparities in the Criminal Justice System*. May 24. https://www.ncsl.org/civil-and-criminal-justice/racial-and-ethnic-disparities-in-the-criminal-justice-system.

National Institute of Corrections. 2021. "Corrections State Statistics Information." https://nicic.gov/resources/nic-library/state-statistics.

Nellis, A. 2021. "No End in Sight: America's Enduring Reliance on Life Imprisonment." The Sentencing Project, February. https://www.sentencingproject.org/app/uploads/2022/08/No-End-in-Sight-Americas-Enduring-Reliance-on-Life-Imprisonment.pdf.

Nellis, A. 2024. "Mass Incarceration Trends." The Sentencing Project, May 21. https://www.sentencingproject.org/reports/mass-incarceration-trends/.

New York Mayor's Office of Criminal Justice. 2024. "System Data: Making Criminal Justice System Data Available to All New Yorkers." https://criminaljustice.cityofnewyork.us/system-data/.

New York Police Department. 2021. "Stop, Question and Frisk Data." https://www.nyc.gov/site/nypd/stats/reports-analysis/stopfrisk.page.

New York Times Editorial Board. 2014. "End Mass Incarceration Now." *New York Times*, May 24. https://www.nytimes.com/2014/05/25/opinion/sunday/end-mass-incarceration-now.html.

Newport, F. 2014. "Gallup Review: Black and White Attitudes toward Police." Gallup, August 20. https://news.gallup.com/poll/175088/gallup-review-black-white-attitudes-toward-police.aspx.

Newport, F. 2020. "Affirmative Action and Public Opinion." Gallup, August 7. https://news.gallup.com/opinion/polling-matters/317006/affirmative-action-public-opinion.aspx.

Novak, W. 2008. "The Myth of the 'Weak' American State." *American Historical Review* 113, no. 3: 752–72.

Nussbaum, M. C. 2001. *Upheavals of Thought: The Intelligence of Emotions*. New York: Cambridge University Press.

NYCLU. 2019. "Stop-and-Frisk in the De Blasio Era." March 14. https://www.nyclu.org/en/publications/stop-and-frisk-de-blasio-era-2019.

Obert, J. 2018. *The Six-Shooter State: Public and Private Violence in American Politics.* Cambridge and New York: Cambridge University Press.

Obert, J., A. Poe, and A. Sarat, eds. 2019. *The Lives of Guns.* New York: Oxford University Press.

OECD. 2017. "OECD Child Well-Being Data Portal Country Factsheet: United States." November. https://www.oecd.org/els/family/CWBDP_Factsheet_USA.pdf.

Ofer, U. 2021. "50 Years into the War on Drugs, Biden-Harris Can Fix the Harm It Created." ACLU, January 6. https://www.aclu.org/news/criminal-law-reform/50-years-into-the-war-on-drugs-biden-harris-can-fix-the-harm-it-created.

O'Flaherty, B., and R. Sethi. 2019. *Shadows of Doubt: Stereotypes, Crime, and the Pursuit of Justice.* Cambridge: Harvard University Press.

O'Flaherty, B., and R. Sethi. 2024. "Stereotypes, Crime, and Policing." *Annual Review of Criminology* 7: 383–401.

Our World in Data. n.d. *Public Social Spending as a Share of GDP, 1880 to 2016.* https://ourworldindata.org/grapher/social-spending-oecd-longrun.

Page, J. 2011. *The Toughest Beat: Politics, Punishment, and the Prison Officers Union in California.* New York: Oxford University Press.

Page, J., P. Goodman, and M. Phelps. 2017. *Breaking the Pendulum: The Long Struggle over Criminal Justice.* New York: Oxford University Press.

Page, J., H. Schoenfeld, and M. Campbell. 2020. "To Defund the Police, We Have to Dethrone the Law Enforcement Lobby." *Jacobin*, July 4. https://jacobin.com/2020/07/defund-police-unions-law-enforcement-lobby.

Page, J., and J. Soss. 2017. "Criminal Justice Predation and Neoliberal Governance." In *Rethinking Neoliberalism: Resisting the Disciplinary Regime,* ed. S. F. Schram and Marianna Pavlovskaya. New York: Routledge.

Pager, D. 2007. *Marked: Race, Crime, and Finding Work in an Era of Mass Incarceration.* Chicago: University of Chicago Press.

Parker, K., J. M. Horowitz, and M. Anderson. 2020. "Amid Protests, Majorities across Racial and Ethnic Groups Express Support for the Black Lives Matter Movement." Pew Research Center, June 12. https://www.pewresearch.org/social-trends/2020/06/12/amid-protests-majorities-across-racial-and-ethnic-groups-express-support-for-the-black-lives-matter-movement/.

Paskov, M., and C. Dewilde. 2012. "Income Inequality and Solidarity in Europe." *Research in Social Stratification and Mobility* 30, no. 4: 415–32.

Peterson, R. D., and L. J. Krivo. 2005. "Macrostructural Analyses of Race, Ethnicity, and Violent Crime: Recent Lessons and New Directions for Research." *Annual Review of Sociology* 31: 331–56.

Petruzzello, M. 2024. "List of Race Riots and Massacres in the United States." *Encyclopedia Britannica.* https://www.britannica.com/topic/list-of-race-riots-and-massacres-in-the-United-States.

Pew Research Center. 2022. "Americans' Views of Government: Decades of Distrust, Enduring Support for Its Role." June 6. https://www.pewresearch.org/politics/2022/06/06/americans-views-of-government-decades-of-distrust-enduring-support-for-its-role/.

Pew Research Center. 2024. "What the Data Says about Crime in the U.S." April 24. https://www.pewresearch.org/short-reads/2024/04/24/what-the-data-says-about-crime-in-the-us.

Pfaff, J. F. 2017. *Locked In: The True Causes of Mass Incarceration and How to Achieve Real Reform.* New York: Basic Books.

Phelps, M. 2020. "Mass Probation from Macro to Micro: Tracing the Expansion and Consequences of Community Supervision." *Annual Review of Criminology* 3: 261–79.

Phelps, M. S. 2024. *The Minneapolis Reckoning: Race, Violence, and the Politics of Policing in America.* Princeton: Princeton University Press.

Pickett, J. T. 2019. "Public Opinion and Criminal Justice Policy: Theory and Research." *Annual Review of Criminology* 2: 405–28.

Pickett, J., A. Graham, and F. Cullen. 2021. "The American Racial Divide in Fear of the Police." *Criminology* 60, no. 2: 291–320.

Pierson, P. 2010. *Dismantling the Welfare State? Reagan, Thatcher, and the Politics of Retrenchment.* New York: Cambridge.

Pildes, P. H. 2011. "Why the Center Does Not Hold: The Cause of Hyperpolarized Democracy in America." *California Law Review* 99, no. 2: 273–333.

Polanyi, K. 1944. *The Great Transformation: The Political and Economic Origins of Our Time.* Repr. 2001. Boston: Beacon Press.

Police Executive Research Forum. 2013. "COMPSTAT: Its Origins, Evolution, and Future in Law Enforcement Agencies." Bureau of Justice Assistance, United States Department of Justice. https://www.ojp.gov/ncjrs/virtual-library/abstracts/compstat-its-origins-evolution-and-future-law-enforcement-agencies.

Porter, C., and C. Méheut. 2023. "Riots in France Highlight a Vicious Cycle between Police and Minorities." *New York Times*, July 17. https://www.nytimes.com/2023/07/17/world/europe/france-riots-police-poor.html.

Porter, N. D., and M. McLeod. 2023. "Expanding the Vote: State Felony Disenfranchisement Reform, 1997–2023." The Sentencing Project, October 18. https://www.sentencingproject.org/reports/expanding-the-vote-state-felony-disenfranchisement-reform-1997-2023/.

Powell, L. F. 1971. "Confidential Memorandum: Attack on American Free Enterprise System." August 23. https://reclaimdemocracy.org/powell_memo_lewis/.

Prasad, M. 2016. "American Exceptionalism and the Welfare State: The Revisionist Literature." *Annual Review of Political Science* 19: 187–203.

Pratt, T. C., and F. T. Cullen. 2005. "Assessing Macro-Level Predictors and Theories of Crime: A Meta-Analysis." *Crime and Justice* 32: 373–450.

Press, E. 2021. *Dirty Work: Essential Jobs and the Hidden Toll of Inequality in America.* New York: Farrar, Straus and Giroux.

Prison Policy Initiative. 2024. *Mass Incarceration: The Whole Pie 2024.* https://www.prisonpolicy.org/reports/pie2024.html.

Prison Policy Initiative. n.d. *Data Toolbox.* https://www.prisonpolicy.org/data/.

Prospects. 2024. "Probation Officer Job Profile." https://www.prospects.ac.uk/job-profiles/probation-officer.

Putnam, R. D. 2000. *Bowling Alone: The Collapse and Revival of American Community.* New York: Simon and Schuster Paperbacks.

Putnam, R. D. 2015. *Our Kids: The American Dream in Crisis.* New York: Simon and Schuster Paperbacks.

Quadagno, J. 1996. *The Color of Welfare: How Racism Undermined the War on Poverty.* New York: Oxford University Press.

Rabin, R. C. 2023. "Why Some Americans Buy Guns." *New York Times*, July 26. https://www.nytimes.com/2023/06/23/health/gun-violence-psychology.html.

Ramesh, R. 2010. "More Black People Jailed in England and Wales Proportionately Than in US." *The Guardian*, October 10. https://www.theguardian.com/society/2010/oct/11/black-prison-population-increase-england.

Ramirez, M. D. 2013. "Americans' Changing Views on Crime and Punishment." *Public Opinion Quarterly* 77, no. 4: 1006–1031.

Ramsay, D. 2023. *When Crack Was King: A People's History of a Misunderstood Era.* New York: One World.

Rank, M. R., L. M. Eppard, and H. E. Bullock. 2021. *Poorly Understood: What America Gets Wrong about Poverty.* New York: Oxford University Press.

Ransby, B. 2018. *Making All Black Lives Matter.* Oakland: University of California Press.

Raphael, S., and M. A. Stoll, eds. 2009. *Do Prisons Make Us Safer? The Benefits and Costs of the Prison Boom.* New York: Russell Sage Foundation.

Reardon, S. F., and A. Owens. 2014. "60 Years After *Brown*: Trends and Consequences of School Segregation." *Annual Review of Sociology* 40: 199–218.

Reaves, B. A. 2013. "Felony Defendants in Large Urban Counties, 2009—Statistical Tables." Bureau of Justice Statistics, United States Department of Justice, December. https://bjs.ojp.gov/library/publications/felony-defendants-large-urban-counties-2009-statistical-tables.

Reed, T. F. 2020. *Toward Freedom: The Case against Race Reductionism.* London: Verso.

Refslund, B., and J. Arnholtz. 2021. "Power Resources Theory Revisited." *Economic and Industrial Democracy* 43, no. 4: 1958–1979.

Reinarman, C., and H. Levine. 1997. "The Crack Attack: Politics and the Media in the Crack Scare." In *Crack in America*, ed. C. Reinarman and H. Levine. Berkeley: University of California Press.

Reiter, K. 2016. *23/7: Pelican Bay Prison and the Rise of Long-Term Solitary Confinement.* New Haven: Yale University Press.

Reiter, K. 2023. "Is the Sun Setting on Solitary Confinement?" *Only Sky*, March 8. https://onlysky.media/kreiter/is-the-sun-setting-on-solitary-confinement/.

Reitz, K. R., ed. 2018. *American Exceptionalism in Crime and Punishment.* New York: Oxford University Press.

Reitz, K. R., ed. 2020. "Parole Release and Supervision." *Annual Review of Criminology* 3: 281–98.

Rios, V. 2011. *Punished: Policing the Lives of Black and Latino Boys.* New York: New York University Press.

Roeder, O., L-B. Eisen, and J. Bowling. 2015. "What Caused the Crime Decline?" Brennan Center for Justice, February 12. http://www.brennancenter.org/our-work/research-reports/what-caused-crime-decline.

Rogers, D., ed. 1992. *Voting and the Spirit of American Democracy.* Urbana: University of Illinois Press.

Rogers, D. 2018. "The Uses and Abuses of Neoliberalism." *Dissent Magazine*, Winter.

Rose, D. R., and T. R. Clear. 1998. "Incarceration, Social Capital, and Crime: Implications for Social Disorganization Theory." *Criminology* 36, no. 3: 441–80.

Rosenfeld, J. 2014. *What Unions No Longer Do*. Cambridge: Harvard University Press.
Rosenfeld, R., and R. Fornango. 2007. "The Impact of Economic Conditions on Robbery and Property Crime: The Role of Consumer Sentiment." *Criminology* 45, no. 4: 735–69.
Rosenfeld, R., and S. F. Messner. 2013. *Crime and the Economy*. Los Angeles: Sage.
Rostker, B. D., L. M. Hanser, W. M. Hix, C. Jensen, A. R. Morral, G. Ridgeway, and T. L. Schell. 2008. "Evaluation of the New York City Police Department Firearm Training and Firearm-Discharge Review Process." RAND Center on Quality Policing. Santa Monica, California.
Roth, R. 2009. *American Homicide*. Cambridge: Harvard University Press.
Rothstein, B. 2011a. "Creating a Sustainable Solidaristic Society: A Manual." QoG Working Paper Series, University of Gothenburg, Gothenburg, Sweden. https://www.gu.se/sites/default/files/2020-05/2011_7_rothstein.pdf.
Rothstein, B. 2011b. *Quality of Government: Corruption, Social Trust, and Inequality in International Perspective*. Chicago: University of Chicago Press.
Rothstein, B., and D. Stolle. 2003. "Social Capital, Impartiality, and the Welfare State." In *Generating Social Capital: Civil Society and Institutions in Comparative Perspective*, ed. M. Hooghe and D. Stolle. New York: Palgrave Macmillan.
Rovner, J. 2023. "Youth Justice by the Numbers." The Sentencing Project, May 16. https://www.sentencingproject.org/policy-brief/youth-justice-by-the-numbers/.
Rowthorn, R., and R. Ramaswamy. 1997. *Deindustrialization—Its Causes and Implications*. Washington, DC: International Monetary Fund.
Rucker, J. M., and J. A. Richeson. 2021. "Toward an Understanding of Structural Racism: Implications for Criminal Justice." *Science* 374, no. 6565: 286–90.
Safier, R., and A. Harrison. 2024. "Student Loan Debt—Averages and Other Statistics in 2024." *USA Today*, June 24. https://www.usatoday.com/money/blueprint/student-loans/average-student-loan-debt-statistics/.
Sampson, R. J. 1987. "Urban Black Violence: The Effect of Male Joblessness and Family Disruption." *American Journal of Sociology* 93, no. 2: 348–82.
Sampson, R. J. 2011. "Neighborhood Effects, Causal Mechanism, and the Social Structure of the City." In *Analytical Sociology and Social Mechanisms*, ed. P. Demeulenaere. New York: Cambridge University Press.
Sampson, R. J. 2012. *Great American City*. Chicago: University of Chicago Press.
Sampson, R. J. 2019. "Neighborhood Effects and Beyond: Explaining the Paradoxes of Inequality in the Changing American Metropolis." *Urban Studies* 56, no. 1: 3–32.
Sampson, R. J., and W. B. Groves. 1989. "Community Structure and Crime: Testing Social-Disorganization Theory." *American Journal of Sociology* 94, no. 4: 774–802.
Sampson, R. J., and C. Loeffler. 2010. "Punishment's Place: The Local Concentration of Mass Incarceration." *Daedalus* 139, no. 3: 20–31.
Sampson, R. J., and S. W. Raudenbush. 2001. "Disorder in Urban Neighborhoods—Does It Lead to Crime?" National Institute of Justice, Research in Brief, February.
Sampson, R. J., and S. W. Raudenbush. 2005. "Social Anatomy of Racial and Ethnic Disparities in Violence." *American Journal of Public Health* 95, no. 2.
Sampson, R. J., S. W. Raudenbush, and F. Earls. 1997. "Neighborhoods and Violent Crime: A Multilevel Study of Collective Efficacy." *Science* 277, no. 5328: 918–24.

Sampson, R. J., and L. A. Smith. 2021. "Rethinking Criminal Propensity and Character: Cohort Inequalities and the Power of Social Change." *Crime and Justice* 50: 13–76.

Sampson, R. J., and W. J. Wilson. 1995. "Toward a Theory of Race, Crime, and Urban Inequality." In *Crime and Inequality*, ed. J. Hagan and R. Peterson. Stanford: Stanford University Press.

Sampson, R., W. J. Wilson, and H. Katz. 2018. "Reassessing 'Toward a Theory of Race, Crime, and Urban Inequality.'" *Du Bois Review* 15, no. 1: 14–34.

Savage, J., R. R. Bennett, and M. Danner. 2008. "Economic Assistance and Crime: A Cross-National Investigation." *European Journal of Criminology* 5, no. 2: 217–38.

Savelsberg, J. J. 1994. "Knowledge, Domination, and Criminal Punishment." *American Journal of Sociology* 99, no. 4: 911–43.

Savolainen, J. 2000. "Inequality, Welfare State, and Homicide: Further Support for the Institutional Anomie Theory." *Criminology* 38, no. 4: 1021–1042.

Sawyer, W., and P. Wagner. 2024. *Mass Incarceration: The Whole Pie 2024*. Prison Policy Initiative, March 14. https://www.prisonpolicy.org/reports/pie2024.html.

Schaeffer, K. 2023. "Key Facts about Americans and Guns." Pew Research Center, September 13. https://www.pewresearch.org/short-reads/2023/09/13/key-facts-about-americans-and-guns.

Schartmueller, D. 2015. *Mass Imprisonment in Scandinavia: The Ultimate Punishment in the Penal Environments of Denmark, Finland, and Sweden*. Doctoral dissertation, Northern Arizona State University, August. https://www.epea.org/wp-content/uploads/LIFE-IMPRISONMENT-IN-SCANDINAVIA.pdf.

Schiraldi, V. 2023. *Mass Supervision: Probation, Parole, and the Illusion of Safety and Freedom*. New York: The New Press.

Schoenfeld, H. 2018. *Building the Prison State*. Chicago: University of Chicago Press.

Schumpeter, J. 1942. *Capitalism, Socialism, and Democracy*. Repr. 2008. New York: Harper Perennial.

Schwartz, J. 2023. *Shielded: How the Police Became Untouchable*. New York: Viking.

Schwartzapfel, B. 2015. "Life Without Parole: Inside the Secretive World of Parole Boards, Where Your Freedom May Depend on Politics and Whim." The Marshall Project, July 10. https://www.themarshallproject.org/2015/07/10/life-without-parole.

Schwenk, K. 2024. "Dark Money Is Paying for the Police's High Tech Weapons." *Jacobin*, March 29.

Sedgh, G., L. B. Finer, A. Bankole, M. A. Eilers, and S. Singh. 2015. "Adolescent Pregnancy, Birth, and Abortion Rates across Countries: Levels and Recent Trends." *Journal of Adolescent Health* 56, no. 2: 223–30.

Selznick, P. 1994. *The Moral Commonwealth: Social Theory and the Promise of Community*. Berkeley: University of California Press.

The Sentencing Project. 2024. "U.S. Criminal Justice Data." https://www.sentencingproject.org/research/us-criminal-justice-data/.

Shalev, S. 2015. "Solitary Confinement: The View from Europe." *Canadian Journal of Human Rights* 4, no. 1: 143–65.

Shammas, V. L. 2015. "A Prison without Walls: Alternative Incarceration in the Late Age of Social Democracy." *Prison Service Journal*, no. 217: 3–9.

Shammas, V. L. 2017. *Prisons of Welfare: Incarceration, Social Democracy, and the Sociology of Punishment*. Doctoral dissertation, University of Oslo.

Shanahan, J., and Z. Kurti. 2022. *States of Incarceration: Rebellion, Reform, and America's Punishment System*. London: Reaktion Books.

Shanahan, L., and W. Copeland. 2023. "A Deadly Drop in the Rankings: How the United States was Left Behind in Global Life Expectancy Trends." *American Journal of Public Health*, September. https://ajph.aphapublications.org/doi/full/10.2105/AJPH.2023.307367.

Sharkey, P. 2008. "Ending Urban Poverty: The Inherited Ghetto." *Boston Review*, January 1. https://www.bostonreview.net/articles/ending-urban-poverty-the-inherited-ghetto/.

Sharkey, P. 2018. "The Long Reach of Violence: A Broader Perspective on Data, Theory, and Evidence on the Prevalence and Consequences of Exposure to Violence." *Annual Review of Criminology* 1: 85–102.

Sharkey, P. 2018. *Uneasy Peace: The Great Crime Decline, the Renewal of City Life, and the Next War on Violence*. New York: W. W. Norton and Company.

Sharkey, P., and M. Kang. 2023. "The Era of Progress on Gun Mortality: State Gun Regulations and Gun Deaths from 1991–2016." *Epidemiology* 34, no. 6: 786–92.

Sharkey, P., and A. Marsteller. 2022. "The Compounding Relationship Between Violence and Urban Inequality." *Gotham Gazette*, March 4. https://www.gothamgazette.com/130-opinion/11143-relationship-between-violence-urban-inequality.

Sharkey, P., G. Torrats-Espinosa, and D. Takyar. 2017. "Community and the Crime Decline: The Causal Effect of Local Nonprofits on Violent Crime." *American Sociological Review* 82, no. 6: 1214–1240.

Shatz, A. 2020. "America Explodes." *London Review of Books* 42, no. 12: 4–8.

Shelby, T. 2022. *The Idea of Prison Abolition*. Princeton: Princeton University Press.

Sherman, L. W. 2018. "Reducing Fatal Police Shootings as System Crashes: Research, Theory, and Practice." *American Review of Criminology* 1: 421–49.

Sherman, L. W., D. Gottfredson, D. MacKenzie, J. Eck, P. Reuter, and S. Bushway. 1997. *Preventing Crime: What Works, What Doesn't, What's Promising*. Washington, DC: United States Department of Justice, Office of Justice Programs.

Sierra-Arévalo, M. 2020a. "Gun Victimization in the Line of Duty: Fatal and Nonfatal Firearm Assaults on Police Officers in the United States, 2014–2019." *Criminology and Public Policy* 19, no. 3: 1041–1066.

Sierra-Arévalo, M. 2020b. "Police, Culture, and Inequality." *ASA Footnotes*, July/August.

Sierra-Arévalo, M. 2021. "American Policing and the Danger Imperative." *Law and Society Review* 55, no. 1: 70–103.

Sierra-Arévalo, M. 2024. *The Danger Imperative: Violence, Death, and the Soul of Policing*. New York: Columbia University Press.

Simmons-Duffin, S. 2023. "'Life Free and Die?' The Sad State of U.S. Life Expectancy." NPR, March 25. https://www.npr.org/sections/health-shots/2023/03/25/1164819944/live-free-and-die-the-sad-state-of-u-s-life-expectancy.

Simon, J. 1993. *Poor Discipline: Parole and the Social Control of the Underclass, 1890–1990*. Chicago: University of Chicago Press.

Simon, J. 2007. *Governing Through Crime: How the War on Crime Transformed American Democracy and Created a Culture of Fear*. New York: Oxford University Press.

Simon, J. 2014. *Mass Incarceration on Trial: A Remarkable Court Decision and the Future of Prisons in America.* New York: The New Press.

Simon, S. 2021. "Opinion: After George Floyd's Death, a Press Release Obscured a Police Murder." NPR, April 24. https://www.npr.org/2021/04/24/990376231/opinion-after-george-floyds-death-a-press-release-obscured-a-police-murder.

Simon, S. 2024. *Before the Badge: How Academy Training Shapes Police Violence.* New York: New York University Press.

Simonson, J. 2023. *Radical Acts of Justice: How Ordinary People are Dismantling Mass Incarceration.* New York: The New Press.

Skeen, C. E. 1999. *Citizen Soldiers in the War of 1812.* Lexington: University Press of Kentucky.

Sklansky, D. A. 2021. *A Pattern of Violence: How the Law Classifies Crime and What It Means for Justice.* Cambridge: Harvard University Press.

Skogan, W. G. 1990. *Disorder and Decline: Crime and the Spiral of Decay in American Neighborhoods.* Berkely and Los Angeles: University of California Press.

Skogan, W. G. 2023. *Stop and Frisk and the Politics of Crime in Chicago.* New York: Oxford University Press.

Small Arms Survey. 2018. *Global Firearms Holdings: There Are More Than One Billion Firearms in the World, the Vast Majority of Which Are in Civilian Hands.* https://www.smallarmssurvey.org/database/global-firearms-holdings.

Smeeding, T. M., L. Rainwater, and G. Burtles. 2001. "U.S. Poverty in a Cross-National Context." In *Understanding Poverty*, ed. S. H. Danziger and R. H. Haveman. Cambridge: Harvard University Press.

Smit, Van Zyl, D., and C. Appleton. 2019. *Life Imprisonment: A Global Human Rights Analysis.* Cambridge: Harvard University Press.

Smit, Van Zyl, D., and A. Corda. 2018. "American Exceptionalism in Parole Release and Supervision: A European Perspective." In *American Exceptionalism in Crime and Punishment*, ed. K. R. Reitz. New York: Oxford University Press.

Smith, C., T. Ireland, and T. Thornberry. 2005. "Adolescent Maltreatment and Its Impact on Young Adult Antisocial Behavior." *Child Abuse and Neglect* 29, no. 10: 1099–1119.

Smith, M. D. 2015. "Abolish the Police. Instead, Let's Have Full Social, Economic, and Political Equality." *The Nation*, April 9. https://www.thenation.com/article/archive/abolish-police-instead-lets-have-full-social-economic-and-political-equality/.

Smith, M. D. 2020. "Incremental Change is a Moral Failure." *The Atlantic*, September 15. https://www.theatlantic.com/magazine/archive/2020/09/police-reform-is-not-enough/614176/.

Social Capital Project. 2017. "What We Do Together: The State of Associational Life in America." *An Overview of Social Capital in America*, May. https://www.jec.senate.gov/public/_cache/files/8cb559c4-3764-4706-9009-b4d8565ec820/scp-volume-1-digital-final.pdf.

Soifer, H., and M. vom Hau. 2008. "Unpacking the Strength of the State: The Utility of State Infrastructural Power." *Studies in Comparative International Development* 43: 219–30.

Soss, J., and V. Weaver. 2017. "The Police are Our Government: Politics, Political Science, and the Policing of Race-Class Subjugated Communities." *Annual Review of Political Science* 20: 563–91.

Spelman, W. 2006. "The Limited Importance of Prison Expansion." In *The Crime Drop in America*, ed. A. Blumstein and J. Wallman. New York: Cambridge University Press.

Stahly-Butts, M., and A. Akbar. 2022. "Reforms for Radicals? An Abolitionist Framework." *UCLA Law Review* 68: 1544–83.

Stanglin, D. 2020. "Fact Check: 1994 Crime Bill Did Not Bring Mass Incarceration of Black Americans." *USA Today*, July 3. https://www.usatoday.com/story/news/factcheck/2020/07/03/fact-check-1994-crime-bill-didnt-bring-mass-incarceration-black-people/3250210001/.

Stansbury, A., and L. Summers. 2020. "The Declining Worker Power Hypothesis: An Explanation for the Recent Evolution of the American Economy." NBER Working Paper 27193, National Bureau of Economic Research, May.

Starr, P. 2023. "The Life-and-Death Cost of Conservative Power." *American Prospect*, December 8. https://prospect.org/health/2023-12-08-life-death-cost-conservative-power/.

Statista Research Department. 2023. "Poverty Rate in the United States in 2022, by Race and Ethnicity." *Statista*, November 3. https://www.statista.com/statistics/200476/us-poverty-rate-by-ethnic-group.

Statista Research Department. 2024a. "Homicide Rate in Europe by Country, 2022." https://www.statista.com/statistics/200476/us-poverty-rate-by-ethnic-group.

Statista Research Department. 2024b. "Rate of Fatal Police Shootings in the United States from 2015 to March 2024, by Ethnicity." *Statista*, March 11. https://ww.statista.com/statistics/1123070/police-shootings-rate-ethnicity-us/.

Statistics Canada. n.d. *Historical Statistics of Canada*. Archived content. https://www150.statcan.gc.ca/n1/pub/11-516-x/sectionz/4147446-eng.htm#3.

Staudt, S. 2024. "Zombie Politics: The Return of Failed Criminal Legal System Policies in 2023—And How to Fight Back." Prison Policy Initiative, January 24. https://www.prisonpolicy.org/blog/2024/01/24/zombie-politics/.

Stemen, D. 2017. *The Prison Paradox: More Incarceration Will Not Make Us Safer*. New York: Vera Institute of Justice. https://www.vera.org/publications/for-the-record-prison-paradox-incarceration-not-safer.

Stjernø, S. 2005. *Solidarity in Europe: The History of an Idea*. New York: Cambridge University Press.

Strauss, V. 2020. "US Ranks near the Bottom of Advanced Nations in Childhood Wellness, New Report Finds." *Washington Post*, October 6. https://www.washingtonpost.com/education/2020/10/06/us-ranks-near-bottom-advanced-nations-child-wellness-new-report/.

Streeck, W. 2010. "E Pluribus Unum? Varieties and Commonalities of Capitalism." MPIfG Discussion Paper 10/12, Max Planck Institute for the Study of Societies, Cologne, Germany.

Streeck, W. 2012. "How to Study Contemporary Capitalism." *European Journal of Sociology* 54, no. 1: 1–28.

Stroud, H. D., and T. King. 2020. "How Electronic Monitoring Incentivizes Prolonged Punishment." Brennan Center for Justice, July 26. https://www.brennancenter.org/our-work/analysis-opinion/how-electronic-monitoring-incentivizes-prolonged-punishment.

Stubbs, T. 2018. *Masters of Violence: The Plantation Overseers of Eighteenth-Century Virginia, South Carolina, and Georgia*. Columbia: University of South Carolina Press.

Stuntz, W. J. 2001. "The Pathological Politics of Criminal Law." *Michigan Law Review* 100, no. 3: 505–600.

Sturge, G. 2024. "UK Prison Population Statistics." House of Commons Library, July 8. https://researchbriefings.files.parliament.uk/documents/SN04334/SN04334.pdf.

Subramanian, R., R. Delaney, S. Roberts, N. Fishman and P. McGarry. 2015. *Incarceration's Front Door: The Misuse of Jails in America*. Vera Institute of Justice, February. https://www.vera.org/publications/incarcerations-front-door-the-misuse-of-jails-in-america.

Subramanian, R., J. Fielding, L.-B. Eisen, H. D. Stroud, and T. King. 2022. "Revenue over Public Safety: How Perverse Financial Incentives Warp the Criminal Justice System." Brennan Center for Justice, July 6. https://www.brennancenter.org/our-work/research-reports/revenue-over-public-safety.

Subramanian, R., and A. Shames. 2013. "Sentencing and Prison Practices in Germany and the Netherlands." Vera Institute of Justice, October. https://www.vera.org/publications/sentencing-and-prison-practices-in-germany-and-the-netherlands-implications-for-the-united-states.

Sugrue, T. 2005. *The Origins of the Urban Crisis: Race and Inequality in Postwar Detroit*. Princeton: Princeton University Press.

Sutton, J. R. 2000. "Imprisonment and Social Classification in Five Common-Law Democracies, 1955–1985." *American Journal of Sociology* 106, no. 2: 350–86.

Sutton, J. R. 2004. "The Political Economy of Imprisonment in Affluent Western Democracies, 1960–1990." *American Sociological Review* 69, no. 2: 170–89.

Swedler, D. I., C. Kercher, M. M. Simmons, and K. M. Pollack. 2014. "Occupational Homicide of Law Enforcement Officers in the US, 1996–2010." *Injury Prevention* 20: 35–40.

Tatum, B. D. 2017. "Segregation Worse in Schools 60 Years After Brown v. Board of Education." *Seattle Times*, September 14. https://www.seattletimes.com/opinion/segregation-worse-in-schools-60-years-after-brown-v-board-of-education/.

Taub, J. 2020. *Big Dirty Money: The Shocking Injustice and Unseen Cost of White Collar Crime*. New York: Viking.

Taylor, K.-Y. 2021a. "Did Last Summer's Black Lives Matter Protests Change Anything." *The New Yorker*, August 6. https://www.newyorker.com/news/our-columnists/did-last-summers-protests-change-anything.

Taylor, K.-Y. 2021b. "The Emerging Movement for Police and Prison Abolition." *The New Yorker*, May 7. https://www.newyorker.com/news/our-columnists/the-emerging-movement-for-police-and-prison-abolition.

Terrill, W., and M. D. Reisig. 2003. "Neighborhood Context and Police Use of Force." *Journal of Research in Crime and Delinquency* 40, no. 3: 291–321.

The Economist. 2018. "Segregation in America: Where a Divided Nation Stands, Half a Century After Martin Luther King's Death." The Data Team, April 4. https://www.economist.com/graphic-detail/2018/04/04/segregation-in-america.

The Economist. 2021. "How America Compares to the World when Split by Race." May 21. https://www.economist.com/graphic-detail/2021/05/21/how-america-compares-to-the-world-when-split-by-race.

The Guardian. 2015. "Walter Scott Shooting Footage Synced with Police Scanner Audio—Video." April 8. https://www.theguardian.com/us-news/video/2015/apr/09/north-charleston-shooting-police-scanner-video.

The Guardian. 2023. "The Guardian View on El Salvador's Crime Crackdown: A Short-Term, High Cost Fix." July 2. https://www.theguardian.com/commentisfree/2023/jul/02/the-guardian-view-on-el-salvadors-crackdown-a-short-term-high-cost-fix.

Thelen, K. 2012. "Varieties of Capitalism: Trajectories of Liberalization and the New Politics of Social Solidarity." *Annual Review of Political Science* 15: 137–59.

Thelen, K. 2014. *Varieties of Liberalization and the New Politics of Social Solidarity*. New York: Cambridge University Press.

Thelen, K. 2019. "The American Precariat: U.S. Capitalism in Comparative Perspective." *Perspectives on Politics* 17, no. 1: 5–27.

Therborn, G. 1986. *Why Some People Are More Unemployed Than Others*. London: Verso.

Thompson, A., and S. Tapp. 2023. "Just the Stats: Violent Victimization by Race of Hispanic Origin, 2008–21." Bureau of Justice Statistics, US Department of Justice, July. https://bjs.ojp.gov/violent-victimization-race-or-hispanic-origin-2008-2021.

Thompson, D. 2022. "Six Reasons the Murder Clearance Rate Is at an All-Time Low." *The Atlantic*, July 7. https://www.theatlantic.com/newsletters/archive/2022/07/police-murder-clearance-rate/661500/.

Tierney, J. 2013. "Prison Population Can Shrink When Police Crowd Streets." *New York Times*, January 25. https://www.nytimes.com/2013/01/26/nyregion/police-have-done-more-than-prisons-to-cut-crime-in-new-york.html.

Tilly, C. 1998. *Durable Inequality*. Berkeley: University of California Press.

Todd-Kvam, J. 2022. "Probation Practice, Desistance, and the Penal Field in Norway." *Criminology and Criminal Justice* 22, no. 3: 349–66.

Tonry, M. 2009. "Explanations of American Punishment Policies." *Punishment and Society* 11, no. 3: 377–94.

Tonry, M. 2012a. "Prosecutors and Politics in Comparative Perspective." *Crime and Justice* 41: 1–33.

Tonry, M. 2012b. *Punishing Race: A Continuing American Dilemma*. New York: Oxford University Press.

Tonry, M. 2016a. *Sentencing Fragments: Penal Reform in America, 1975–2025*. New York: Oxford University Press.

Tonry, M., ed. 2016b. "Sentencing Policies and Practices in Western Countries." In *Crime and Justice*, vol. 45. Chicago: University of Chicago Press.

Tonry, M. 2023. "Why Americans Are a People of Exceptional Violence." In *Crime and Justice*, vol. 45. Chicago: University of Chicago Press.

Tonry, M., and T. Lappi-Seppala, eds. 2011. *Crime and Justice in Scandinavia*. Crime and Justice series, vol. 40. Chicago: University of Chicago Press.

Travis, J. 2002. "Invisible Punishment: An Instrument of Social Exclusion." In *Invisible Punishment: The Collateral Consequences of Mass Imprisonment*, ed. M. Mauer and M. Chesney-Lind. New York: The New Press.

Travis, J., B. Western, and S. Redburn, eds. 2014. *The Growth of Incarceration in the United States: Exploring Causes and Consequences*. National Research Council. Washington, DC: National Academies Press.

Trump-Vance 2024 campaign. 2024. *Big Ideas, Bold Ambitions, and Daring Dreams for America's Future*. https://www.donaldjtrump.com/issues.

Ugelvik, T., and J. Dullum, eds. 2012. *Penal Exceptionalism? Nordic Prison Policy and Practice*. New York: Routledge.

USA Facts. 2023. "How Many Police Officers Die in the Line of Duty?" *USA Facts*, November 30. https://usafacts.org/articles/how-many-police-officers-die-in-the-line-of-duty/.

USA Facts. 2024. *How Much Do States Spend on Prisoners.* https://usafacts.org/articles/how-much-do-states-spend-on-prisons/.

United States Department of Justice. 1992. *The Case for More Incarceration.* Office of Policy Development. https://www.ojp.gov/ncjrs/virtual-library/abstracts/case-more-incarceration.

United States Department of Justice. 2011. *Plea Bargaining and Charges: Research Summary.* Bureau of Justice Statistics. https://bja.ojp.gov/sites/g/files/xyckuh186/files/media/document/pleabargainingresearchsummary.pdf.

United States Department of Justice. 2013. *Compstat: Its Origins, Evolution and Future in Law Enforcement Agencies.* Bureau of Justice Assistance.

United States Department of Justice. 2015. *The Ferguson Report: Department of Justice Investigation of the Ferguson Police Department.* Civil Rights Division. New York: The New Press. https://bja.ojp.gov/sites/g/files/xyckuh186/files/Publications/PERF-Compstat.pdf.

United States Department of Justice. 2019. *Local Police Departments, Policies and Procedures, 2016.* Bureau of Justice Statistics. https://bjs.ojp.gov/library/publications/local-police-departments-policies-and-procedures-2016.

United States Department of Justice. 2021. "State and Local Law Enforcement Training Academies, 2013." Bureau of Justice Statistics, July. https://bjs.ojp.gov/library/publications/state-and-local-law-enforcement-training-academies-2013.

United States Department of Labor. 2024. "Union Members—2023." Bureau of Labor Statistics, January 23. https://www.bls.gov/news.release/pdf/union2.pdf.

Usmani, A., and C. Lewis. Forthcoming. *What's Wrong with Mass Incarceration?*

Vallier, K. 2020. "Why Are Americans So Distrustful of Each Other?" *Wall Street Journal,* December 17. https://www.wsj.com/articles/why-are-americans-so-distrustful-of-each-other-11608217988.

van de Rijt, J., E. van Ginneken, and M. Boone. 2023. "Lost in Translation: The Principle of Normalisation in Prison Policy in Norway and the Netherlands." *Punishment and Society* 25, no. 3: 766–83.

Vanstone, M., and P. Priestley. 2022. *The Palgrave Handbook of Global Rehabilitation in Criminal Justice.* Cham, Switzerland: Springer.

Venkatesh, S. A. 2002. *American Project: The Rise and Fall of a Modern Ghetto.* Cambridge: Harvard University Press.

Vieraitis, L., T. Kovandzik, and T. Marvel. 2007. "The Criminogenic Effects of Imprisonment." *Criminology and Public Policy* 6, no. 3: 589–622.

Violence Prevention Project. 2023. "Search the Database: Mass Public Shootings in the United States, 1966–Present." Hamline University, Saint Paul, Minnesota. https://www.theviolenceproject.org/mass-shooter-database/.

Vitale, A. S. 2017. *The End of Policing.* Brooklyn: Verso.

Vogel, D. 1978. "Why Businessmen Distrust Their State: The Political Consciousness of American Corporate Executives." *British Journal of Political Science* 8, no. 1: 45–78.

Vogler, J. 2020. "Access to Healthcare and Criminal Behavior: Evidence from the ACA Medicaid Expansion." *Journal of Policy Analysis and Management* 39, no. 4: 1166–1213.

Wacquant, L. 2009. *Punishing the Poor: The Neoliberal Government of Social Insecurity.* Durham: Duke University Press.

Wacquant, L. 2022. *The Invention of the "Underclass": A Study in the Politics of Knowledge.* Medford, MA: Polity.

Wagner, P., and B. Rabuy. 2017. *Following the Money of Mass Incarceration.* Prison Policy Initiative, January 25. https://www.prisonpolicy.org/reports/money.html.

Walker, S., and C. M. Katz. 2017. *The Police in America: An Introduction.* 9th ed. New York: McGraw Hill.

Wallace-Wells, D. 2023. "It's Not 'Deaths of Despair.' It's Deaths of Children." *New York Times,* April 6. https://www.nytimes.com/2023/04/06/opinion/deaths-life-expectancy-guns-children.html.

Walmsley, R. 2014. *World Pre-Trial/Remand Imprisonment List.* 2nd ed. International Centre for Prison Studies.

Wang, L., W. Sawyer, T. Herring, and E. Widra. 2022. "Beyond the Count: A Deep Dive into State Prison Populations." Prison Policy Initiative, April 2022. https://www.prisonpolicy.org/reports/beyondthecount.html.

Weaver, R. K. 2000. *Ending Welfare as We Know It.* Washington, DC: Brookings Institution Press.

Weaver, V. M. 2017. "The Untold Story of Mass Incarceration: Reform." *Boston Review,* October 23. https://www.bostonreview.net/articles/vesla-m-weaver-black-washingtonians/.

Weber, M. 1905. *The Protestant Ethic and the "Spirit" of Capitalism.* Translated by Peter Baehr and Gordon C. Wells. Repr. 2002. New York: Penguin Classics.

Weigend, T. 2016. "No News is Good News: Criminal Sentencing in Germany Since 2000." In *Crime and Justice,* vol. 45, ed. M. Tonry, 83–106.

Welsh, B. C., and R. D. Pfeffer. 2013. "Reclaiming Crime Prevention in an Age of Punishment: An American History." *Punishment and Society* 15, no. 15: 534–53.

Western, B. 2009. *Punishment and Inequality in America.* New York: Russell Sage Foundation.

Western, B. 2018. *Homeward: Life in the Year After Prison.* New York: Russell Sage Foundation.

Western, B. 2019. "The Challenge of Criminal Justice Reform." *Square One Project,* January. https://squareonejustice.org/paper/the-challenge-of-criminal-justice-reform/.

Western, B. 2023. "Slash Poverty and the Rest Will Get Easier." *Vital City,* April 4. https://www.vitalcitynyc.org/articles/slash-poverty-and-the-rest-will-get-easier.

Western, B., and C. Muller. 2013. "Mass Incarceration, Macrosociology, and the Poor." *Annals of the American Academy of Political and Social Science* 647: 166–89.

Western, B., and C. Wildeman. 2009. "The Black Family and Mass Incarceration." *Annals of the American Academy of Political and Social Science* 621: 221–42.

White, D. 2016. "America's Gun Homicide Rate Is 25 Time Higher Than Other Rich Countries." *Time,* February 3. https://time.com/4206484/america-violent-death-rate-higher/.

White, G. B. 2015. "Stranded: How America's Failing Public Transportation Increases Inequality." *The Atlantic,* May 16. https://www.theatlantic.com/business/archive/2015/05/stranded-how-americas-failing-public-transportation-increases-inequality/393419/.

Whitman, J. Q. 2003. *Harsh Justice: Criminal Punishment and the Widening Divide between America and Europe.* New York: Oxford University Press.

Widra, E. 2023. "Ten Statistics About the Scale and Impact of Mass Incarceration in the U.S." Prison Policy Initiative, October 24. https://www.prisonpolicy.org/blog/2023/10/24/ten-statistics/.

Widra, E. 2024. "States of Incarceration: The Global Context, 2024." June. https://www.prisonpolicy.org/global/2024.html.

Wildeman, C., M. D. Fitzpatrick, and A. W. Goldman. 2018. "Conditions of Confinement in American Prisons and Jails." *Annual Review of Law and Social Sciences* 14: 29–47.

Wilensky, H. 2018. *American Political Economy in Global Perspective.* New York: Cambridge University Press.
Wilkinson, R., and K. Pickett. 2010. *The Spirit Level: Why Equality is Better for Everyone.* New York: Bloomsbury Press.
Williams, C. 2019. "Black Workers Had Long History with Fed Jobs Before Shutdown." AP News, January 26. https://apnews.com/article/55792de5cc4946b1844c028469389c9f.
Wilson, J. Q. 1975. *Thinking about Crime.* New York: Basic Books, 1983.
Wilson, W. J. 1987. *The Truly Disadvantaged: The Inner City, the Underclass, and Public Policy.* Chicago: University of Chicago Press.
Wilson, W. J. 1996. *When Work Disappears: The World of the New Urban Poor.* New York: Alfred A. Knopf.
Wilson, W. J. 2002. "Foreword." In S. A. Venkatesh, *American Project: The Rise and Fall of a Modern Ghetto.* Cambridge: Harvard University Press.
Wilson, W. J. 2011. "Being Poor, Black, and American: The Impact of Political, Economic, and Cultural Forces." *American Educator,* Spring.
Winkler, A. 2011. *Gunfight: The Battle over the Right to Bear Arms in America.* New York: W. W. Norton.
Woodhill, L. 2014. "The War on Poverty Wasn't a Failure: It Was a Catastrophe." *Forbes,* March 19. https://www.forbes.com/sites/louiswoodhill/2014/03/19/the-war-on-poverty-wasnt-a-failure-it-was-a-catastrophe/.
Woodly, D. 2021. *Reckoning: Black Lives Matter and the Democratic Necessity of Social Movements.* New York: Oxford University Press.
Wootson, C. R., and M. Berman. 2017. "U.S. Police Chiefs Blast Trump for Endorsing 'Police Brutality.'" *Washington Post,* July 30. https://www.washingtonpost.com/news/post-nation/wp/2017/07/29/u-s-police-chiefs-blast-trump-for-endorsing-police-brutality/.
Wright, J. P., and M. DeLisi. 2016. *Conservative Criminology: A Call to Restore Balance to the Social Sciences.* New York: Routledge.
Wrong, D. H. 1994. *The Problem of Order: What Unites and Divides Society.* New York: Free Press.
Yaname, D. 2019. "The First Rule of Gunfighting is *Have a Gun*: Technologies of Concealed Carry in Gun Culture 2.0." In *The Lives of Guns,* ed. J. Obert, A. Poe, and A. Sarat. New York: Oxford University Press.
Zelizer, J. E. 2015. *The Fierce Urgency of Now: Lyndon Johnson, Congress, and the Battle for the Great Society.* New York: Penguin Books.
Zeng, Z. 2022. "Jail Inmates in 2021—Statistical Tables." Bureau of Justice Statistics, US Department of Justice, December. https://bjs.ojp.gov/library/publications/jail-inmates-2021-statistical-tables.
Zimring, F. E. 2006. *The Great American Crime Decline.* New York: Oxford University Press.
Zimring, F. E. 2013. *The City That Became Safe: New York's Lessons for Urban Crime and Its Control.* New York: Oxford University Press.
Zimring, F. E. 2017. *When Police Kill.* Cambridge: Harvard University Press.
Zimring, F. E. 2019. "The Death of the Unarmed Assailant: On Racial Fears, Ambiguous Movement, and the Vulnerability of Armed Police." In *The Lives of Guns,* ed. J. Obert, A. Poe, and A. Sarat. New York: Oxford University Press.
Zimring, F. E. 2020. *The Insidious Momentum of American Mass Incarceration.* New York: Oxford University Press.

Zimring, F. E., and G. Hawkins. 1991. *The Scale of Imprisonment*. Chicago: University of Chicago Press.

Zimring, F. E., and G. Hawkins. 1997. *Crime Is Not the Problem: Lethal Violence in America*. New York: Oxford University Press.

Zimring, F. E., G. Hawkins, and S. Kamin. 2001. *Punishment and Democracy: Three Strikes and You're Out in California*. New York: Oxford University Press.

INDEX

abolition (abolitionists, abolitionism): defined, 120; efforts at abolishing slavery, 112; idealism, low expectations, 125; institutional abolition, 121, 125; of the police (as an idea), 8, 12, 121, 123–124; politics of, 125; practical abolition, 125; of prisons (as an idea), 122; of slavery, racial segregation, 112; strategies for success of, 120–121

Abt, Thomas, 80, 131, 168n42

activists/activism/advocacy groups: for changing the penal state, 125, 130–131, 134; civil rights movements, 2, 112; in communities, for improved public safety, 48; for defunding the police, 12, 166n2; localism and, 32; pre-2020 protests, 106; protests against stop and frisk searches, 8; support for ending mass incarceration, 7–8. *See also* Black Lives Matter movement; Floyd, George, murder of

African Americans. *See* Black Americans

Alexander, Michelle, 131

American bandwidth, description, 26

Asian Americans, 2

bandwidth: concept of, 24–26; possibilities enabled by, 133–135

Bill of Rights (US), 2

Black Americans: collapse of the two-parent family, 67; disparities with White people, 45; family-related incarceration data, 32–33; government's abandonment of, 76; health outcomes comparison, 66; homicide rates (2019), 68–69; murder rates in majority-Black cities, 69; overpolicing, underprotection of, 102; penal state's use against young Black men, 48; Pickett on indifference toward, 106; police violence, incarceration, penal control against, 14, 45; political economy's impact on, 61; segregation of Black families, 68; state-supported segregation, racial discrimination against, 2; Wilson's characterization of, 2. *See also* segregation (racial segregation)

Black Lives Matter movement: attacks by right-wing groups on demonstrators, 11; historical background, 139n2, 140n10; positive enabling influence on citizens, 7; protests by, 4–6. *See also* Floyd, George, murder of

Blue Lives Matter signs, 11

Book of Job (Bible), 4

Braga. A. A., 98

Breivik, Anders Behring, 37

broken windows policing, 10, 33, 54

Browder, Kalief, 140n4

Brown, Michael, 10, 105, 140n4

Brown v. Board of Education, Supreme Court decision, 113

Brown v. Plata, Supreme Court decision, 39

capitalism: America's penal Leviathan and, 4; disruptive influence of, 75; free-market capitalism, 4, 9, 114, 126, 131; Keynesian-style intervention and, 9; penal state

capitalism (*continued*)
arrangements and, 8; real world social contexts of, 62; Schumpeter's observation on, 44; social disruption caused by, 3–4; ultraliberal form, in the US, 119; welfare capitalism, 60
capital punishment. *See* death penalty
Carter, Jimmy, 70
Chauvin, Derek, 7, 10, 141n22. *See also* Floyd, George, murder of
children: benefits of poverty reduction for, 129; Black vs. White, poverty rates, 66, 156n72; building of solidarity for, 111; impact of poverty on, 86, 157n81, 160n47; incarceration of fathers, 46; penal state's adverse effect on, 48; reasons for criminal activity by, 86; in segregated neighborhoods, 113; in single-/no parent homes, 67–68, 156n67; welfare state limitations for, 156n49
Civil Rights Acts (1960s), 2–3, 70, 157n83
civil rights movements, 2, 112
Clinton, Bill, 65
collateral consequences: defined/described, 42–43, 51, 103; institutional distinctness of, 52; modifications of, 149n86; origin of, 104
communities: failures of social controls in, 23, 28, 44–45; impact of political economy on, 17–19; intermediating-level processes in, 21, 26, 29; lethal violence, poverty, and, 15; mass incarcerations in, 38; police activities in, 33; state penal controls in, 21–22; stop and frisk, of young men of color, 34; urging of authorities to control violent crime by, 94; use of correctional supervision in, 41–42
comparative analysis: of American difference, 139n9; comparative date, 154n30; comparator group, 142n1
Congress: challenges in enacting/implementing social policy, 59; cutbacks in federal prison programs by, 40;

enactment of positive economic measures, support of working people, 9
Constitution (US): allocation of responsibility for policing, 16; gun problem and constitutional rights, 132; Second Amendment (right to bear arms), 72; unconstitutionality of stop and frisk, 141n26
control imperative, description, 29, 49–52. *See also* penal control
Cook, P. J., 98
correctional supervision, 41–42, 52, 151n36
COVID-19 pandemic: government efforts to control the spread of, 6; impact on social, economic life, 6–7, 11; implementation/dismantling of European-style welfare measures, 9; Klinenberg's comment on America's reactions to, 13; neoliberalism and, 9; New Jersey prisoners release during, 41; surge in gun crimes and sales during, 12; uniqueness of America's reaction to, 13
crime control: criminal justice system and, 22; efficacy of nonpenal interventions, 48, 132, 135; global comparison, 92, 95, 103; growing need for, 12; influence of socioeconomic conditions, 28, 94–95, 101; law and order covenant, 4; left-vs.-right debates about, 15; limits on social approaches to, 95; loose link with political economy, 133; polarizing quality of, 132; political institutions and, 88–101; politics of, 18; social democratic institution-building for, 129; success of penal control assumed, 94; urgency of, for lethal violence, 131. *See also* stop and frisk searches
criminal justice legal system: challenges to the legitimacy of (2020), 6; global comparison of, 57, 97; governmental responsibility for, 89–91; gun violence and, 5; hyper-local character of, 129; indifference toward justice-involved people, 108–109; influences on the conduct of, 97; "less-eligibility" principle, 92–03; operational background of, 5;

political economy's link with, 127; predatory practices of, 93–94; principles and purposes of, 56–57; racialization of, 1, 107; rapid decision-making by officials, 88; scandal of, 124–125; social dislocation and, 56; socioeconomic context/material conditions of, 5; split-second judgments, 10, 91, 125 , 141n21; underfunding of, 90, 92. *See also* prosecution; sentencing

criminal violence: community activism's positive influence on, 48; link of the political economy with, 15–16; material causes of, 18; multiple causes of, 16, 18; neoliberalism's influence on, 119; 1960s and 1970s triggers of an upsurge in, 14; political economy's role in, 119; roots of, in socioeconomic circumstances, 27–28. *See also* police violence; violence

criminogenic processes: causes/origins of, 21, 71; consequences of, 77; penal state contributions, 47; political economy and, 21, 26, 53; role in determining outcomes, 20; social disorganization and, 79–82

Crutchfield, Robert, 83

cultural codes, 22, 81

danger: and decision-making, 97–101; perceptions of, 99

Davis, Angela, 148n58

death penalty (capital punishment), 50, 109; comparison with corporal punishment, 123; comparison with imprisonment, 123; custodial measures alternative, 122–123; life imprisonment vs., 122; vs. other forms of punishment, 151n36; persistence of, 139n9; role of activists in challenging, 125; Trump administration's use of, 36–37; unevenness in abolition, 129

deindustrialization: impact on US cities, 4, 19; neoliberalism and, 69–70

Democratic Party: blended policy promises by, 70; left wing political activism, 12; possible future firearm controls, 133; Republican Party comparison, 130; social democratic phase, 69–70, 129–130; support for egalitarian racial policies, 144n33; welfare state establishment by, 64. *See also* Republican Party

Denton, Nancy, 78

Denzel, Mychal, 120

Department of Justice, 32, 146n22, 147n35, 151n19

deviance: inadequacy of social controls in containing, 55; role of social services in managing, 96, 115; social disorganization and, 80; social norms normalization of, 82

Diallo, Amadou, 140n4

Dinkheller, Kyle, 99

disorganization. *See* social disorder/disorganization

drugs/drug offenses, 39, 46, 67, 79, 82. *See also* War on Drugs

Durkheim, Émile, 109, 110, 121

economy. *See* political economy

Fair Housing Act, 70

family/families: collapse of two-parent family, 67; crimes of survival by, 83; economic disadvantage, violent crime, and, 67; extorting of revenues from, 52, 93, 102–103; flight from poor neighborhoods, 76; impact of economic hardship on, 55, 64, 67, 77–81, 86; impact of 1970s rightward shift on, 44; incarceration-related data, 32–33; law-abiding behaviors of, 21; negative impact of political economy, 17–19, 28, 75; penal state's adverse effect on, 48; role in shaping children, 86; single-parent households, 67–68; social disorganization and, 97; welfare state help for, 22, 96. *See also* single-parent households

Federal Bureau of Investigation (FBI), 32, 160n51

Federal Bureau of Prisons, 32

federal penitentiaries, 40

Ferguson Report (2015), 105

fines: as add-on to sentences, 51; indebtedness from, 43; penal power and, 31; revenue policing and, 35; stand-along fines, 51

Floyd, George, murder of: cell phone capture of, 7, 104; false statement by police department on, 104; influence on penal state debate, 12; influence on policing and punishment, 102; influence on public attitudes, 9–11, 102

free-market capitalism, 4, 9, 114, 126, 131

free-market deregulation, 117

free-market fundamentalism, 69–70, 114

free-market liberalism, 69

Garner, Eric, 10, 140n4

G.I. Bill, 114

Gilmore, Ruth, 122

Gottschalk, Marie, 93

government (US): citizens' "law and order" covenant with, 4; limited investment in crime control, 94; responsibility for criminal justice, 89; social infrastructure limitations, 96–97; US citizens' distrust of, 3. *See also* Democratic Party; penal state; political development; political economy; Republican Party

GPS monitors, 42

Gray, Freddie, 140n4

Great Society programs, 2, 69, 126

Great Transformation, The (Polanyi), 54

guns/gun crime: Constitutional right to bear arms, 72; dangers created by the possession of, 98–100; global comparison, 2, 19; historical debate on possession, 73–74; impact in disorganized neighborhoods, 23; impact of incarcerations on, 47; impact of "stop and frisk" on gun carrying, 48; as impediment to public safety, 132; influence on penal state, 15; ownership control in most developed nations, 72; surge in ownership, 11–13, 17, 19; US gun ownership data, 71–72

healthcare: benefits of government funding for, 12; benefits of universal healthcare, 65, 114, 128; global comparison of, 40, 65–67; imprisonment's facilitation of, 123, 167n14; Medicare's subsidizing of, 65; for middle-class vs. poor people, 112; political economy's impact on, 20; public support for, 94; vs. punishment, for low-level offenders, 40; welfare states impact on, 62, 65, 116

Hobbes, Thomas, v, 4, 24

homelessness: affordable housing solution for, 128; agencies and social services for, 96; crimes of survival and, 83; economic distress and, 80; expectations of police management of, 96–97; of low-level offenders, 40; rates of, 67

homicides: global comparison of, 2, 12, 139n3; in poor, segregated communities, 71; prevalence of, in the US, 71; rate surge (mid-1960s to mid-1990s), 3, 10, 55

imprisonment. *See* incarceration; jails; prisons

incarceration: bipartisan politics and, 129–130; correctional supervision comparison, 41–42; efforts at limiting the use of, 36, 39; facilitation of healthcare in, 123; Gilmore's comment on, 122, 140n3; global comparison of rates, 31, 38, 92; historical background, 122; inconclusive causal links of, 47; increasingly negative view of, 10; influence of New Deal politics on, 25; "million-dollar blocks" of, 38; parsimony and, 52; penal state's overuse of, 14, 38, 131; political economy and, 20; racial disparity characteristic of, 45–46. *See also* mass incarceration; prisons (prison system)

indifference, social sources of, 102–118; anti-Black sentiments and, 107; criminal legal systems, 108–109; de facto segregation and, 112–115; penal state's enabling of, 14, 30; Pickett, on indifference toward

Blacks, 106; public indifference, in America, 102–108, 107–108; race and the limits of solidarity, 107–109; visibility, acceptability, and, 104–107; welfare states, solidarity, and, 115–118

inequality: association with violence, social disorganization, 143n13; benefits of reducing, 134; global comparison of, 2, 17; negative impact on solidarity, 111, 166n52; political economy's role in creating, 24, 61, 113, 154n29; role in criminal violence, 16; role of rightward shift in creating, 70; segregation and, 112; strategy for reducing, 117, 127, 129; US ranking of, 155n46

institutional abolition, 121, 125

jails: cash bail/for-profit bail bond system, 39–40; COVID-19 emergency release from, 39; institutional difference with prisons, 39; numbers/types of, in the US, 39; prosecutorial control of, 35–36; racial complexion of, 46; racially-imposed commercial profits of, 8. *See also* incarceration; prisons

Jim Crow era, 3, 61

Johnson, Lyndon, 69. *See also* Great Society programs; War on Poverty

journalists: on abolishing/defunding police, 8; on the "broken system," 102; coverage of police killings, 7; documenting of penal state harms by, 106

Kaba, Mariame, 121
Katz, H., 81
King, Rodney, 140n4
Klinenberg, Eric, 13
Kolakowski, Leszek, 121

labor markets: America's outlier status, 18; characteristics of, 63–64; comparison of, 63–64, 66; consequences of low wages, 55; influence of organized labor on, 60; outlier status of, in America, 18; penal state involvement with, 44; political economy and, 24, 55, 58; racialization of, 61; social control and, 23

labor unions: benefits of strengthening of, 116–117, 127–128; efforts at crushing, 3; neoliberalism's antagonism toward, 117; political economy's effect on, 58, 62; solidarity in, 110–111, 115; welfare capitalism and, 60

law and order covenant, 4

law enforcement (criminal law enforcement): impact of America's polity on, 88; operation in disorganized, gun-laden environments, 98; racialization of, 8; structural explanation of, 14–30. *See also* crime control; criminal justice legal system

"less-eligibility" principle, 92–03

Leviathan: definition as used by Hobbes, 4; usage in the Bible, 4

LGBTQ people, 2

localism, policing and, 91–92

Luxembourg Income Survey (2000), 65

market fundamentalism, 1

Martin, Trayvon, 140n2

Massey, Doug, 78

mass incarceration: anti-mass incarceration movement, 142n40; Black Lives Matter movement protests against, 6–7, 12; challenges of unwinding, 167n19; citizen demand for ending, 6; comments on the practice of, 151n20; description, 32, 38, 103–104, 145n7; deterrent/incapacitation effects of, 47; disproportionate use vs. Blacks, 38, 104; ideological dissonance and, 3; impact on White, well-to-do Americans, 104; limited voter opposition to, 102; link with low levels of equality, social provision, 18; mid-1970s run-up of, 31; *New York Times* editorial on, 141n26; opposition to/efforts at reducing, 10, 12, 36, 80, 141n27; prosecutorial role in enabling, sustaining, 24, 31, 35–36, 51, 56;

mass incarceration (*continued*)
racial disparity feature of, 46; support for ending, 7–8, 12; tension with America's social arrangements, 3. *See also* incarceration; jails; prisons
Medicaid, 64, 65, 114, 163n38, 167n24
Medicare, 64, 65, 110, 114, 142n44
mental illness: agencies and social services for, 96; expectations of police management of, 96–97; of low-level offenders, 40; penal state and, 17; rate of America's jailed inmates, 163n38; rates of, 67; survival crime and, 80; universal healthcare as solution for, 128
Messner, S. F., 85–86
minimum-security prisons, 40, 57
Morone, James, 114
multiracial democracy, 2–3, 131

Native Americans, 2, 3, 107
neoliberalism: COVID-19 pandemic and, 9; deindustrialization and, 69–70; description of, 70; hallmarks of, 117; impact on criminal violence, penal controls, 119; New Deal politics transition to, 18, 25; penal state arrangements and, 8
New Deal: decline/collapse of, 1, 19, 30, 70; "Four Freedoms," 131; racial injustices of, 157n83; state capacity transformations during, 162n33; successes of, 2, 69, 70, 114, 126, 168n25; transition to neoliberalism, 18, 25
New Federalism, 70, 157n88
New Jim Crow, 8
New Right agenda, 139n8
Nixon, Richard, 70, 76. *See also* New Federalism

Obert, Jonathan, 73
O'Flaherty, B., 99

penal codes, 32
penal control: control imperative, 49–52; description/goals of, 50; expansiveness of, 45; government officials support for, 49; influence on mass incarceration, 51; influence on sentencing legislation, 51–52; mass incarceration and, 31; overuse against Black Americans, 14; overuse in poor neighborhoods, 15; political economy's impact on, 17–18, 20–21; probation/parole, as measures of, 42; reasons for the emphasis on, 53; sentencing patterns, 51; social controls and, 21–23, 26; state capacity and, 94–97; vengeful, degrading, cheap and mean practices, 50–51; voter consent for, 4, 24
penal state, 31–43: activation in well-regulated communities, 22; America's polity and, 89–91; causes of, 5, 26; correctional supervision, 41–42; criminal violence link with, 15; description, 23, 44, 144n22; disproportionate use against young Black men, 48; distinguishing features of, 4; expansion of prosecutions, prosecutors, 35–36; fees and "user-pays" charges on offenders, 43; franchise quality of, 93; functional adaptation of social systems, 53–56; global comparison of, 38–39, 46, 49–50, 119; historical background, 32–33; illiberalism of, 3; impacts of, 46–49; imposition of justice fees/"user-pays" charges on offenders, 43; incarceration growth rates, 38–39; influence of socioeconomic circumstances, 27; limited successful challenges against, 12; localism as a defining feature, 32; material causes of repression in, 18; neoliberalism's influence on, 119; penal and social controls, 21–23; political economy's links with, 25–26, 119; possible future directions of, 133–136; profile of the clientele in, 46; projection of penal control by, 21–23, 32–33; public indifference toward, 107–108; racial disparity in, 46; role in enabling indifference, 14, 30; rooted in/shaped by political economy, 58; sentencing in criminal courts, 36–38;

sentencing patterns, 51; social controls and, 21–23; social science's view on, 44; spillover onto children of offenders, 48; steps necessary for dismantling of, 131–132; structural limits to reform of, 125–126; subcontracting of functions, 90; ultraliberal political economy's influence on, 17; use of collateral consequences, 42–43, 51–52, 103–104, 149n86; use of correctional supervision, 41–42, 52, 151n36; view of radicals on, 8; welfare state link with, 17–18

Pickett, Justin, 106

Polanyi, Karl, 54

police/policing: broken windows policing, 10, 33, 54; categories of, 90; Constitution's allocation of responsibility for, 16; "danger imperative" emphasis in training, 90; deadliness of, 2; deaths in the line of duty, 34–35, 98; fear of being killed of, 98–99; federal law enforcement agencies, 33; as a fundamental institution, 6; global comparison of killing of civilians, 99; influence of anti-Black sentiments on, 107; influences on the conduct of, 97; invisibility of the conduct of, 104; Kaba on the abolition of, 121; killing of Brown, 10, 105, 140n4; killing of Garner, 10, 140n4; localism and, 91–92; municipal, county-level departments, 33; qualified immunity for, 91–92; rank-and-file officers, 90; revenue policing, 35, 92–93; role of racism in shaping, 27; snap decisions made by, 88; split-second judgments, 10, 91, 125, 141n21; support for abolishing/defunding, 8, 12; underdevelopment of accountability of, 91–92; underfunding of, 90, 97; use of aggressiveness in "hot spots," 33; warrior-style demeanor of, 98; zero tolerance policing, 54–55. *See also* Floyd, George, murder of; stop and frisk searches; War on Drugs

police violence: in the aftermath of Floyd's murder, 102; data on 2023 killings, 12; impact of, on Americans, 11; pre-2020 excesses of, 7; public indifference toward, 106; victim social status and, 11. *See also* criminal violence

political development (in the U.S.), 15–19; influence of federal polity, 16; negative social indicators, 17; twentieth century, middle years, 16–17; US Constitution and, 16

political economy, 58–74; comparison to other nations, 19; criminal legal system's link with, 127; defined, 58; deindustrialization, neoliberalism, and, 69–70; description/features of, 19–21, 59–61; emergence of American bandwidth, 26; glimpses of possible remedies for, 9; impact of the COVID-19 pandemic, 13; impact on violence, 71–74; influence on criminal justice system, 5; insecurities caused by, 4; interaction of macro-level forces with community-level processes, 14–15; labor markets and, 63–64; lack of a strong labor movement, 60; limited support for the public sector, 59–60; macro-structures of, 20; modern-day "varieties of capitalism" framework, 62–63; negative impact on poor communities, families, 17–18; penal state's links with, 25–26, 119; possible future directions of, 133–136; racialization of, 14–15, 19–21, 60–61, 80, 103, 117, 119; role of community-level social processes in determining outcomes, 20; role of criminogenic processes in determining outcomes, 20; role of intermediating processes in determining outcomes, 21, 29; social democratic, 129; social disorder and, 58, 75–87; structural explanation of, 14–30; structural foundations of, 58; support for the private sector, 59–60; of the United States, 58–74; valued features of, 61; weakening influence on informal social controls, 15–16; welfare state and, 64–66 political institutions: backfiring of welfare policy claim, 94; "cheap and mean" regimes, 92–94; connection to political economy, 28, 58, 62; crime control and, 88–101; enabling of gun ownership by, 74; "less-eligibility" principle, 92–93; limited resources for local authorities, 92; localism and policing, 91–92; penal state and, 89–91; racialization/racial hierarchy of, 17, 60; slaveholding South's influence on shaping, 3; underfunding of criminal justice, 90, 92

poverty: association with racial segregation, social dislocation, 79; Black vs. White children in, 66; complexity of causation of, 83–84; global rate comparison, 66. *See also* homelessness; worklessness

prisons (prison system), 40–41; abolition of, 122; absence of "normalization" rights (US), 41; calibration of sentences, 123; commercial profits from, 8; comparison with corporal, capital punishment, 123; COVID-19 emergency release from, 39; cruelty and neglect conditions in, 40; Davis's comment on, 148n58; federal penitentiaries variation, 40; federal system components, 32; global officer-to-inmate comparison, 41; global size comparison, 2; idea/support for abolishing, 8, 12; incarceration rates, 31–32; institutional difference with jails, 39; "less-eligibility" principle, 92–93; limited provisions for prisoners in, 41; minimum-security, 40, 57; Nordic system comparison, 129; population data (2022), 12; potential transformative improvements, 124; racial complexion of, 46; racial controls in, 8; racialized penal segregation, 102; severity of conditions in, 40; societal reliance on, 123; Southern prison farms, 31; supermax prisons, 40; Tocqueville on, 1; uniqueness of Nordic systems, 129. *See also* incarceration; mass incarceration

prosecution: Black Lives Matter movement and, 6; expansion and aggressiveness of practices, 24, 31, 35; impact of tough-on-crime legislation, 35; political association of prosecutors, 36; "progressive prosecutors" movement, 36; socioeconomic context of, 18; US Constitution and, 16. *See also* criminal justice legal system

punishment (state punishment): comparison with other affluent nations, 18; as a fundamental institution, 6, 121; inevitability of, 121; micro-structures of, 20; pre-2020 excesses of, 7; role of racism in shaping, 27; roots of, in socioeconomic circumstances, 27–28

Putnam, Robert, 67

race/racism: American's abhorrence of explicit, 11; Black Lives Matter movement and, 6; institutional racism, 20; limits of solidarity and, 107–109; penal state and, 5; political economy and, 19; public indifference toward, 107; role in criminal violence, 16; role in shaping policing, punishment, 27; structural racism, 20; toward Asian Americans, 2; toward Native Americans, 2

racialization: of criminal legal system, 1, 8, 106–107; of labor markets, 61; of law enforcement, 8; of political economy, 14–15, 19–21, 60–61, 80, 103, 117, 119; of political institutions, 17, 60; of public opinion on crime, punishment, 165n17; of ultraliberal market economy, 84. *See also* Black Lives Matter movement

rapid response tactical units, 33

Reagan, Ronald, 65, 70, 76, 168n43

Reconstruction, successes of, 2

Republican Party: blended policy promises by, 70; complaints about criminal justice costs, 10; opposition to decarceration, 130; opposition to egalitarian racial policies, 144n33; opposition to social spending by, 94; role in building a

neoliberalized economy, 70. *See also* Democratic Party
revenue policing, 35, 92–93
riot squads, 33
Roosevelt, Franklin D., 69. *See also* New Deal
Rosenfeld, R., 85–86

Sampson, R., 81, 158n1
Schumpeter, Joseph, 44
segregation (racial segregation), 18–19, 24, 75; global comparison of, 165n44; homicide rates and, 71; ignorance/stereotyping, as results of, 109; impact on Black families, 2, 18–19, 24, 68, 75, 113; influence on cross-class, cross-race solidarity, 30, 103; negative effects on solidarity, 111, 112–115; 1960s illegality of, 78–79; Nixon/Reagan's abandoned efforts at reducing, 76; in penal confinement, 78–79, 102; political economy's support for, 14, 17, 60, 78, 103; social disorganization, failure, and, 68, 79; strategy for reducing, 116–117; structural arrangements role in creating, 84; violent crime rates and, 86
Selznick, Philip, 23, 132
sentencing: death penalty, 36–37; for drug offenses, 37; global comparisons, 37; global imprisonment comparison, 37–38; increasing severity in, 36; life imprisonment with/without parole, 36–37; in Norwegian law, 37; patterns of, 51; penal control's influence on, 51–52; proportionality principle of, 52; role of penal power in, 31; suspended sentences, 51; Trump's use of the death penalty, 36–37; truth in sentencing laws, 36
Sethi, R., 99
sexual offending, 37
Sierra-Arévalo, Michael, 99
Simon, Jonathan, 22
single-parent households: association with poverty, child detriment, 67; available benefits for, 66; conditions leading to, 77–78; consequences for children in, 86; penal state and, 17; rate in America, 67–68; Sawhill's comment on, 156n67
slavery: efforts at abolishing, 112, 120–121; political economy and, 60; support for, in the South, 3; toleration of violence in, 71
social control: breakdown in poor neighborhoods, 18; economic exclusion's influence on, 80–81; influence of deindustrialization, 22; interaction of macrostructures in creating, 14–15; material circumstances and, 26–28; penal controls and, 21–23; political economy's link with, 19; political economy's weakening of, 15–16; Selznick's comment on, 23
social democracy programs. *See* War on Poverty
social dislocation, 5, 56–57, 79
social disorder/disorganization, 5, 17, 97–101; complex causation of, 82–87; criminogenic processes and, 79–82; dangers of, in poor neighborhoods, 100; decline of inner cities, 76; economic stress and, 77–79; government's abandonment of Black Americans, 75–76; impact of capitalist markets, 75; impact of economic stress, 77–79; political economy and, 58, 75–88; worklessness and, 2, 55, 70, 76–77, 79, 82
social order: in affluent vs. poor neighborhoods, 14, 80; community-level processes of, 14; creation of group norms of, 121; Hobbesian account of, 4, 24; Lockean theory of, 23–24; 1980s-1990s, spontaneous informal controls, 45; penal controls and, 97; Rousseau's account of, 23; sources of, 23–24
social problems: drugs/drug offenses, 39, 46, 66, 67, 79, 82; global comparison of, 66; health outcomes, 66; homelessness rates, 40, 67, 80, 96; homicide rates/lethal violence, 68–69; life expectancy, Blacks vs. Whites, 66; male obesity, 66;

social problems (*continued*)
  mental illness, 17, 40, 67, 80, 96, 100, 128; poverty rates, 66; segregation of Black families, 68; single-parent households, 67–68; substance dependency, 67, 128. *See also* homelessness; worklessness
social science: political economy and, 15–16; theoretical models of, 20; view of the penal state in, 44
Social Security, 64, 65, 110, 114, 116, 142n44
solidarity: absence of, between punished and punisher, 109; consequences of deficiency of, 53; cross-class, cross-racial, 103, 114; defined, 109–110; Durkheim's description of, 110; emotional connections, shared practices of, 110–111; global comparison of, 114; political economy's effect on, 16; race and the limits of, 107–109; reasons for failures of, 111; segregation's negative effect on, 14, 30, 111, 112–115; slavery-related deficits, 113; strategy for enhancing, 117; Thelen's observation about, 114; types/variations of, 110; in the United States, 111–112; welfare states and, 115–118
split-second judgments, 10, 91, 125, 141n21
state capacity: definition, 95, 162n33; limitations of, 14, 18–19, 27, 30, 59, 88, 101; penal control and, 94–97, 95; strategy for building, 117; welfare states' expansion of, 96
stop and frisk searches: activism against, 8; data on NYPD's usage of, 134, 141n26, 150n4, 151n19; fear of police recruits in using, 98; ineffectiveness of, 10; police use in high-crime neighborhoods, 33, 47; racial disparities in, 45; ruling of unconstitutionality of, 141n26; success as a gun control tactic, 48; use as a gun control tactic, 48; use in Great Britain (stop and search), 146n18
structural analysis, 5, 14–30; explanation (of criminal law enforcement), 14–30; structures and actions, 28–29

supermax prisons, 40
Supreme Court: *Brown v. Board of Education*, 113; *Brown v. Plata*, 39; decisions on gun ownership, possession, 132; *Graham v. Connor*, 141n21; rejection of appeal of Chauvin's appeal, 141n22
SWAT teams, 33

Taylor, Breonna, 140n4
Temporary Assistance for Needy Families program, 66
Thelen, Kathleen, 114
Tocqueville, Alexis de, 1, 111
Trump, Donald: tweeting of law and order messages, 11; 2024 law and order platform of, 12; use of the death penalty, 36–37

United States (US): distinct governing style of, 59; global comparison of incarceration rates, 31, 38, 92; global leadership in lethal violence, 68; gun ownership data, 71–72; high-crime decades (1980s, 1990s), 10; inequality comparison, 2; labor markets, 63–64; lack of a strong labor movement, 60; lack of support for the public sector, 59–60; mass incarceration in, 1; modern-day economy of, 62–63; narratives about, 1–2; nineteenth-century union movement, 60; as outlier in lethal violence, 68; outsourcing of public functions to private, quasi-public organizations, 72–73; political development in, 15–19; social problems comparison, 66–69; solidarity in, 111–112; state repression in, 3; sympathetic/supportive of business sector, 59; ultraliberalism capitalism in, 119; variations in policing, criminal punishment, 24; War on Drugs, 10, 34, 37, 91, 147n46, 150n8; welfare state, 64–66
universal healthcare, 65, 114, 128

Valjean, Jean, 83
Vallier, Kevin, 112–113

Vietnam War, 69
violence: childhood experiences of, 81; community-based initiatives against, 132; criminological explanations for high levels of, 79–82; gang-related, 82; global comparison of, 38–39, 49–50, 71, 119; gun-related, 5, 131; linked causal mechanisms for, 76–77; political economy's impact on, 71–74; retaliatory violence, 82; sentence enhancements for, 37; stereotypical identification of Black people and, 108; US as outlier in lethal violence, 68. *See also* criminal violence; police violence
Voting Rights Acts (1960s), 2–3, 70, 157n82

War on Drugs, 10, 34, 37, 91, 147n46, 150n8
War on Poverty, 19, 69, 94, 107, 114, 157n83
Weber, Max, 73
welfare state(s): backfiring of welfare policy claim, 94; capitalism's impact on, 53; COVID-19 pandemic and, 1, 9; description, 22, 96; functions of, 23; global comparison of, 2, 19, 41, 67, 69, 86, 93; impact on social disorder, 75; influence on state power, government, 96; of liberal market economies, 62; limitations of, 95–96; neoliberalism's antagonism toward, 117; organized labor and, 60; penal state relation with, 17–18, 44; political economy's impact on, 19, 64–66; post-1940s comparison to OECD countries, 65; Reagan's attack on, 70; role in state capacity expansions, 96; solidarity and, 115–118; US development of, 64–66
Western, Bruce, 129
White supremacy, 8, 60, 128
Wilson, William Julius, 2, 81
worklessness, 2, 55, 70, 76–77, 79, 82

zero tolerance policing, 54
Zimmerman, George, 140n2

A NOTE ON THE TYPE

This book has been composed in Arno, an Old-style serif typeface in the classic Venetian tradition, designed by Robert Slimbach at Adobe.